PROCESS IMPROVEMENT FOR EFFECTIVE BUDGETING AND FINANCIAL REPORTING

PROCESS IMPROVEMENT FOR EFFECTIVE BUDGETING AND FINANCIAL REPORTING

NILS H. RASMUSSEN

CHRISTOPHER J. EICHORN

COREY S. BARAK

TOBY PRINCE

WILEY

John Wiley & Sons, Inc.

CONTENTS

PREFACE

We decided to write this book when we discovered that a majority of the companies we talked to had dysfunctional and low-value added processes for budgeting, forecasting, and financial reporting. And, as financial executives come and go, typically little is done to streamline these processes. Even when large amounts of money are invested in new financial software, the solutions are usually put in place based on the old, inefficient routines. This locks a company into its past planning and reporting habits, when changes really need to be taken to realign the processes with the current management team, company, industry, and economical situation. Such problems were apparent in the many failed business process improvement (BPI) and reengineering projects during the 1990s.

Process Improvement for Effective Budgeting and Financial Reporting combines methodologies and systems from general business process improvement and business reengineering theories and applies them specifically to budgeting and reporting processes. Our goal for this book is to help you to be realistic about the outcomes you can deliver with your available time and resources. To that end, we have applied the well-known 80/20 principle, meaning that we aim to help you improve 80 percent of all inefficient processes, and in 20 percent of the time it would take to attempt to fix 100 percent of all processes (which we believe is close to impossible due to the frequently changing nature of organizations and technologies).

This book focuses on using business process improvement (BPI) to help you analyze your company's current inefficiencies and to create a strategy to improve your planning and reporting and management decision-making processes. In short, the book will help you to address the issues shown in Exhibit P.1.

Another objective for this book is to provide a tool for anyone who sees a need to improve their company's budgeting and reporting processes, not just by buying new software or adding interesting reports, but by addressing the broader underlying organizational process issues. The point is to achieve long-term improvement that will have a significant positive impact on the business.

Probably many of you have been involved in or have observed business process reengineering projects that have failed or at least failed to live up to their promise. We do not want this to be like other BPI projects; rather we want to provide an efficient and reusable tool that you can take with you in different financial jobs and that you can feel comfortable using to streamline any company's budgeting and reporting processes.

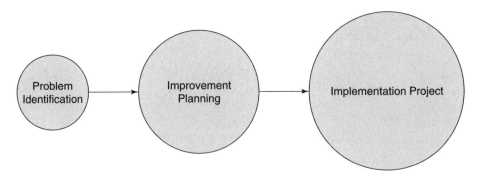

EXHIBIT P.1   Major BPI Areas Addressed in This Book

Our combined years of consulting experiences, across all major industries and in organizations of different sizes, with widely different management styles and cultures, have taught us that a process redesign needs to be the following to be successful:

- *Specific.* Addresses the most important issues
- *Simple.* Provides easy-to-understand tools for analyzing issues and creating the change needed
- *Achievable over a fairly short time frame.* Keeps cost low, ensures complete implementation, and provides readily measurable results
- *Sustainable.* Enables the redesigned budgeting and reporting processes to easily adapt to changes in the business and industry
- *Achievable with or without outside consulting assistance.* Avoids overly ambitious projects, which tend not to get completed.
- *Worthwhile.* Delivers an attractive return on investment (ROI), so the effort put into the project is clearly measurable and proving it is worth the time and energy invested

Because you are reading this book, it is safe to assume you are probably already involved in a budgeting and/or reporting process that you want to improve. We believe this book will provide you with many of the ideas and tools you need to "sell" your peers a project to improve your organization's budgeting and reporting processes and to successfully undertake such a project from start to finish.

A word on the use of terms in this book: We frequently use the word "organization" to mean any department, company, corporation, division, or field office that is part of the business. The word "budgeting," unless otherwise stated, also includes planning and forecasting. The word "analytics" we use to cover budgeting, reporting, and analysis.

The book consists of five parts plus appendices:

- Part One: Introduction to Business Process Improvement
- Part Two: The Business Process Improvement Project

- Part Three: Designing the Ultimate Chart of Accounts
- Part Four: Interviews
- Part Five: Software Tools and Resources
- Appendices

PART ONE: INTRODUCTION TO BUSINESS PROCESS IMPROVEMENT

This part introduces you to financial business process analysis. Here you'll read about the trends financial managers must be aware of today if they are to effectively manage their companies' planning and reporting processes and the tools necessary to implement those processes. The following topics are covered:

- About BPI
- When BPI is valuable
- Small and large projects and the associated costs
- ROI of BPI projects
- Best practices, trends, and technology
- Selling change to your organization

PART TWO: THE BPI PROJECT

In this part we cover the business process improvement project itself. You will be guided through the following BPI activities:

- Preparing for the project
- Profiles of budget models and approaches
- Your company's budgeting and reporting diagnostics
- Key budgeting and reporting process criteria
- Key budget process building blocks
- Financial reporting process improvement
- Recommendations for implementation

PART THREE: DESIGNING THE ULTIMATE CHART OF ACCOUNTS

Most companies with an accounting system are continuously modifying, redoing, adding to, and deleting items from their chart of accounts. And, every few years, most accounting departments have the same goal: to finally clean up that old, messy chart of accounts and create a new one so that they can:

- Easily adapt to changes and/or additions in the business (departments, products, etc.).
- Write reports easily because the COA is clean and structured.
- Incorporate a code system to better capture relevant management information.

Usually, however, after weeks or even months of planning and systemizing, and many thousands of dollars later, the ultimate chart of accounts remains a fantasy. In this part we review myths, pitfalls, tips, and tricks to help you create an optimal—if not ultimate—chart of accounts that, among other things, will support effective budgeting and reporting.

PART FOUR: INTERVIEWS

In this part you will read interviews with experts who have analyzed and improved budgeting and reporting processes. We asked them such questions as:

- What are your current budgeting and reporting processes?
- What do you suggest to do to improve budgeting and reporting processes?
- Which obstacles did you have to overcome in your BPI project?
- How did you overcome these obstacles?

PART FIVE: RESOURCES AND SOFTWARE TOOLS

This part provides you with an in-depth look at the different software tools available for automating and enhancing budgeting, reporting, and analysis functions in a company. Topics covered include:

- Ideas and tools for the software selection process
- Software evaluation and request for proposals
- Software buyer's guide
- Other tools and resources

APPENDICES

We have included a number of value-added documents in the appendices of the book. You can use these documents as examples or templates for your own BPI project; you can also copy information from the examples provided.

The appendices consist of the following documents:

- Sample nondisclosure contract
- Sample consulting contract
- Software vendor addresses
- Sample chart of accounts

In order to save you time and money in your software selection and implementation process, several useful documents from the appendices are provided on the Web. Please visit *www.wiley.com/go/processimprovement*. The user password is *process*. These documents are in Word format and you will be able to download and adjust them as necessary.

PART ONE

INTRODUCTION TO BUSINESS PROCESS IMPROVEMENT

1

ABOUT BUSINESS PROCESS IMPROVEMENT

INTRODUCTION

What is business process improvement (BPI)? It is a systematic methodology developed to help an organization make significant advances in the way its business processes operate. Business process improvement is not a new concept (See Exhibit 1.1). It has been around for as long as there have been businesses whose owners/managers have consciously (or unconsciously) pursued changes to improve the way different activities in their business were handled. Modern BPI projects can range from the very extensive and expensive, involving everyone in the organization, to short-term and highly focused, involving just a few people.

Improving budgeting and reporting processes does not have to be a major undertaking but the payoff should make the effort well worthwhile. That said, if you intend to achieve major and highly visible improvements, plan to spend significant amounts of time, money, and resources on the project. If you are in a midsized to a large company, you will have to involve a number of people in the project, and no doubt many "political" opinions will have to be heard along the way.

As the popularity of modern analytics software and related Web-based technologies has grown since the end of the 1990s and into the millennium, there has been a lot of talk about workflow. Too many organizations today mistakenly think that such software itself can take care of their necessary workflow changes, hence they do not put enough effort into revamping their internal organizational processes before implementing new technology.

Few, if any, corporations can claim to have perfect processes, and by carefully breaking down budgeting and reporting processes into small components, each activity can be analyzed, then improved. The three major objectives of BPI are:

1. To make processes more effective by providing the desired results.
2. To make processes more efficient by minimizing the resources used.
3. To make processes more adaptable by changing when businesses and customer needs change.

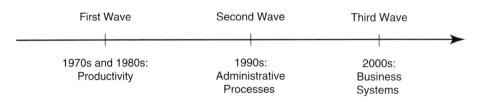

First Wave	Second Wave	Third Wave
1970s and 1980s: Productivity	1990s: Administrative Processes	2000s: Business Systems

EXHIBIT 1.1   Progression of Business Process Improvement

WHY FOCUS ON BUDGETING AND REPORTING PROCESSES?

This book covers BPI for budgeting and reporting. No company yet can claim a perfect score in these two areas. Throughout the years, many organizational processes (e.g., manufacturing, customer relationship management (CRM), etc.) have received considerable attention and resources for improvement. But, the processes that drive a company's budgeting and reporting activities have not changed much, except for more recent technology advances. Consequently, a large number of companies have invested in new budgeting and reporting software without giving any thought to also improving their internal processes. Many people even think that new technology alone will streamline their business. In most cases, this mind-set will dramatically reduce the return on investment (ROI) in any technology and it will *not* contribute to an analytical environment necessary to enhance a company's competitiveness.

For any improvement project to be successful, the goals should be clearly established before undertaking any activities, and that goes for budgeting and reporting process improvement as well, for these reasons:

- It helps prepare the organization to address future challenges.
- It aids in preparing a financial and statistical measurement system.
- It provides guidance in setting realistic targets that the organization can work toward, as well as a road map of how to reach them.
- It puts the budgeting and reporting activities in a system.
- It helps explain how budget input eventually leads to report output.
- It offers guidance as to why errors are made and how to avoid them.
- It provides a means to predict and manage change.
- It improves the company's competitiveness by improving key aspects of the planning and decision-making process.

POSITIVE EFFECTS OF BPI

A number of positive effects of BPI are clearly identifiable:

- Improved reliability of business processes
- Improved response times (e.g., ad hoc reports and on-the-fly forecasts)

- Lower costs
- Improved customer (i.e., users of reports/budgets) satisfaction
- Improved employee morale
- Reduced bureaucracy
- Improved quality of reporting
- Better financial control

IMPLEMENTING CHANGE

Change equals opportunity, but bringing about change is not easy, as it often is met with skepticism and resistance. However, as the positive effects of a successful budgeting and reporting process improvement become visible, the resulting benefits will far outweigh the initial difficulties of implementing the change. According to James Harrington, by many considered the father of BPI, there are 10 rules to follow to guide a change process:

1. There must be a vision of a desired future state that everyone sees and understands.
2. The organization must believe that change is important and valuable to its future.
3. Existing and potential barriers must be identified and removed.
4. The whole organization must be behind the strategy to achieve the vision.
5. Management has to model the process and set an example.
6. Training must be provided for the required new skills.
7. Measurement systems must be established so that results can be quantified.
8. Continuous feedback must be provided to everyone involved.
9. Coaching must be provided to correct undesirable behavior.
10. A recognition and reward system must be established to effectively reinforce desirable behavior.

Though these items were written to apply to full, organizationwide BPI and reengineering efforts, they can be applied to the budgeting and reporting process as well. This effort simply takes less time and resources than an organization wide change.

PHASES OF A BPI PROJECT

A BPI project can be divided into five logically organized phases (see Exhibit 1.2):

1. *Research.* Research current processes, and document the improvement opportunities so that the level of improvement achieved by the BPI project can be measured later. Wherever the research phase uncovers significant improvement opportunities, these will be documented and used in the "sales pitch" to the organization in phase 2.

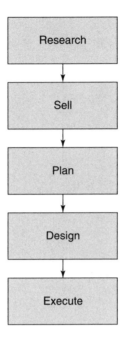

EXHIBIT 1.2   BPI Methodology

2. *Sell.* If the research phase uncovers enough improvement opportunities to make it worthwhile to go ahead with the BPI project, this phase focuses on creating a sales pitch to achieve management buy-in, and then to sell the project to the rest of the organization.

3. *Plan.* Create a detailed project plan that describes each activity in the project, including the people involved.

4. *Design.* Streamline old processes and design new ones, as required. An important part of this phase is to document any new processes.

5. *Execute.* Implement the new and improved processes, measure and record improvements, and make necessary adjustments.

Much of this book will focus on phase 4, the design of the business processes, as this is usually the greatest challenge for a company. The following delineates the methodology employed in the design phase:

1. Break up each process in subprocesses, activities, and tasks (see Exhibit 1.3).

2. Identify improvement opportunities:
   - By focusing on obviously weak areas.
   - By observing best practices, competitors, outside consultants, and other resources.

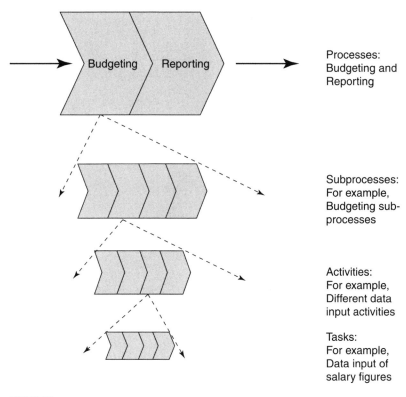

EXHIBIT 1.3   Business Process Components

3. Select changes to implement.
4. Adapt changes to own administrative processes and needs.
5. Document the new processes.

All the project phases come together in a BPI project plan and the accompanying documentation.

CORE BUDGETING AND REPORTING PROCESSES

Following the introductory chapters, this book discusses in detail how to improve your budgeting and reporting processes. But, before delving into a more detailed analysis of these processes, it is necessary to present an overview of the core activities typically involved in budgeting and reporting processes (see Exhibit 1.4). And as you start analyzing and redesigning your own processes, remember that a key part of BPI is to assign an individual as owner of each critical business process.

Strategic Planning

Reporting Workflow   Target Setting

Users Definition   Allocations

Integration Requirements
and Data Sources

Assumptions/Drivers

Defining Security

Deadlines

Budget Workflow

Type of Reports

Defining Corporate
Information Needs

Model and Process
Documentation

Defining Input Form
Layout and Functionality

Training Needs
for Users

Defining Version Control

Integrations to
Other Systems

Setting Deadlines

Forecasts

Defining Approvals and
Routing (approval workflow)

Budget Reports

EXHIBIT 1.4   Budgeting and Reporting Activities

CLOSING REMARKS

Finally, before moving on, it's important to look at some of the key factors that will be important to the success of your project. In particular, if you have already decided to go ahead with a BPI project, the following items should be on your mind as you start planning:

- *Ongoing support from management.* Don't start, or continue, a BPI project without first assuring that key decision makers are with you and will provide the necessary support.
- *Long-term commitment.* The last thing you want is to start a project and then discover that the people involved are not committed. This can be avoided or minimized by putting the right people on the team, as well as by good planning and information flow.
- *Effective implementation methodology.* All successful projects start with a plan. Don't underestimate the value of thinking about the big picture as well as the details, in terms of:
  - What you want to achieve
  - How it is going to be done
  - Timeline for implementation

- *Assigned process owners.* For each process that is part of the project, a process owner should be assigned. This will help ensure that there is one person to go to for related questions and information.

- *Measurement and feedback systems.* This is more important for larger BPI projects in which a significant investment is being made and for which it is important to measure the return on investment and the level of improvement achieved. Creating a feedback system through which information about progress and issues flow back and forth easily will help ensure success of the project.

- *Focus on the process.* During a BPI project, many issues and problems will come up. Software solutions, interpersonal conflicts, and so on can easily overshadow the objectives. Along the way, don't lose sight of the processes that you have set out to improve.

You will read more about the these items in Chapter 7.

2

WHEN BPI IS VALUABLE

A BPI project will require a commitment of time and resources from the people on the process improvement team, so before you decide to implement a BPI project, you should make sure that the desired outcome of the project outweighs the cost and efforts necessary to implement it (see cost-benefit study in Chapter 28).

PRECONDITIONS FOR BPI

These examples of typical preconditions are good indicators that a financial business process improvement project may be worthwhile:

- *Too much dependence on IT staff to manage data and to write reports.* Most people will have experienced this. Valuable financial data sits more or less unavailable in corporate databases because only one or two IT people (or other technically inclined employees) understand the report writer formulas and can change existing reports or write new ones. And, if data needs to be deleted or copied, the financial staff has to call on their counterparts in the IT departments. The results of this inefficient process are:
  - Wasted time
  - Higher costs
  - Frustrated employees
  - Slower decision-making

  This precondition is easily identifiable, and if found to be a problem in your company, should earn a prominent place on your BPI to-do list.

- *Lack of functional budgeting and reporting software.* This is a technology issue. Beginning in the 1990s, software in this area has come a long way. Today, many commercially available solutions offer powerful functionality for everything from workflow to budget input screen customizations, report writing and Web-based access (see Appendix C for a list of software and vendors). However, the majority of companies still do not have highly efficient budgeting and reporting software in place. Or, in some cases, companies have acquired a great budgeting solution, but have not made it part of—or integrated it well with—the reporting package. Some of the resulting inefficiencies are:
  - Manual data transfer between databases
  - Manual report distribution

- Wasted time
- Delayed reporting

If a software upgrade is identified as one of the components for improvement, typically it will raise a cost-benefit question; and if affordable, it should most likely be part of the BPI project.

- *Lack of good reports and analytical views for decision makers.* Independent of how good or bad a company's current budgeting and reporting software is, managers still complain that they don't get the right type of reports, and that they lack highly analytical views (graphs with drill-down, ranking, and other needed capabilities). Best practices have shown that top management should be spending more time studying key performance indicators (KPIs) and exception reports than lengthy financial statements. And a lot of financial information (e.g., a 12-month trend) is better presented as a graphical line chart than as 12 columns of numbers "hidden" in a financial report. Lack of good analytical reports and charts usually leads to:

- Lack of managerial interest in reports
- Harder-to-find trends
- Reduced understanding of how the business is doing and where it is going.

Addressing these issues requires first, defining key performance indicators and, second, developing a set of graphs and charts that are truly helpful.

- *Poor access to budgets and reports.* It doesn't matter how efficient and streamlined other parts of the budgeting and reporting are if there are major roadblocks to submitting budgets and forecasts or monthly management comments. Another access-related bottleneck occurs in the distribution of reports to managers across the organization. For many companies, collection and distribution of information is a major headache, yet no major initiatives have yet been undertaken to improve the situation. The results include:

- Frustrated employees
- Lengthier budget cycles
- Lengthier reporting cycles
- Slower decision making

Improving access to budgets and reports can, today, usually be taken care of by utilizing Web-based budgeting and reporting software (if employees are in multiple locations) or by streamlining formats for input, reports, and the process for data collection and distribution.

- *Poor integration of strategies and planning process.* The problem with most planning and budgeting processes is that they are poorly integrated with the corporate strategy. In many companies, a clearly defined strategy has been developed by top management, and involves an extensive bottom-up budgeting process that eventually returns consolidated numbers to top management, where they are then compared to the targets set by the corporate strategy (see Exhibit 2.1). If the numbers are not satisfactory, department managers are typically

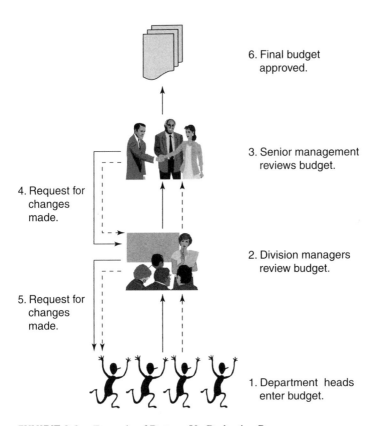

6. Final budget approved.

3. Senior management reviews budget.

4. Request for changes made.

2. Division managers review budget.

5. Request for changes made.

1. Department heads enter budget.

EXHIBIT 2.1   Example of Bottom-Up Budgeting Process

asked to adjust their budgets and resubmit them. This can happen multiple times before top management targets are met and the budget is eventually frozen. These inefficiencies can lead to:

• Demotivated and frustrated line managers
• Delayed budgets
• Reduced interest and participation from line managers

The solution is a best practices approach called *top-down/bottom-up budgeting* (see Exhibit 2.2), whereby corporate strategy is communicated to all parties involved in the budgeting process and cascaded down to division/departments so that lower-level managers have specific targets to work toward as they create their budgets.

• *Poor integration and coordination between financial functions and systems.* This is both a people and a systems problem. The first issue refers to the fact that a major communications gap exists between people in different departments and positions across the company. Managers whose responsibilities lie in one area, such as budgeting, often don't want to, or are not encouraged to, discuss

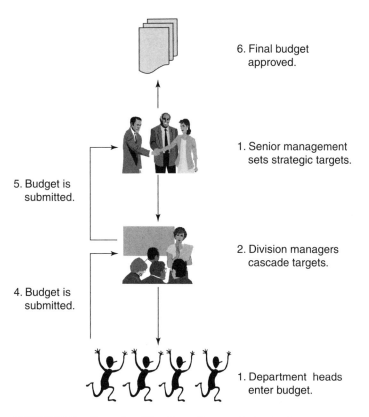

6. Final budget
approved.

1. Senior management
sets strategic targets.

5. Budget is
submitted.

2. Division managers
cascade targets.

4. Budget is
submitted.

1. Department heads
enter budget.

EXHIBIT 2.2   Example of Top-Down/Bottom-Up Budgeting Process

improvements, problems, and so on with managers responsible for other areas, such as month-end closing and reporting. This often also relates to the second issue mentioned, the fact that there is poor integration between different software systems (e.g., between general ledger, budgeting, consolidation, and analysis tools). The resulting inefficiencies can cause:

- Retyping of data from one system to another
- Lack of rich information from different operational areas in management reports
- Poorly integrated budgeting and reporting processes
- No common vision for streamlined and high-value analytics

This situation can be improved when top managers provide stronger leadership in the financial area. They can also offer incentives and encourage coordination and improvements between the different finance functions. The IT department can assist in the integration of systems and in selecting software platforms and packages that can easily "talk" to each other.

- *Disconnect between corporate and local processes.* This relates to organizations with multiple entities managed by a corporate headquarters. In terms of budgeting and reporting processes, the focus of this book, problems typically relate to two different situations:

  1. Corporate enforces too much of its own analytics requirements (e.g., corporate chart of accounts, specific budget line items, etc.) to the local entities. Resulting inefficiencies can be seen in:
     - Demotivated and uncooperative local financial managers
     - Corporate numbers that are often incorrect and unsupported
  2. Corporate executes too little influence on the analytics processes in the organizational entities. Resulting inefficiencies can be seen in:
     - Lack of information about local operations
     - Poorly consolidated views of the business (for both actual reporting and budgets)
     - Difficulties in communicating because of inconsistent use of terminology (trying to compare "apples and bananas" in consolidated financial statements)

  The goal is to find a "middle road" between two much and too little influence on local operations. To that end, some companies have put all organizational entities on the same software system(s), to simplify data integration and reporting.

WHAT BPI CAN DO FOR A COMPANY

The rule of thumb is not to embark on any BPI project until you have convinced both yourself and other key people in the organization that the project will be well worth the invested time and effort (see Chapters 4 and 6). To do this, look beyond whether or not you should pursue a BPI project for your analytics processes, and consider the potential benefits of such a project. The following are examples of typical BPI benefits:

Benefit (Output)	Improvement Activity (Output)
Establish analytics processes that reflect and support management planning, control and decision making.	• Link strategies to budgeting and reporting processes. • Link compensation to performance in budgeting and reporting processes.
Maximize ROI for resources, such as people and technology.	• Offer adequate training. • Document key processes. • Invest in the right software for the job.
Speed up budgeting, reporting and decision-making processes by optimizing access to information.	• Utilize Web-enabled software. • Offer a Web-based portal for budget input, reports, data mapping, and loading.

Benefit (Output)	Improvement Activity
	• Offer automated e-mail distribution of reports and related messages when more convenient for users.
Optimize time spent on data input and report analysis by focusing managers and users on key information.	• Improve budget input screen format and content. • Improve report format and content. • Provide graphics and ad hoc reporting tools. • Create a chart of accounts that captures the information needed.
Save time and money by improving workflow for analytics processes.	• Implement top-down/bottom-up budgeting processes. • Automate and streamline adjustments and eliminations. • Remove unnecessary budget iterations and report formats.
Provide managers with information that is timely, accurate, and from relevant data sources.	• Optimize process to load and (if necessary) convert/transform from original data source to reporting tool. • Automate validation and/or approval of data from different sources.

The BPI project will become increasingly valuable to your organization for each of these items in the budgeting and reporting processes that you need to improve:

Improvement Item	Enabler
Support superior control and decision making, to give the organization a competitive advantage.	• Technology • Control elements • Improve reports
Effectively use available resources.	• Training • Right people • Workflow • Best practices
Speed up budget process and financial reporting (and meet all deadlines).	• Technology • Chart of accounts • Detail • Structure • Bottlenecks/workflow
Eliminate or reduce errors.	• Technology • Control reports • Business rules

Improvement Item	Enabler
Increase understanding of budgeting and reporting processes.	• Communication • Training • Documentation
Put tools in place that will automate and simplify process.	• Technology • Workflow
Put tools and models in place that are easy to use and understand.	• Design • Training
Create budgeting and reporting processes that can easily be altered to adapt to the organization's changing information needs.	• Account structure (chart of accounts) • Technology • Communicate needs and measure

BPI OVERVIEW

In order to achieve a business process improvement objective, you need to take three steps:

1. Divide your budgeting and reporting processes into individual components.
2. Identify the particular areas where improvement can be achieved with the resources you have available.
3. Apply process enablers to improve the targeted activities.

In the following list, these three steps were used to create a simplified example that shows processes, improvement opportunities, and enablers:

Processes	Improvement Opportunities	Enablers
Open budget	Reduce input errors	Technology
Target setting	Improve speed	Best practices
Data entry	Increase detail	Process workflow
Control	Decrease detail	Human resources
Approval	Reduce keystrokes	
Close budget	Improve ease of use	
Revisions	Increase value of information	
Run reports	Provide targets	
Distribute reports	Improve communication	
Analysis	Increase ownership	
Action	Provide documentation	

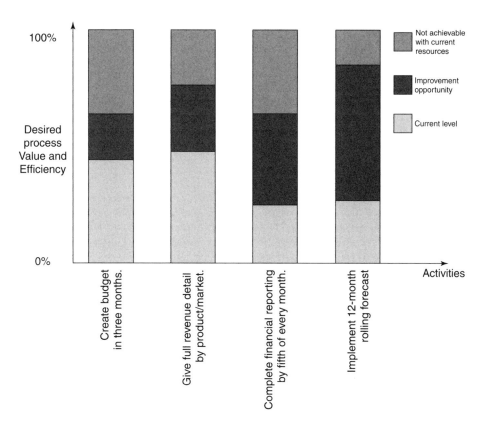

EXHIBIT 2.3   Example of Identification of Improvement Opportunities

For each of the processes in the first column it is possible to analyze the improvement opportunities (goals) that apply, and graphically represent them (see Exhibit 2.3).

This type of diagram can illustrate to people in the organization where you are now and where you want to be after the project. When you do this, however, it is important to be realistic. Aim for obtainable targets, somewhere between current performance and absolute perfection.

In Part Two, you will find a detailed analysis of typical budgeting and reporting processes that will give you good ideas for conducting your own analysis, which will subsequently help you to identify improvement opportunities.

3

SMALL AND LARGE PROJECTS AND ASSOCIATED RESOURCES

Busy financial managers today do not have the time to take on a BPI project that is too long and complex; and if they try, chances are, it will not be completed. Therefore this chapter introduces three BPI project categories to provide examples of projects that can fit the needs and resources of various types of organizations:

1. *Short project*, for those with very little time (a few weeks) and few resources.
2. *Medium project*, for those with a month or more available and a reasonable amount of resources.
3. *Long project*, for those with several months to a year to spend, and a solid resource base.

Most likely you are not undertaking this BPI project because you have too much time on your hands or because senior management has expressed that it would be "nice" to improve certain budgeting- and reporting-related processes. Probably there are some fairly significant problems or inefficiencies in the company today that are slowing down your budget process, delaying implementation of new analytics software, or causing other issues mentioned earlier in Part One. The question at this point is not whether you need to make improvements, but rather which improvements to make; how to undertake them; and how much time, money, and effort you should (or can) put into it.

It is important to be aware of the constraints that can limit the scope of your project, so that you can choose the project type that will most likely succeed for you. Be realistic with yourself! One of the most common reasons a project fails to reach its objectives is that it grows too large, time-consuming, and complex. It is much better to identify one or a few processes to improve, and fully succeed with the project, than to try to "change the world" and fail at it. For example, if you have limited time and resources, and the major problem the finance department is facing is an old, messy chart of accounts that can't properly support current budgeting and reporting needs, then make this item your first project. If there are other improvements you would also like to make to support better analytics processes, you can always create other projects later.

With the preceding discussion in mind and armed with realistic expectations, let us look at some high-level examples of what we define as short-, medium-, and long-term projects (see Exhibits 3.1, 3.2, and 3.3).

Improvement Goal	Project Activities	Time Commitment	Resources
Create a chart of accounts (COA) that properly supports current and future budgeting and needs.	1. Form a project group. 2. Define detailed goals. 3. Create new COA. 4. Test new COA. 5. Make adjustments. 6. Get approval.	5–10 days	*Small Company* Could comprise as few as one or two people who are highly familiar with both the accounting system and analytics needs.
			Larger Company Need to include key people from each related area: accounting, finance, analytics, senior management. Can also be beneficial to include an outside consultant with additional expertise.

EXHIBIT 3.1   Short Project Example

Improvement Goal	Project Activities	Time Commitment	Resources
Chart of Accounts (see Exhibit 3.1) Best Practices	1. Form a project group (include outside consultant if additional skills and ideas are needed). 2. Implement changes. 3. Document new practices.	15–20 weeks	*Small Company* If knowledgeable staff are available, the project can be handled by two to three people.
			Larger Company Expect to include 5 to 10 people at different stages, and most likely an outside consultant to drive the project, mediate, advise, and so on.

EXHIBIT 3.2   Medium Project Example

Improvement Goal	Project Activities	Time Commitment	Resources
Chart of Accounts (see Exhibit 3.1) Best Practices (see Exhibit 3.2) Automation with software	1. Software selection process 2. Model planning 3. Software implementation 4. Training	18–25 weeks	*Small Company* A minimum of two people should be involved in the software selection, implementation, and training processes.
			Larger Company Representatives from top-level financial management, accounting staff, and department heads should be involved in the selection process, to ensure solid buy-in from the organization. Include two to four power users in the training.

EXHIBIT 3.3   Long Project Example

4

RETURN ON INVESTMENT OF BPI PROJECTS

In the previous chapter, we looked at examples of projects of different duration for companies of different sizes. Exhibit 4.1 illustrates the potential investment and ROI of a BPI project.

So many variables (including expertise and dedication of involved employees) can affect the level of success and ROI of a project that it can be extremely difficult to accurately predict specific dollar amounts. Depending on your company size and the scope of the BPI project, you should create a more detailed ROI calculation. The ROI calculation for a medium-length project in a large company can be seen in Exhibit 4.2.

Based on Exhibit 4.2, the accumulated return on the BPI investment over a number of years could be as follows:

	Year 1	Year 2	Year 3	Year 4	Year 5
ROI	–25%	50%	125%	200%	267%

Armed with this type of ROI analysis, it can be a lot easier to validate the cost of a BPI project when presenting it to top management.

Project Category	Company Size	
	Small	**Large**
Short	Investment: $10,000 ROI: $30,000	Investment: $30,000 ROI: $90,000
Medium	Investment: $50,000 ROI: $150,000	Investment: $150,000 ROI: $450,000
Long	Investment: $150,000 ROI: $450,000	Investment: $1,000,000 ROI: $3,000,000

EXHIBIT 4.1   Project Categories

	Number of hours	Average Dollars per Hour	Cost
Expenses			
Project Management	400	$100	$40,000
COA Improvement	200	$100	$20,000
Best Practices for Budgeting	300	$100	$30,000
Software Evaluation	100	$100	$10,000
Software Purchase	—	—	$100,000
Software Implementation	400	$200	$80,000
Documentation	200	$100	$20,000
Total	**1,600**	—	**$300,000**
Annual ROI			
Faster Budgeting Process	150	$100	$15,000
Quicker Decision-Making	—	—	$100,000
Better Information in Reports (due to new COA, redesign, etc.)	—	—	$100,000
Easier to Write and Maintain Reports	100	$100	$10,000
Total Annual ROI	—	—	**$225,000**

EXHIBIT 4.2 ROI Example

5

BEST PRACTICES, TRENDS, AND TECHNOLOGY

TECHNOLOGY TRENDS

Technology is a key enabler for most business process improvement projects. Major advances took place in the budgeting and reporting software space in the 1990s; now, in the twenty-first century, a number of new and promising technologies are available to further help automate and streamline analytics processes. The following sections describe some of the technology trends that will impact budgeting and reporting activities, as well as other activities in most businesses.

Prebuilt Business Intelligence Tools

Analytics tools, especially online analytical processing (OLAP) software, have been around for many years. However, in the late '90s and in the early part of the new millennium, this technology saw a surge in popularity. Much of this increased interest was no doubt caused by the fact that a large number of companies were finishing up their implementations of a new enterprise resource planning (ERP) system and came to the realization that they could not get good visibility of all the valuable data they were now capturing in the new system. The virtual nonexistence of user-friendly, yet powerful report writers and analytical tools as an integral part of new ERP systems led financial managers and analysts right back to the analytical tool they had been using for years—Excel spreadsheets.

However, as they deal with larger volumes of data with more information attached to each transaction, spreadsheet users all over the world are discovering that spreadsheets were not built to analyze data from large ERP systems. This, coupled with new and improved business intelligence technologies, has led to a surge in interest in OLAP tools and powerful report writers.

Already, many very successful business intelligence (BI) software implementations have opened up a whole new world of analysis capabilities for their users (see Exhibit 5.1). Unfortunately, many of these implementations have come at a high cost to the customer because of the challenges of properly integrating a third-party BI tool with an ERP system. Further, these challenges have led to less than optimal data availability and integrity in the BI tools, meaning that even though the result is many

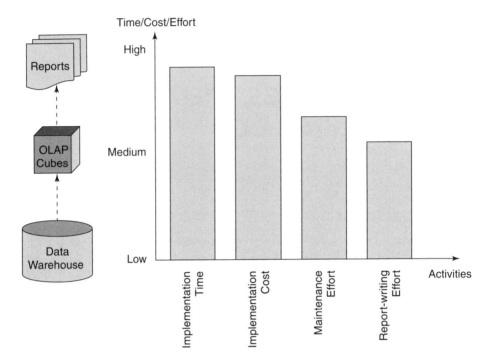

EXHIBIT 5.1   Traditional Approach to BI for ERP

times better than without the analytical platform, more is still needed to see full-blown use of both the data in the ERP system and the features available in the BI software.

The potential solution to these issues is now available from an increasing number of ERP vendors, BI vendors, and system integrators. The solution can be labeled *pre-built business intelligence*, or PBI, (the term has already been used by a number of vendors and experts in the BI industry). What is PBI? In simple terms, it means that the integration of the ERP system (or any other valuable data sources for that matter) and the business intelligence tool, and in many cases also the reports or views that users typically desire, have been prebuilt before the implementation (see Exhibit 5.2). In other words, much of the tedious and error-prone work of former BI implementations has been eliminated. How is this possible? In many cases, the ERP vendors themselves have entered into an OEM agreement with a BI software vendor, and then sat down and linked the tool to the different ERP modules. And, because ERP vendors are already familiar with the typical reports and graphs customers want to use to analyze data, (for example, accounts receivable or sales order processing modules), they can also predefine a number of these and deliver them with the BI tool. In other words, the customer can get BI "out-of-the-box," instead of BI four months and $100,000 in consulting charges later. Obviously, customizations and other work will be required to get a good PBI solution up and running, but the main

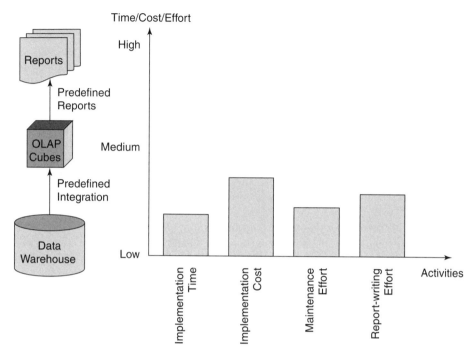

EXHIBIT 5.2   PBI Approach to BI for ERP Systems

advantage is that you will get it a lot sooner and for a lot smaller investment in consulting than for a nonintegrated BI solution.

Because of the apparent attractiveness of PBI solutions, ERP vendors, along with systems integrators and other technology companies, are rapidly developing standard integrations, scheduling devices, and predefined reports that make a BI tool into a PBI tool.

In summary, a large number of companies can now analyze their ERP data with powerful business intelligence software at a lower cost than ever before, and with better integrations to the data sources, thanks to the emergence of PBI solutions.

Open Databases

One of the most important technology trends affecting BPI is the movement of vendors toward commercial database platforms for their business applications. Because analytics software is only as good as the data available to it, it is of key importance that data can be accessed easily and directly via analytical tools, or transferred to a data warehouse.

Though there is no industry-standard definition of what an *open database platform* is, most technical people would agree that an open database is software that facilitates structured data storage and that can be populated or read from by using one or more commonly known data extraction tools (you can read more about modern ETL tools later in this chapter).

For more than a decade, it has been (and still is) common to transfer data between databases, such as between a general ledger and a consolidation and reporting or a budgeting tool, by using a standard text file (often referred to as a *flat file*). As long as both the source and destination database can accept the text file format, it should be possible to transfer data. Most modern databases, such as Oracle, Microsoft SQL Server, Sybase, and DB2 (you can find a list of popular databases in Part Five), support more sophisticated data transfer procedures than simply producing and loading text files.

Perhaps the most common underlying technology standard for data integration is Online Database Connectivity (ODBC). If a database supports this standard, it is relatively easy to make a direct connection between two systems (although usually it will still be necessary to do a data conversion before the data can be loaded into the source database). In addition, most modern databases that we consider "open" and easy to read from, support Standard Query Language (SQL). Using SQL, a technical consultant can write or customize an integration between two open databases and facilitate a direct and automated data transfer process.

Budgeting and reporting tools might depend on updates from the data source(s) as frequently as several times per day, and in the future, close to real-time access. This means that it is critical that data transfer (and possible conversions) be fully automated and that they only trigger manual (human) intervention when there are exceptions or issues that cannot be handled by the business rules in the extraction, transformation, and loading program. This type of automation lacked integration capabilities in the past, hence it was very labor-intensive to keep them up to date. Today, however, an increasing number of companies have replaced their old proprietary transaction systems with new ones that allow for automated integration with data warehouses and data marts, thereby opening up their data for easy and automated integration with analytics software.

Common Data Exchange Formats

The main obstacle to providing decision makers with a single report writer interface that has direct access to all the information that resides in their company's financial databases is that different software vendors have never been good at extracting data and delivering it to each other's databases. Historically, it has been the job of the company's IT department to move data from one system to another. In its simplest sense, this job has consisted of creating an export file from the data source and importing it to the other system.

The most common file format that has been (and still is) used is the text file. In this context, a text file is a list transactions, wherein each transaction is a row, and each row consists of a number of information fields (such as account number, period, amount, cost center, currency code, etc.) separated by a common character such as a comma, space, or semicolon. In many cases, however, moving data from one database to another is not as simple as exporting and importing files. Often, systems have conflicting codes; for example, the same account number can refer to two different revenue or expense categories in two systems. In particular, this is a common problem in large companies with multiple subsidiaries that use systems from different vendors. In the case of conflicting code systems, a data conversion (sometimes referred to as *data cleansing* in data warehouse projects) is necessary to make it possible for two or more systems to exchange information. In a worst-case scenario, data has to be manually reentered from one system to another (see Exhibit 5.3).

In most companies, the IT department will write conversion programs to automate the conversion of data files. In a better scenario, one of the two systems exchanging data can convert the data file to the other system's required format as the file is being exported or imported. Also, a number of third-party data conversion tools are available today that have predefined or user-defined links to popular systems and that can save a company's IT department a lot of time and money (see the ETL product and vendor list in Appendix C).

ETL Tools

Increasingly, software vendors (in particular, budgeting software, financial reporting software, OLAP software, and data warehouse vendors) recognize the need of organizations today to move large volumes of data smoothly and efficiently among databases; and in recent years, a number of powerful new tools have become available. Many of these tools have been referred to as extraction, transformation, and

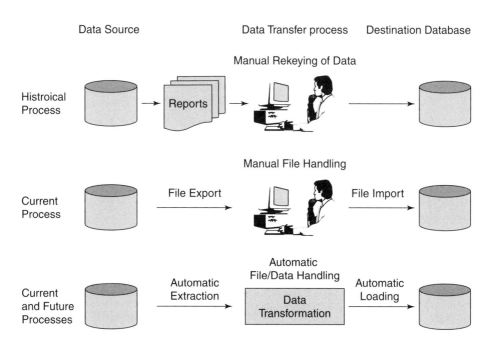

EXHIBIT 5.3 Evolution of Data Transfer

loading tools (ETL). Setting up an effective data extraction, transformation, and loading process can take up to 70 to 75 percent of the time spent on a typical warehousing project.

ETL tools automate the sometimes extremely laborious (manual) job of moving data from one data source/data base (e.g., a transaction database like the general ledger) to another (e.g., a data warehouse or data mart). In general, an ETL tool does the following:

1. It reads data from an input source (relational table, flat file, etc.).
2. It passes the information through a business-rule-based process to modify, enhance, or eliminate different data elements.
3. It writes the output result out to another relational table (e.g., in a data warehouse), flat file, and so on.

A number of tools perform the ETL functions with greater or less functionality in a certain area, such as extraction, transformation, or loading; but true ETL tools are strong in all three areas.

A good example of an ETL tool is the Data Transformation Services (DTS) utility, which is included with the Microsoft SQL Server database management system (DBMS). The tool comes with a number of prebuilt links to make it faster and easier to connect to other popular databases such as Oracle, Sybase, UNIX-based databases, and Microsoft Access. This capability makes it faster and easier to set up integrations; it also allows for scheduling, so the ETL process can take place automatically at any given point in time and with a predefined frequency.

More recently, we have seen the emergence of common data exchange languages, on which governments, information standards organizations, software companies, and different interest groups from all major industries are cooperating. Probably one of the most significant of these data exchange languages is the eXtensible Markup Language (XML) and eXtensive Business Reporting Language (XBRL), a subset of XML specifically developed to ease exchange of *business* information among different applications. The formal definition of XBRL is: "A standards-based electronic language for business information, financial reporting, and analysis." Standards like XML and XBRL take data handling a major step forward from the HyperText Markup Language (HTML), the current Web standard also used for web-enabling formatted reports or other financial information. With the new XML standard, plus the related ones specifically developed for accounting and financial information, it will be possible search and extract for sample industry or competitor information from across the Web. Because a layer of business logic can be applied to a search, instead of returning information from *all* of your competitors, it can, for example, filter out only those that have a market capitalization higher than $500 million or total revenues higher than $200 million (see Exhibit 5.4).

XBRL standards (which describe the business language) have been, or are currently being, developed for the following areas:

- Assurance schedules
- Authoritative literature

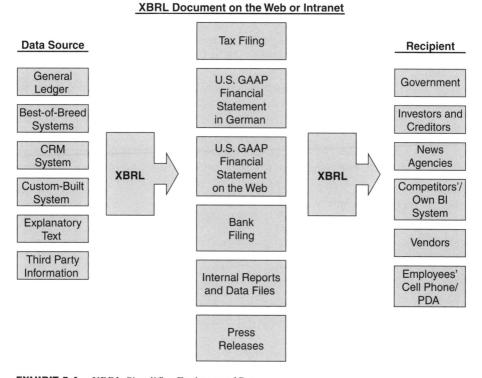

EXHIBIT 5.4   XBRL Simplifies Exchange of Data

- Business reporting (balanced scorecard, benchmarking, etc.)
- Credit line reporting
- Economic indicators and demographics
- Financial statements
- General Ledger
- Journal entry reporting
- Mutual fund performance
- Performance-related Press Releases
- Risk reporting
- Regulatory filings
- Tax filings

The positive impact of XBRL on financial reporting can be very significant. Imagine decision makers in a company being able to turn on their computers (or handheld devices) in the morning and see fresh information on their screens that has automatically been extracted (thanks to XBRL) from competitors' or partners' press releases and regulatory filings. And because XBRL contains specific information about the type of data being extracted, the BI software can take the data and put it into the right context. In other words, if a manager is looking at a key performance indicator report with actual-to-budget variances and actual-to-industry or -competitor variances, the industry and competitor information can be included automatically thanks to XBRL (see Exhibit 5.5).

Further, because of the specific information contained within an XBRL tag (part of the XBRL code that is linked to financial or text information), it is possible to automatically locate and retrieve pieces of information within a report/document and pull it out to use it somewhere else, for example in a BI system (see Exhibit 5.6).

All major industries now have international organizations that develop XBRL tags specific to their industries' financial and other information. These industry-specific tags are known as *taxonomies*.

Some key benefits of XBRL include:

- Enables faster access to external information.
- Makes it easier to create integrations to third-party systems and documents.

KPI—Key Performance Indicators
Company: SPORTY Manufacturing
June 2001

	Actual Jun-01	Budget Jun-01	Variance in $	Variance in %	Industry Average	Competitor XYZ
Net Revenue	$1,300	$1,100	$200	15%	$922	$875
Average Revenue per Employee	$260	$220	$40	15%	$85	$80
Gross Margin	$400	$350	$50	13%	$280	$200
Average Gross Margin per Product	$25	$20	$5	20%	$22	$15
Online Sales as a % of Total Sales	$15	$20	($5)	–33%	$5	$10
Cash Flow	$35	$30	$5	14%	$28	$15
Sales Pipeline	$3,000	$4,000	($1,000)	–33%	na	na

EXHIBIT 5.5   Sample KPI Report

Financial Report Example

Balance Sheet
Company XYZ

	Period Ending 12/31/2001	Period Ending 11/30/2001
Cash and Cash Equivalents	$235,000	$238,000

Conversion to XBRL

Simplified XBRL Example

```
<group>
<group type="currentAssets.cashandCashEquivalents">
<item period="2001-12-31">$235,000 </item>
<item period="2001-11-30">$238,000 </item>
</group>
```

EXHIBIT 5.6   XBRL Example

- Saves cost by reducing development time.
- Saves costs and potential errors by eliminating manual data entry.

In the coming years, as legacy applications are phased out and new software and integration standards are adopted, it will be easier to move data between a company's own systems or between the databases of different organizations. For business intelligence, this means that decision makers and analysts will have easier and faster access to frequently updated information, which ultimately should support quicker and better decision making.

Using Data Marts and Data Warehouses to Enhance Business Intelligences

Chief financial officers, controllers, analysts, and other high-end users of financial information in a company will agree that their ERP software was not built with easy budgeting and reporting in mind. More than a decade ago, it was common to have isolated financial modules for each accounting area, to use multiple report writers to get information out of the different modules, and, typically, to do budgeting in Excel.

Today, most companies have an ERP system in place that provides highly integrated accounting databases. Report writers can access data from multiple modules and integrate it in information-rich reports. Many vendors now also have budgeting and reporting tools that can directly access several, or all, of their accounting modules (see Exhibit 5.7).

1. The Past — "Data"
Isolated Financial Systems

2. Today — "Information"
ERP-Focused Integrations

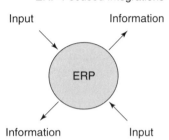

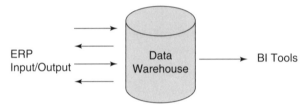

3. The Future — "Knowledge"
Data Warehouse-Focused Integrations

EXHIBIT 5.7   Evolution of Financial Systems

It is now increasingly popular to gather all the significant data from the ERP system and load it into a data warehouse or a data mart and then connect report writers and analysis tools to these to create a more consistent and knowledge-oriented environment.

For many years now companies have been deploying data warehouses as a means to facilitate common data storage for better reporting and analysis. A data warehouse can be defined as a collection of data designed to support management decision making. In the past, a majority of these implementation projects have been known to be slow, complex, and often very expensive. Data warehousing activities have, therefore, for the most part, been found only in large companies with a particularly strong need for the technology and with enough resources to build and support it. Now, many recent trends and technology developments are making data warehousing a hot topic in a wider variety of companies. Some of these trends are:

- *Business intelligence push.* The popularity of BI tools (here referring to reporting and analysis software) are pushing data warehouse initiatives to provide a common, easily accessible data source.
- *Technological advances.* Adoption of open database platforms and powerful integration tools makes it easier and less expensive to build and maintain data warehouses.

- *Reduced prices.* Increased competition (from large database vendors like Oracle and Microsoft) and easier-to-use technologies are lowering the cost of data warehousing.

Data warehouses contain a wide variety of data that present a coherent picture of business conditions at a single point in time. Development of a data warehouse includes development of systems to extract data from operating systems, plus installation of a warehouse database system that provides data storage and gives managers flexible access to the data. In sum, the term *data warehousing* generally refers to combining many different databases across an entire enterprise.

Data mart is another term frequently used in connection with analytics tools. A data mart (also spelled datamart) can be defined as a database, or collection of databases, designed to help managers make strategic decisions about their business. Whereas a data warehouse combines databases across an entire enterprise, data marts are usually smaller and focus on a particular subject or department. Some data marts, often called *dependent data marts,* are subsets of larger data warehouses.

In order to provide coherent, rich and timely data to a company's BI tool, many organizations—in particular larger ones—have found it essential to gather all the data from different transactional sources in a data warehouse that can feed their BI tool. Advantages of gathering data in a data warehouse include:

- A single source for important data
- Consistent definitions
- Well-documented relationships
- Coordinated cut-off times

Your company's reporting capabilities are going to be only as good as the data available to the front-end analysis tools in place (see product and vendor list in Appendix C). Most modern financial analysis tools use OLAP data cubes as their database, to provide flexible views and fast drill-down and querying capabilities. These OLAP cubes (often called data marts because each contains a specific set of related data) either can be built or populated directly from the transaction source (e.g., a budgeting and reporting database, accounts payable, sales order processing, accounts receivable, customer relationship management, etc.), or they can be fed from a full-fledged data warehouse.

Depending on the size and scope, a data warehouse project can take as little as an hour's work and a few thousand dollars in software, to build a specific data mart from a transaction system that has out-of-the-box OLAP cube generation features, to a multiyear effort that can cost millions of dollars and entail loading data from all core enterprise databases into a very large data warehouse. Exhibit 5.8 shows how data warehouses have changed to become much more effective information stores for BI tools.

Vendors and companies have realized that to link a front-end reporting tool directly to each different transactional database (such as the general ledger, accounts payable, accounts receivable, sales order entry, budget software, etc.) can be a daunting task, so many opt for putting a data warehouse "on top" of the transaction systems,

Past	Present
Decentralized system	Centralized and integrated
Static users	Scaleable
Low security concerns	High security concerns
Mostly batch updates	More real time
Noncritical availability	More critical availability (24 hours a day/7 days a week)
Internal data sources	Includes external data sources

EXHIBIT 5.8   Evolution of Data Warehouses

and then integrating the reporting software with the data warehouse. The following are the different integration options (see Exhibit 5.9):

- Integrate a single reporting tool directly with the transaction sources.
- Integrate several different reporting tools with the different transaction sources (often based on which technology or reporting tool a transaction system vendor supports).
- Use several different reporting tools with the different transaction sources and provide the user with a single, portal-based interface to all the analytics tools.
- Use the reporting tools that come with the transaction systems you have (e.g., your CRM system might offer graphing and querying, and your ERP solution might come with its own analytics tools).
- Use a single (or more) report writer that integrates with all your data through the use of a data warehouse that links to all transaction systems.

Because it is the goal of most companies to take better advantage of all their rich data sources by providing employees easy and fast access to data, to enable them to make optimal decisions, in many cases it will make the most sense to gather and organize all the data in a single data warehouse (often with many smaller data marts feeding off it). This approach allows companies to implement on a single database platform (the data warehouse), to standardize on one or two tools for analytics, and use a portal as a single, web-based front end (see Exhibit 5.10). Doing so will save costs, reduce training requirements, provide faster access to corporate information, and more.

Merging Report Writers and Analysis Tools

Financial reporting has gone through several phases since its inception half a century ago. This has resulted in three different types of reporting tools still in use today.

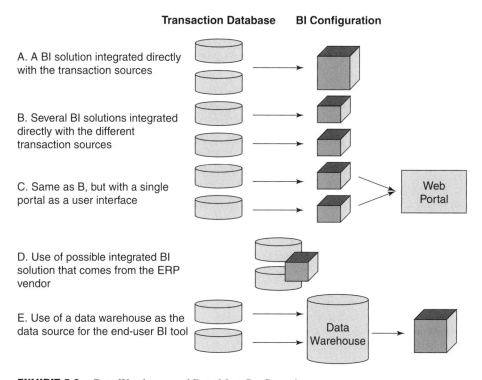

Transaction Database **BI Configuration**

A. A BI solution integrated directly with the transaction sources

B. Several BI solutions integrated directly with the different transaction sources

C. Same as B, but with a single portal as a user interface

Web Portal

D. Use of possible integrated BI solution that comes from the ERP vendor

E. Use of a data warehouse as the data source for the end-user BI tool

Data Warehouse

EXHIBIT 5.9   Data Warehouse and Data Mart Configurations

These can be categorized by the type of end-user interaction they allow (see Exhibit 5.11):

- Standard reports (static, specific format)
- Semicustom reports (customizable with parameters and variables)
- Ad hoc reports (allows drill-down and customization on the fly)

For years, the common way of retrieving and organizing data from a financial database has been to write (or "code," as many people call it, due to the technical expertise required to use many report writers) reports. If your system has a strong report writer, this approach will take you far in supplying the organization with good, informative reports upon which to base control and decision making. However, the problem with a typical financial report (such as a profit and loss report, a balance sheet, or a sales report) is that it is *static*. This means that you can, for example, read from your report that salary expenses for the company are 20 percent above budget this month; but the question that should immediately follow is *why*? With the typical financial report writer at your disposal, you would, in this case, have to run a more detailed report for each department to find out which department(s) have caused the high salary expense variance—that is, of course, if someone has already written such

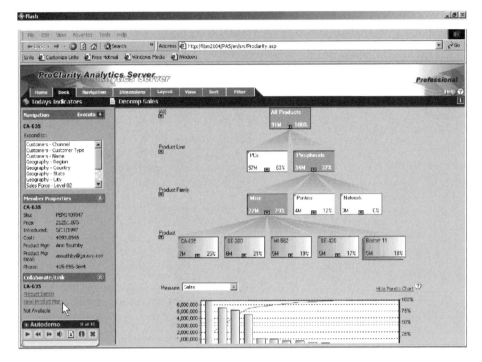

EXHIBIT 5.10   Example of a BI Web Portal

a report for you; otherwise you hopefully know how to write reports so you can create one yourself. Once you run the report for each department, and discover that department 100 caused the high variance, the next step is to figure out what lies hidden behind the salary account in this department. At this point, most users will have to move over to the payroll system and run a detailed employee level report there—that is, of course, if you know how to run reports in the payroll software.

All the wasted time and effort just exemplified, which has been true for so many financial software users, is becoming history for an increasing number of companies. A new breed of analytics tools that can be categorized as financial ad hoc report writers are entering the market. The tools offer such functionality as:

- *Drill-down, drill-around, and drill-through.* Enabling report users to get their questions answered without running additional reports
- *Direct spreadsheet integration.* Providing a high level of formatting and end-user friendliness (see Exhibit 5.12)
- *Fully web-based interface.* For both report writing and report processing, and for drill-down from a Web browser
- *Intelligent tree hierarchies.* These are becoming increasingly popular to automate report writing and drill-down. Intelligent trees can also provide formatting, automatic maintenance of hierarchies, and more.

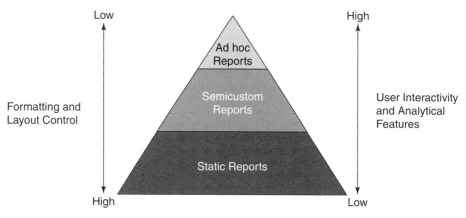

EXHIBIT 5.11   Report Writer Categories

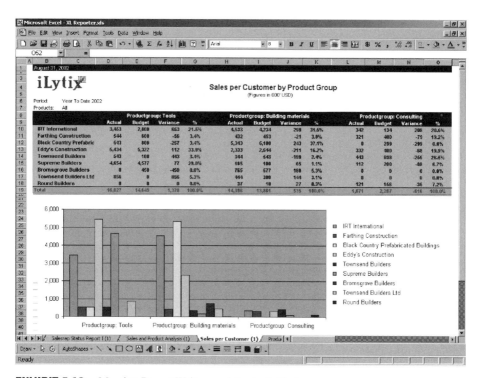

EXHIBIT 5.12   Merging Report Writers and Analysis Tools

Source: Used with permission, iLytix Systems. All rights reserved.

- *Automatic generation of OLAP cubes.* For low-cost and easy-to-implement OLAP analysis that complements highly formatted financial reports

Drill-down capability enables you to double-click on a row, column, or number in a report and the system automatically generates a new report/view for you, which provides the underlying detail. With *drill-around*, you can also drill sideways (instead of down in a hierarchy) to a neighboring department, account, period, and so on. When you are at the lowest level of information in your database (e.g., salary expense for department 100 in February 2003), some report writers now offer a direct link to the other database(s) that supplied the detail underlying the lowest transaction level in the current report and database. This is referred to as a *drill-through.* It enables users with little training to look at reports and investigate numbers of interest without using multiple reports or report writers and multiple software packages. The result should be better, faster decision making, as well as time and cost savings for the company.

Traditionally, interactive functionality, such as the drill-down features just described, has been the domain of executive information systems, spreadsheet pivot tables, and online analytical processing (OLAP). While a new breed of report writers are providing strong analytical features, OLAP software packages are becoming better at producing formatted reports, as compared to more rigid data grids with few financial reporting formatting features. The result is a blurring of the traditional lines between report writers and analysis tools, so that, increasingly, end users can enjoy the best of two worlds: powerful formatting and flexible report writing, as well as strong analysis features. The ultimate result is what analytical software vendors have been promising for several years: you should be able to spend 80 percent of your time on analysis and decision making and 20 percent on preparing the information (e.g., uploading data, writing reports, etc.), rather than the opposite. Though most companies don't yet have the systems in place to get anywhere close to this ratio, as the different technologies involved improve, this capability should be reality for most people in the coming years. The companies that are first to enable themselves to spend most of their time on analysis and decision making will certainly come out on top in tomorrow's marketplace.

Real-Time Reporting

Especially in financial management, you will start to hear the term *real-time reporting* more often. It refers to a process whereby a user will get a report at the same time the underlying transactional data is entered and saved somewhere else. According to this definition, most likely we will never be able to experience "real" real-time reporting, but we will get so close that the seconds or milliseconds we have to wait for our financial reports will not matter.

Up-to-the-second current information has traditionally been the privilege of only professional stock brokers and traders; but, now, many web-based information services deliver stock quotes and other information that is updated every 15 minutes or less, straight to the office or home computer of anyone who wants it.

In regard to a company's own internal financial reporting activities, it is still not uncommon to have to wait days for weekly or bimonthly sales reports, or a week or more for monthly or quarterly financial statements (such as profit and loss, balance sheet, and cash flow reports). This obviously is a far cry from real-time reporting, so it is the goal of most financial managers to drastically reduce this delay from the time information is entered until it is available to decision makers in both summarized and detailed reports.

There are several reasons why most organizations wait days or weeks for their vital financial information. One major factor is the lack of good integration between software solutions; for example, to get information from a sales order entry system and into a business intelligence data mart or into an Excel spreadsheet. (Integration issues were described in more detail in the "Common Data Exchange Formats" section earlier in this chapter.) Another reason is the need for human intervention to make adjustments to data, or to check that the data is correct before it is given to decision makers.

New reporting tools that support the concept of real-time (or near real-time) reporting are coming to the market. These tools typically offer the following features:

- *Real-time "dashboard"*. A combination of key figures and graphs based on essential business information from across a company's ERP modules (see Exhibit 5.13).

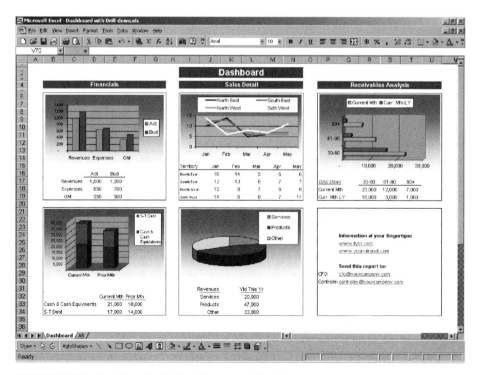

EXHIBIT 5.13 Dashboard with Key Figures and Graphs

- *Scheduled processing and delivery of reports.* People who don't have online access to the reporting tool and the ERP system can instead, based on automatic scheduling, receive their reports by e-mail. Depending on how rapidly the underlying data changes, reports can be sent out, for example, every hour or every day at a certain time (see Exhibit 5.14).

- *Drag-and-drop report design.* Whenever there is a need to look at the company's information from a new perspective, using simple drag-and-drop functionality, the user can design new reports on the fly. In contrast, with many traditional reporting tools, it can take hours to design reports, and the user often needs knowledge of table names, as well as special formulas.

For most financial systems, data entry is moving online as these systems become Web-enabled, or by other means are directly connected to each other. This is evident across a number of applications, from point-of-purchase scanners in stores to customers entering orders themselves directly through an e-commerce store front; moreover, it is automatically updating the enterprise resource planning (ERP) system.

Also, many software packages are becoming better at providing automatic entries (e.g., allocations, currency adjustments, or elimination entries) to reduce manual entries as financial information is rolled up to company or corporate group levels. An

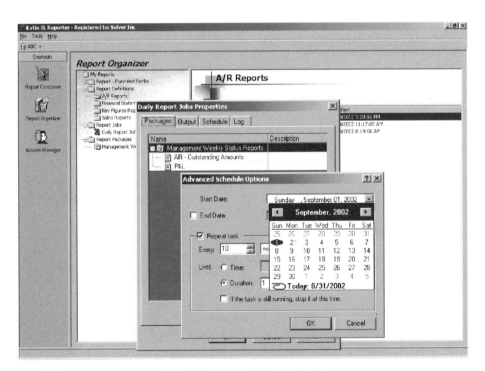

EXHIBIT 5.14   Automation of Report Scheduling and Distribution

Source: Used with permission, iLytix Systems. All rights reserved.

increasing number of companies have also introduced rules for accepting certain, less significant, variances or errors, in preliminary reports to avoid human-related delays. If, for example, a sales or inventory report at Company A is 97 percent accurate, and they can get it one hour after the last data was entered, it means that employees can make decisions quicker, thereby getting a clear competitive advantage on Company B, which may read the same type of report two days later.

This *preclosing* of the accounting books is often referred to as real-time reporting (if the time delay is very short) or *virtual closing*. It normally means that the necessary manual control procedures and adjustments are done later, and a final closing for legal and control purposes takes place later, without delaying initial key decision making. John Chambers, CEO at Cisco, a company known to be an industry leader in fast financial reporting turnaround, made the following statement during Cisco's year-end earnings release call on August 10, 1999: "What excites the CEO is the ability to know what the business is doing at any given point in time, react quickly to market shifts and competitive threats, and remain in tight control while empowering employees to make informed decisions more quickly." He further stated: "The virtual close . . . has, in my opinion, just as much impact on a company's future success or lack thereof as the well-published e-commerce area."

An increasing number of organizations will weigh the cost of potential poor decisions, based on absent or erroneous information, against the cost of late decisions. As more of the world goes online every year, and as the global marketplace becomes more competitive, we will see that a large number of companies will strive toward achieving real-time reporting.

ANALYTICS AND BALANCED SCORECARDS

What is a *Balanced Scorecard*? A Balanced Scorecard provides a means for linking the strategies of the different business areas within a corporation to the overall corporate vision. The term and methodology was introduced by David Norton and Harvard Business School Professor Robert Kaplan in 1992. They had found that the typical financial reports most companies were churning out did not provide managers with enough information to run their companies. Instead of reporting just the account numbers in the general ledger, Norton and Kaplan suggested that managers focus on the key performance indicators, whether financial figures or statistical figures, that really drive their business.

In recent years, the Balanced Scorecard methodology has become well accepted. A number of well-known management consulting companies offer implementation services, and software vendors are improving their applications to handle Balanced Scorecard reporting. Even very successful organizations could be more profitable utilizing the resources they have today by developing a set of key performance indicators and a continuous follow-up process. Examples of such indicators might be:

- Average revenue per employee
- Customer satisfaction (as a number on a scale from, for example, 1 to 5)
- Employee retention rate

Most modern analytics software programs now have the capability to allow for loading or entering all the data needed to create a Balanced Scorecard, and they have the report-writing features (for advanced calculations), as well as the analytical functionality (such as drill-down and graphics) needed. Now that Balanced Scorecards are being offered by a number of software vendors, large organizations around the world using applications from multiple vendors are finding it necessary to integrate their scorecards. Vendors are solving this by implementing XML (described earlier in this chapter) and a set of standards for integration.

The Hackett Group (a consulting company that maintains the world's largest and most comprehensive ongoing benchmark studies of different knowledge-worker functions) has found that the information that eventually reaches top management is often in too much general detail and lacks specific focus on the key financial and statistical drivers of the business. The idea behind the Balanced Scorecard is to address this issue and to give decision makers a performance measurement and planning tool that is easy to understand and focused, and that can help the company link its strategic plan with key performance indicators.

Why use Balanced Scorecards in the reporting and analysis process? Simply, because the way we do business is changing (see Exhibit 5.15).

It used to be simpler to keep track of the performance of a business and to create future plans. However, as key business conditions are changing, performance measurement, reporting, and analysis also must change. The idea of the Balanced Scorecard is to focus on the financial and statistical measurement that really drives the company and not waste time and money on planning and reporting for every possible line item in every corner of the business. The Balanced Scorecard approach also encourages management to include general industry comparisons as well as competitive comparisons in the planning and reporting.

Balanced Scorecards versus Standard Reports

The majority of companies utilize the general ledger as their key information source, so management reporting remains largely driven by the accounting close. Two benefits of the Balanced Scorecard are that the reports are very easy to read and every piece of data contains key information about the business. This means that managers

Business Driver	Past	Future
Competitors	Few/Big	Many/Small
Markets	National	Global
Manufacturing	Mass Production	Flexible
Products	Standardized	Innovative
Service	Standardized	Customized

EXHIBIT 5.15   Business Drivers and How They Have Changed

do not get distracted with nonpertinent information, enabling them to spend their time analyzing the real drivers of the business.

Probably one of the most important aspects of the Balanced Scorecard approach is that it is a tool directly linked with the corporate strategy. Whereas most companies today have a reporting process that is not tightly integrated with their strategic objectives, and thus has much less value as a business management tool, the metrics in the Balanced Scorecard are developed to follow the establishment of strategic targets and related tactical plans.

Employee Motivation and Involvement

Another key focus of the Balanced Scorecard approach is to link employee compensation to the performance metrics. This increases the focus and effort spent on achieving the targets set forth in the Balanced Scorecard. And because the reports focus on the key performance indicators, it is easy to follow where the company is going every period, when actual figures are measured against budgets and forecasts.

Potential Problems with the Balanced Scorecard

Almost half of all companies use some type of balanced scorecard, combining operational and financial measures; however, the impact is not pronounced. For those companies claiming to use the faddish tool, almost three-quarters of performance measures still are financial. This is little better than companies not utilizing the Balanced Scorecard, which rely on slightly more than 80 percent financial measures. Furthermore, if too many measures are chosen, the amount of time necessary to capture the data may outweigh the value of the information.

IMPACT OF THE INTERNET

Analytics applications will empower users by enabling them to easily analyze and visualize essential financial and statistical data from the company's different transactional databases. The Internet is making these applications even more powerful, for several reasons:

- *Easy access.* Data sources such as exchange rates, competitive or industry measures, and so on can be accessed online and used by the analytics applications.
- *Convenience.* The analytics application itself can be Web-based, allowing users to access the system from home, while traveling, or from remote offices.
- *Speed of data distribution.* Information is available immediately, from anywhere.
- *Speed of data collection.* Budgets, statistics, comments, and more can be entered from anywhere.
- *Ease of use.* There is no need for software installation and maintenance on users' computers.

Most analytics software vendors now have a Web version of their software, and as long as you have the infrastructure in place (Web server and Internet connection for all users), you should seriously consider making your key information available through a Web-based application. (see Exhibit 5.16). That said, make sure you verify that speed, security, printing quality, and functionality are all compatible with your and your users' systems. Although most vendors still require some of the setup and maintenance work to take place on a regular software client installation, rich functionality is quickly becoming available in their Web versions.

As your analytics applications, as well as many of your other information systems, become available on the Web, the next natural step is to integrate your application to a corporate Web portal (also referred to as an *enterprise information portal* (EIP), or often in the area of financial BI, a *digital dashboard*) (see Exhibit 5.17).

Over the next decade, most employees in any modern organization will access all corporate information through a single Internet or intranet-based portal. EIPs provide employees with a single point of access to corporate information and resources. The technology provides a Web-based interface that channels content so that individuals need to see only the underlying business application modules or information that is most relevant to them. For example, in the context of a company's financial staff members, a CFO might have a customized portal with sales information, cash positions, and actual to budget variance reports, while an accounting clerk might have a portal view that provides access to accounts receivable and general ledger journal entries.

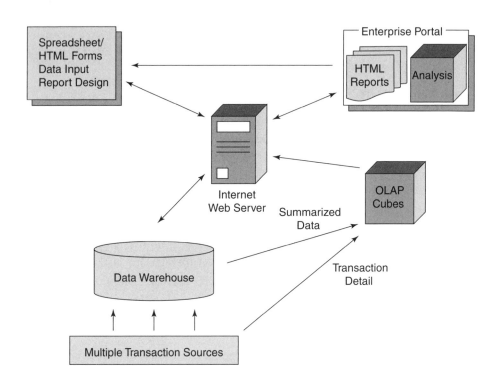

EXHIBIT 5.16   Sample Web-Based System Configuration

EXHIBIT 5.17   Enterprise Information Portal

Source: Used with permission, Microsoft Corporation. All rights reserved.

Applications and information that can make up a portal include:

- Analytics application (budgeting, reporting, analysis)
- ERP application (accounts payable, accounts receivable, general ledger, sales order processing, etc.)
- Customer relationship management (CRM) application
- Company news and policies
- External information

Today, a number of organizations already have enterprise information portals up and running. This means that they have a common Web site that provides access to all the different Web-based software applications in the company. First-generation EIPs were, however, just *links*, not live information or summaries fed directly from the underlying application. Consequently, most software vendors have created, or will have to create, a special front end to enable their solution to plug directly into a portal, instead of being just a link from a portal to a proprietary Web interface for their package.

Recently, a new generation of portal software has arrived that provides functionality such as:

- Display of many sources of data in a single user interface (*dashboard*)
- A single log-in to the portal, with user security linked to all the applications in the portal, to avoid multiple log-ins to different data sources

- Very simple (drag-and-drop and menu-based) customization of the portal so users see only the information most relevant to them

In companies where analytics is a key focus, a portal category that might grow fast is a corporate portal with built-in report writer, graphics, and business rules, and with the additional capability to directly pull information from the transactional data sources. The latter ensures that users always get access to the latest data because there is no temporary storage system (e.g., a data warehouse or data mart). However, a portal that uses third-party, specialized analytics applications to provide data and analytical functionality might be faster and offer more powerful features.

Thanks to the many exciting and useful applications the Internet offers the field of business intelligence and related software, IT and financial managers will have a number of new technologies to choose from in the coming years.

e-Learning: The New Way to Bring Budgeting and Reporting to End Users

What is the point of implementing a powerful new analytics solution to make valuable information available to users if they don't know how to properly use the software? If this book had been written just a few years ago, this topic would not have been included because the term e-learning was not yet in the vocabulary. What is e-learning? The "e," as in so many other new "e"-words in our vocabulary, stands for *electronic*, and generally refers to an educational process wherein the information and instructions typically reside on a data device that is enabled with sound and animation and is accessed through a computer. Examples are:

- Multimedia CD-ROM courses (have been around for many years)
- Self-run or instructor-led Web-based courses

Here we will focus on e-learning as a Web-based process, as this is clearly the trend of the future. Companies frequently introduce new technologies to their workforce, as well as demand that employees stay up to date on new or changing information, such as budgeting requirements, financial reports, and so on. Consequently, training costs are, in many cases, skyrocketing, forcing corporate managers and training providers to look for alternative technologies and methods to support their educational initiatives.

It is not uncommon for companies to get a poor ROI on their software applications due to lack of training. Maybe John Doe went to a three-day training class in Atlanta last year, but what good does that do the company if John left the company last month, and Lisa, who was trained by John half a day before he left, now is sitting there with the frustrating task of running the system? Or what if Company A has 80 users at 30 locations, all of whom need a one-day end-user class so they can start using the great new business intelligence tool you just installed and implemented? Sending a trainer to 30 locations, or sending 80 users to a training session, can quickly become a $100,000 investment. Not only that, but a massive amount of scheduling has to take place to fit this into everyone's busy calendars; and even then, there is a good chance that a few attendees can't come due to sickness or other unexpected events. And last but not least, for all the people who do attend a training session, many will miss out on important information due to:

- Poor attention span
- Interruptions, such as leaving class to check messages, make calls, or to attend to personal needs
- Slow learning abilities

Now imagine that the one-day training session, which probably, in effective presentation time, consisted of about two hours of content dissemination, was available on the Internet. Let's assume your new application is ready to run this week: You could send an e-mail to all your end users and instruct them to go to the Web site where the course files reside. During the next week, they could take the course as many times as they want, and whenever it is convenient for them. Each user would go to the given Web site, probably download the same material that would have been handed out during the off-site training class, and take the course by clicking on the course module on the e-learning Web site.

Normally, e-learning courses are broken up into short modules consisting of 2- to 10-minute sessions with text slides, graphics, screen videos, sound, and so on that are easy to find, quick to finish, and easy to navigate.

But in order for Web-based e-learning to provide a satisfactory learning environment, it is necessary to enable users' computers with sound capability (including headset or loudspeakers) and an Internet connection with reasonable speed (at least 50 kilobytes per second for many e-learning solutions).

e-Learning is also a great tool for repetitive training. Most users, if they don't frequently use all the features of the software, will forget certain parts of it. With all the course modules residing on a Web site, the users can log on and review specific course modules at any time they choose.

Most e-learning providers offer courses on a per-use basis or on a subscription basis. But if you have a customized or homegrown analytics solution, and no e-learning provider yet offers courses for your software, you can create your own online courses and put them on your Web site, intranet, or local area network (LAN). (Chapter 29 contains a list of e-learning software and vendors.) This option can also be of great value if you need to train a large number of users in a few modules, and you need to show them specific features and functionality. Depending on the resources available in your organization and the users' skill level, course development can be handled by your own team or outsourced to an e-learning software vendor or a consultant. And depending on the quality required and the amount of custom animations, graphics, and so on that is used, one hour of online courses can cost from a few thousand dollars to $50,000 to develop. The key is to evaluate the cost/benefit and then pick the best alternative. Some very inexpensive and easy-to-use software is available that you or a power user can utilize to create the courses yourself.

The approach you choose to take should be based on the following:

- How many people will use the courses
- How long the courses can be used before they are out of date
- The time and resources you have available

Software training (e.g., analytics software) lends itself very well to online implementation because trainees will see the actual screens they will be using in real life, with information, buttons, and menus residing on a screen to help them. What could be better than showing the actual screens and a mouse clicking on items while an instructor's voice explains in the background?

A large number of companies are planning to provide modern analytics applications to their users over the next few years, to unlock the information "gold" residing deep in their corporate databases. The new e-learning devices can help make the software investment worthwhile, as well as help end users quickly get up to speed on the application and help them stay that way over the long term.

6

SELLING CHANGE TO YOUR ORGANIZATION

In this chapter we will discuss why it is important to sell the idea of change to the rest of the organization. So far we have introduced you to BPI concepts and new technologies that can help enable successful BPI projects; but more importantly, the previous chapters have prepared you to analyze and plan for a potential BPI project in your organization.

The ideas discussed up to this point all belong to the first step, *research*, in our BPI project methodology (see Chapter 1). The next step is *sell*, that is, the sales phase of the project. At this point you should have a good idea whether you should go ahead with a BPI project, as well as what type of project to expect and the high-level associated costs and resource requirements. Assuming you are ready to pursue your BPI project, the final task in the initial preparation is to sell the importance and validity of the project to the people who will be involved (see Exhibit 6.1). The following list breaks down your target audiences and the sales message you will deliver to each of them:

Target Audience	Sales message
Top Decision Makers	All significant projects need an executive sponsor to show the rest of the organization that the project has top management support. In addition, this person, or persons, should have the power to allocate the necessary money and resources that you will need for the project.
Project Team	The cohesiveness and drive exhibited by the members of the project team will, in many ways, set the energy level for the team; it will also project to the rest of the organization that this is an important initiative with motivated people behind it. Before you dive into details of the project, make sure you thoroughly sell

Target Audience	Sales message
Project Team (*cont.*)	each person on the high-level goals of the project: how it will improve important tasks related to budgeting and reporting and what the rewards of a successful project will be for everyone.
Other Related Parties	Other people in the organization will, at different times during the project (especially in large projects), be interviewed by the project team and asked to contribute their knowledge, share documentation they have, and so on. If, at an early stage, you do a good job at selling them on the benefits (in particular, benefits to the individual person) of the BPI activities that will take place, you are less likely to encounter typical resistance to change, such as:

- Uncooperative attitudes

- Concealing information

- Negative talk about the project

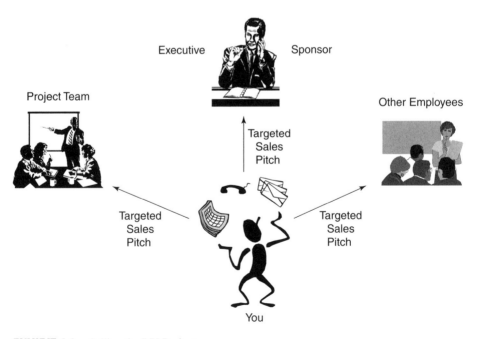

EXHIBIT 6.1   Selling the BPI Project

HOW TO SELL A BPI PROJECT

In the beginning of this chapter, we answered *why* it is important to sell the BPI project to the various audiences in the organization. Now, in Exhibits 6.1, 6.2, and 6.3, we demonstrate *how* to give your sales pitch. Top management, the project team, and the members of the organization each need a customized version of your sales pitch for maximum effect and support.

Small BPI projects (such as changing the chart of accounts) clearly require a lot less involvement from the organization and less preparation to sell the project to decision makers. However, as soon as it is clear that you are confronting a midsized

Main Goals	Main Concerns	Key Elements of Sales Pitch
Cost control Corporate profitability Improved decision making as a result of BPI	Wasted time and resources on failed project Lost focus on other key business activities	Cost-benefit analysis ROI analysis Executive PowerPoint presentation, with reasoning for project, goals, main project information (dates, main activities, cost, etc.)

EXHIBIT 6.2   Selling to Top Decision Makers

Main Goals	Main Concerns	Key Elements of Sales Pitch
Improved personal work tasks (e.g., automated budgeting and reporting processes) Improved work experience and career opportunities with BPI project and best practices Rewards as result of successful project	Lose face as a result of unsuccessful project Job security Workload during peak project activities	Present BPI goals and describe how the organization will benefit. Provide estimates of time and resource requirements. Create and present personal research to team members based on project involvement and duration. Reduce potential risks to team by defining as clearly as possible the scope of the project.

EXHIBIT 6.3   Selling to the Project Team

Main Goals	Main Concerns	Key Elements of Sales Pitch
Improved personal work tasks (e.g., less data entry, earlier reporting)	Job security Wasted time (extra work) Fear of the new and unknown (e.g., new software or routines)	Present the project concisely or distribute information document; have personal conversation that encourages them to assist/ cooperate with project team. Emphasize that life will be better after BPI and that job security will be higher. Explain that they will be updated as to progress as the project moves forward.

EXHIBIT 6.4   Selling to the Rest of the Organization

or large project, proper preparation to effectively sell the idea and benefits of a BPI project can easily mean the difference between no project (because you did not get approval), a failed project (because you didn't get access to enough time and resources during the project), and a highly successful project.

Another important tip is to carefully plan the timing of your sales pitch. Obviously you want to avoid busy periods such as month-, quarter-, and year-end closings, during the budget process, and the like. The best time to target is following a period when the old processes for which you are suggesting improvement have been utilized. Then it will be fresh in people's minds that these processes are manual, slow, error-prone, or ineffective in some other way.

PART TWO

BUSINESS PROCESS IMPROVEMENT PROJECT

7

GETTING STARTED

This book focuses on both the budgeting process and the reporting process. Although the two relate to each other, each is covered in its own chapter. Depending on the existing weaknesses and inefficiencies in each area, you can, of course, combine the budgeting and reporting projects into one project, or you can evaluate them individually, as we do here.

Note: Because of the importance and popularity of a chart of accounts (COA) improvement project, we address it in a separate section. This will allow those of you who are primarily concerned with improving your COA to easily access all the material in one place. If you are considering a more complete BPI project, the COA will just be a subproject, and as such is referred to in numerous places in this part of the book.

BUDGETING AND REPORTING OVERVIEW: SO YOU WANT PERFECT ANALYTICS PROCESSES?

Budgeting and reporting processes are in many ways similar across different companies and industries. Though the underlying ERP systems and chart of accounts may differ, and though there maybe variations in layouts and detail of budget input templates and financial statements, still there are a large number of similarities. For example:

- Detailed budgets are usually produced annually
- A large number of people and effort are assigned in the annual budget.
- Actual figures from the ERP system are compared to the budget for the same period to produce variances that can be used as management controls and performance measurements.
- Forecasts are produced at certain points in time (e.g., monthly, quarterly, or annually) to provide a fresher outlook for the rest of the year than the old annual budget.
- Budgets are collected and "rolled up" using the ERP system itself, spreadsheets, or specialized budgeting systems (see Part Five)
- Financial reports (most of which will include budget figures) are produced monthly, quarterly, and annually, by a few central accounting or IT people who know how to write and execute reports.

- End users either receive reports as hard copies or as e-mail attachments, or they have access to the reporting system locally or through the Web.
- A lot of time and effort is spent on budgeting and reporting, and most companies complain that there is too little time left to analyze the numbers.

These examples represent only a few of the high-level budgeting and reporting processes being used in companies, and in later chapters we will discover more related processes, activities, and tasks.

Many organizations, professional services companies, and even individual "activists" have started to address the many flaws, inefficiencies, and issues related to most companies' analytics processes. Improvement propositions range from small fixes to large, expensive projects that will completely change current procedures. As stated, in this part of the book we take a close look at budgeting and reporting processes and how they can be improved, to arm you with knowledge and a set of useful tools for your own financial BPI project.

PREPARING FOR THE BPI PROJECT

By now you should be ready to roll up your sleeves and kick off the actual project itself. However, before you dive into the budgeting and reporting processes, you should develop a clear picture of the roles that end users, administrators, and managers play in the budgeting and reporting process. By identifying and documenting these roles, it will be easier for everyone involved in the BPI project to comprehend who is doing what, why they are doing it, and when they are doing it. There are also a few other items you should evaluate to create the best possible framework for the project. They are (see Exhibit 7.1):

- Management objectives
- Improvement opportunities and ROI
- Methodology
- BPI enablers ("toolkit")
- Potential obstacles
- Project organization

Management Objectives

Whether you are the manager initiating the BPI project or you have been assigned by someone else to handle the project, it is still of critical importance to involve top-level financial managers and executives at a very early stage. You have to clearly define management's objectives so you know you can validate a BPI project and get buy-in and support throughout the project.

The best forum in which to discuss and document management objectives is a meeting. The people who initially raised the issue of the need for improvement in budgeting and reporting should prepare some basic notes for the meeting and make a high-level presentation of the major issues and how they ultimately affect the business. For example:

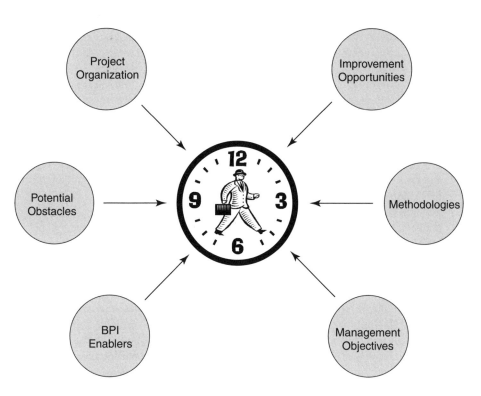

EXHIBIT 7.1   BPI Project Preparation

Problem	Effect on Business
BUDGETING	
Too-lengthy budget cycle	The budget is outdated before it's even completed.
Inflexible tools	Takes weeks to do a reorganization or what-if analysis, thus changes are costly and often not done.
Too much detail or manual input	The Process is demotivating for end users, resulting in lack of participation.
REPORTING	
Too-lengthy monthly closing cycle	Slower decision making because of lack of information.
Lack of easy-to-use, flexible reporting tools	No, or low, analytical activities, resulting in poor decision making.

It is important that the problem areas identified be real and worth pursuing. The last thing you want is to have the BPI project derailed by focusing on insignificant problems or jumping the gun on the methodology deployment. For example, a number of "best practices" methodologies suggested by consulting companies today, which can be costly to implement, might not fit a corporate culture, and ultimately might not improve things much. In other words, make sure the focus of the meeting is not just to change for the sake of trying something different, but to solve actual problems and suggest solutions that will result in a solid ROI for the project.

Once the items/problems have been discussed, get input from the participants, then take a vote on whether you should initiate a project. Depending on the level of preparation and documentation you brought to this first meeting, you might have to call for a second meeting, to which you bring more detailed information on the actual improvement opportunities (including ROI), potential methodologies (if you are going to take a new approach to budgeting and reporting versus what you do today), the key enablers you will utilize, obstacles to success, and organizational plans.

Improvement Opportunities and ROI

Assuming you now have an initial buy-in for the project from top management, it is time to look more closely at current analytics processes and at potential improvements. Many improvement opportunities will probably be obvious and commonly known throughout the organization, based on everyday discussions and complaints about inefficiencies and problems with the budgeting and reporting processes. However, to make sure all the significant opportunities for improvement are uncovered (not just the issues that a few people may be vocal about) and can be fairly ranked according to importance, it is best to take a methodical approach to this research. Some good starting points are:

1. *Map and describe the major steps in both budgeting and reporting processes* (see Exhibit 7.2). This will be very useful when talking to different people about problems and opportunities, as you can always make sure you are describing the same tasks or items in the same part of a process.

2. *Create a list of all the people involved in budgeting and reporting.* This step should include support staff (e.g., IT), end users (input and output), top decision makers (as long as they depend on information from the systems), as well as power users/administrators (the people who initiate and manage the budgeting process, responsible for report writing, closing books, etc.) (Exhibit 7.3).

3. *Assign roles and responsibilities to each person listed.* This ensures that everyone involved in the BPI project knows who is responsible for what and when.

4. *Interview the people on your list.* To encourage as much openness as possible amongst the interviewees, you can let someone with a low political profile in the organization perform the interviews. Get a good sampling from within each similar user group and focus specifically on uncovering key issues, so as not to drown in documenting unimportant detail that will slow down or clutter the BPI project. You might start by describing the purpose of the project and how it can result in a better situation (the reward.) Then ask questions such as:

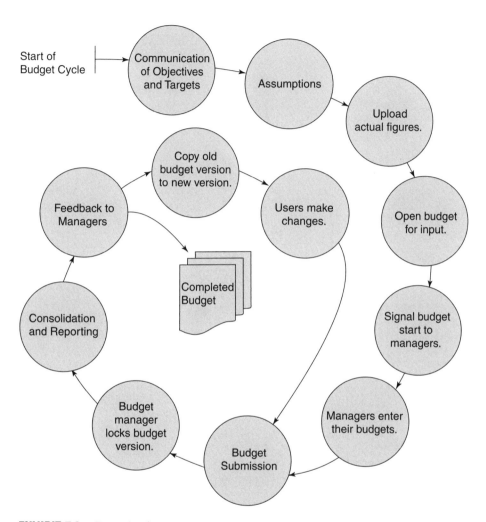

EXHIBIT 7.2   Example of Budgeting Process

- What is your role in the budgeting and/or reporting processes?
- Where do you see major problems?
- How would you propose solving these problems?
- How would improvement make you better able to focus on more important tasks?
- How would you rank each problem based on importance?

5. *Document current issues.* Create a summary document that lists all relevant issues and ranks them based on total score.

Budgeting   **Reporting**

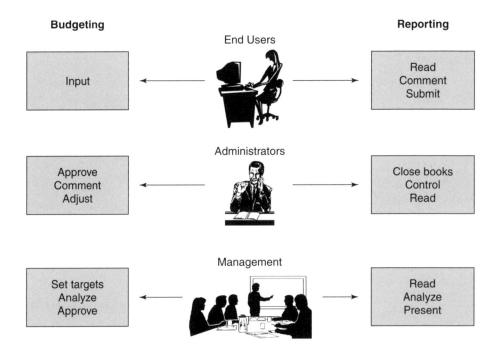

EXHIBIT 7.3   People and Processes

6. *Map improvement opportunities.* Meet with the project group, present ranked improvement opportunities, and gather information (research/interviews) on how many of them are reasonable (based on money/time invested) to determine how each selected item can be improved. Graph each and calculate the ROI (see Exhibit 7.4).

7. *Meet the project group to achieve final buy-in and give the start signal.* Present the findings to the project group and the rest of the management organization, and make a final decision as to whether the project should be launched based on all available information and the current business climate. (Are the right people still here? Are any other projects, such as an ERP implementation, going on that could disturb or impact this one?)

Methodology

There is no perfect methodology to apply to your BPI project. Think of a chef making a five-course gourmet meal flavored with his or her favorite spices and prepared according to his or her preferred workflow in the kitchen, while still satisfying special customer requests. Even though different chefs might create the same meal according to their own kitchen rules and outside influences, the objective is the same: to make the customer happy and to do so without wasting unnecessary time and re-

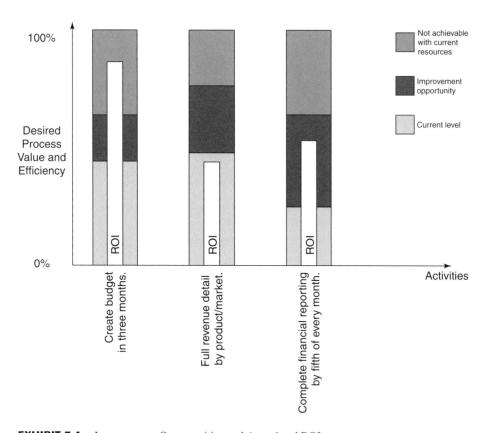

EXHIBIT 7.4   Improvement Opportunities and Associated ROI

sources. And if it is the first time that a specific meal is being made, it is important that the chef write down the recipe (i.e., document the process), so that the restaurant can continue to serve the meal to customers even if the original chef departs and a new one takes his or her place.

It is not hard to analogize this scenario to your own BPI project. You need to have a plan of action and you need to document both the plan and the result. We propose the following methodology (as introduced in Part One):

1. Research
2. Sell
3. Plan
4. Design
5. Execute

We have discussed research and sell; and plan, design and execute will be covered in depth in the budgeting and reporting chapters in this part.

BPI Enablers

There are a number of tools you can utilize to help improve the analytics processes. One of the most common solutions companies apply when they need to streamline their budgeting process is to invest in budgeting software. Technology alone cannot, however, effectively improve analytics processes, but it continues to be the most frequently applied solution to solve problems. There is no doubt that technology will, and should, play an important role in most BPI projects. But if you want to maximize the improvement opportunities that exist, it is very important to both carefully analyze objectives and current problems and to look at a number of other potential enablers. We have identified these enablers as follows:

- *Human resources*. People involved both in the BPI project itself and in ongoing budgeting and reporting activities
- *Best practices*. Budget detail, frequency, report content, linkage to strategy, and so on
- *Technology*. Software and communication platforms that help automate and streamline processes and increase control and decision support
- *Workflow*. Who is doing what? When? In what order? A well-planned workflow is the backbone of an efficient budgeting and reporting infrastructure.

In the rest of the chapters in this part we will first look at the budgeting process, analyze it, and offer suggestions for making improvements; we'll then do the same for the reporting process. As you will see, all of the improvement enablers are important for maximizing the potential results of your BPI project.

Potential Obstacles

If you prepare and plan well for your BPI project, you should face fewer surprises and obstacles along the way. That said, with larger projects, there are more variables and a longer time period during which problems can occur. The following list outlines three typical obstacles you might come across in your project, along with tips on how you can avoid or overcome them:

1. Turnover

   Challenge: A key person might leave the company, such as the manager who sanctioned the project or someone responsible for key activities in the project itself.

   Solution: Document all important parts of the project, so new people can more easily replace those who left. Also document the sales pitch (including ROI, etc.) that you gave the project sponsors, so that new managers can readily take ownership of the project if the original sponsors are gone.

2. Lost focus

   Challenge: Unless you carefully adjust activities to fit the objectives of the BPI project, it can very easily expand in size or shift focus to less important areas.

Solution: Make sure the BPI objectives are documented, easily available, and always referred to when there is any question whether the activities in the project are outside the scope. If a project must be expanded (or decreased) in size, make sure this is formally verified with the manager(s) who sanctioned the project.

3. Lack of planning and project management

   Challenge: If changes must happen quickly, it is tempting to try to fix the obvious problems right away without doing the proper planning and without assigning ownership and responsibilities. Ultimately, this can lead to poor or even failed projects.

   Solution: Use the planning tools described in this book or other tools available to you; and don't underestimate the importance of good project planning and management to keep a BPI project on track.

Project Organization

If your BPI project is a small one, you might be doing most of the work yourself, supplemented by some discussions and meetings with end users and decision makers involved with the budgeting and reporting processes. But, if you are planning to do a major overhaul of all analytics activities, a number of people will have to be involved in different parts of your project. Whichever of the categories best describes your situation—anything from a two-person project team with some assistance from other people to numerous people across multiple departments and locations—will be part of the project. Just as it is important to plan well for your project, it is of key importance to create an effective project organization.

SUMMARY OF CURRENT ISSUES: SIMPLIFIED EXAMPLE

As you begin to map out the different areas that are due for improvement ("improvement opportunities"), it can help to create a table like the one in Exhibit 7.5. For each improvement opportunity, identify which of your BPI enablers can be effectively used to generate an improvement. This table will not only be a good draft document to refer to as you move into more detail in the project, but it will help keep you focused on the key problems and the potential enablers to help resolve them.

USING DIAGRAMS TO VISUALIZE PROCESSES

Before you start your BPI project, we want to provide you with some ideas and tools to help you and the project team visualize both existing and new processes.

Note: This is a brief overview, so if you are planning to create highly advanced diagrams, we suggest you read one of the many diagram-related books on the topic.

By creating graphical diagrams depicting the different steps in a budgeting or reporting process, it is much easier for people to understand all the activities involved and the order in which they should take place.

Improvement Opportunity	Enabler			
	Best Practices	**Workflow**	**Human Resources**	**Technology**
Lack of system knowledge among users			X	
Too lengthy a budget cycle	X	X		X
Too much detail in some areas	X			
Too little detail in other areas	X			
Poor integration with ERP system				X
Lack of access to transaction detail in ERP system				X
Poor report formats (not attractive)				X
Can't produce the reports management wants			X	X
Too many keystrokes to complete tasks				X
Lack of ownership of processes	X	X	X	
Outdated budget (lack of continuous planning)	X			X
Too lengthy a closing (and reporting) cycle	X	X	X	X

EXHIBIT 7.5   Improvement Opportunities and Enablers

To create professional and easily editable diagrams, it is best to use specialized software. For simpler processes, you can use any software with drawing capabilities, like Microsoft PowerPoint. Most people are familiar with this tool and it comes with a number of prebuilt objects (e.g., circles, squares, and arrows) that are easy to integrate to a process diagram. If you have more advanced needs, a tool like Microsoft Visio will give you the functionality you need to create almost any type of diagram. A word of caution here: If you are going to invest in a professional diagram tool, make sure at least a couple of people on your team are willing and interested in adapting it for the project so it doesn't go unused.

The following are three examples of the most popular diagrams used in BPI projects:

1. Organizational hierarchy diagram

   Purpose: This diagram provides important insight to the organizational roll-up of a company, in particular for midsized and large companies, which often have rather complex organizational structures. The organizational hierarchy diagram should not be used to depict budgeting or reporting processes, but rather to clarify the administrative relationship between entities and/or people in the company (see Exhibits 7.6 and 7.7 for examples).

   Comments: The two most common versions of the organizational hierarchy diagram are the vertical and the horizontal. The major difference between them is that a vertical diagram is better used to fit a large organization on paper and/or in computer software (almost all analytics software use vertical organizational hierarchy diagrams).

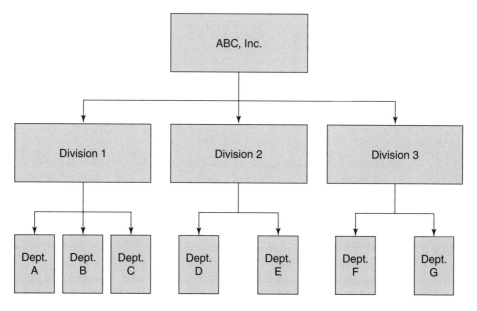

EXHIBIT 7.6   Sample Horizontal Organizational Hierarchy Diagram

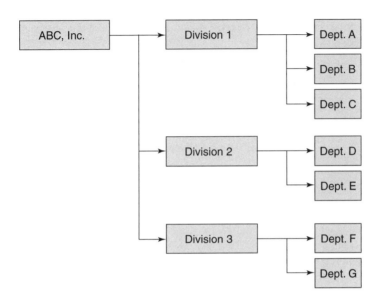

EXHIBIT 7.7   Vertical Organizational Hierarchy Diagram

2. Global overview of processes and divisions diagram

   Purpose: In contrast to the organizational hierarchy diagram, the global overview of processes and divisions diagram offers a good schematic format to show (high-level) processes and the entities/people (divisions) responsible for different parts of each process (see Exhibit 7.8).

   Comments: Although there are a number of ways to design this type of diagram, it often works well to put processes in rows, and departments/functions in columns, especially for layout purposes, as there typically will be more processes than departments/functions; thus it is an easier layout to work with on both paper and a computer screen.

3. Detailed process diagram

   Purpose: This type of diagram is often also called a flowchart. It is a great way to visualize processes. Whether it is used to show detailed tasks and activities or interrelated processes at a higher level, this diagram is easy to understand and can be invaluable in a BPI project (see Exhibit 7.9).

   Comments: Detailed process diagrams provide an excellent means of depicting budgeting and reporting processes. And keep these rules of thumb in mind to make the diagram as clear as possible:

   - Keep the lines between the symbols short to make it easy for people to follow.
   - Draw lines vertically or horizontally; avoid curved or angled lines.
   - Minimize the number of lines and arrows to avoid cluttering the diagrams.

Project: BPI — Budgeting Process		Date: February 15, 2003				
Doc. Version: 1.0		By: Johnny B. Good				
Department/Function:		A	B	C	D	E
Process:		Board	CFO	Account-ing	Budget Mgr.	Dept. Heads
1	Set strategic targets.	I	P			
2	Cascade targets to departments.		C	I	P	I
3	Populate budget system with targets.				P	
4	Distribute current budget instructions.				P	
5	Open budget input process.			I	I	P	I
6	Enter budgets.				C	P
7	Close budget input process.			I	I	P	I
8	Produce reports.			P	P	
9	Validate budgets.			P	P	
10	Approve budgets.	A	A	I	I	I

Example of codes to use in the diagram:
A = Approve
C = Control
I = Inform
P = Perform task

EXHIBIT 7.8 Processes and Divisions Diagram

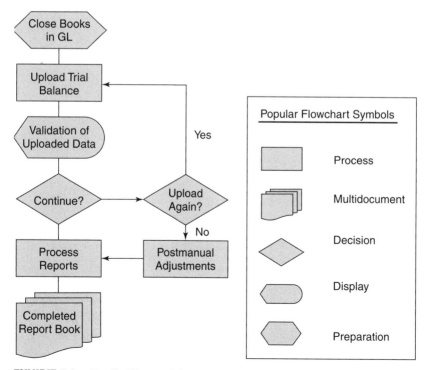

EXHIBIT 7.9 Detailed Process Diagram for Financial Reporting Process (Simplified)

Note: The International Standards Organization (ISO) has proposed ISO 1028, "Information Processing: Flowchart Symbols," (see examples on the right side of Exhibit 7.9) to make it easier for both designers and users to construct and read workflow diagrams. This type of standardization makes it easier to communicate processes in large projects with multinational teams and of various backgrounds.

8

DUE DILIGENCE

As you know by now, the budget process deals with all five levels of the BPI project, but in this chapter we will concentrate primarily on three of them: research, plan, and design. It is important to research the current processes and document the entire process so that you can find the improvement opportunities in the budgeting process. After researching the processes, you need to make a detailed plan that describes each and every activity and that lists the resources involved. Finally, you must design the new budget process, to include the new or streamlined processes (see Exhibit 8.1).

Annual budgeting is a vital activity that is mandatory for most managers. Hence, managers are always looking toward the future, meaning that planning is a key component of any management work. Simply put, the budget is a quantitative and qualitative illustration of the plans for the coming year. The budget is the primary tool that can give authenticity to an organization's objectives, strategies, priorities, and plans. Resources are essential for a company to achieve its goals and so they must be planned for as well. Similarly, goals take on meaning only when they are reflected in the budget.

The first step in budgeting is to determine the right *model* to use for your company. In the simplest form, a model is a relationship among variables articulated in equation form. Models are designed with knowledge, information, and assumptions about elements of a variable. Individuals who do their own personal budgets, always use a model, albeit a simpler one. For example, if you paid, on average, $100 a month for gasoline last year, but you assume that you will drive 50 percent more this year, then you will budget $150 a month for gasoline in the next year. In essence, you would design a *growth curve model* on certain accounts, or use a software program such as Quicken to help you. Companies also use budgeting software to help develop their models.

A model can mean different things to different people. A model can be a database that includes budget forms and reports, or it can be a link among many Excel worksheets. In this chapter, we cover the issues that will enable you to make the right choice of a budgeting model by discussing a company's values, risks it faces, and its strengths and weaknesses.

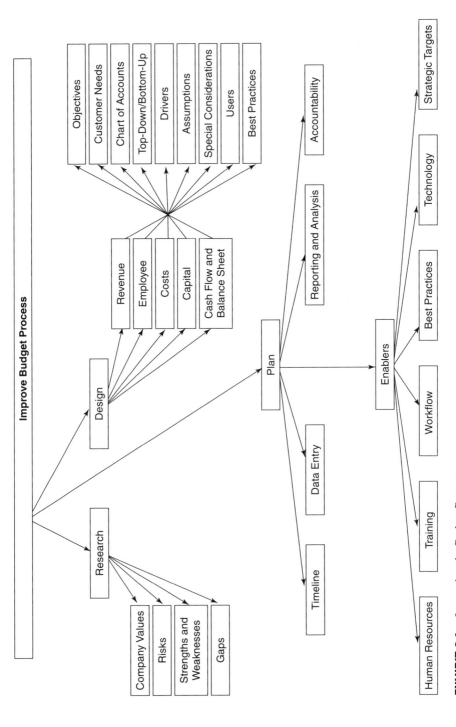

EXHIBIT 8.1 Improving the Budget Process

COMPANY VALUES

Company values are typically written down and are frequently changed, but do they really define the values of a company? Recently, such "value statements" have become very generic at organizations, making them virtually meaningless. Thomas A. Stewart, in his article "Reassessing the Corporate Value Statement"[1], describes a practice among MBA teachers to ask students to retrieve the value statements from their organizations and bring them to class. The teacher has each value statement typed in the same font and then displays printed copies on a wall. Most students have a very difficult time trying to identify their company's statement. Most value statements use all or some of these words: integrity, respect, teamwork, excellence, and communication. These should be staples of all organizations and should not need to be referenced by a company as "values."

Ideally, corporate values should help employees do their jobs more effectively. Values should suggest priorities that guide employees to do the right thing and to feel good about themselves and their company. Does your organization cite integrity as a value, but, in practice actually demonstrates very little integrity in its day-to-day operation of business? Actions are what really define a company's values, just as your actions define your individual values. What you say has little influence over people if you behave in a totally different manner. It works the same for companies. Enron is an example of a company that did not follow its value statement:[2]

> Our values:
> *Communication*—We have an obligation to communicate. Here, we take the time to talk with one another and to listen. We believe that information is meant to move and that information moves people.
>   *Respect*—We treat others as we would like to be treated ourselves. We do not tolerate abusive or disrespectful treatment.
>   *Integrity*—We work with customers and prospects openly, honestly, and sincerely. When we say we will do something, we do it; when we say we cannot or will not do something, then we won't.
>   *Excellence*—We are satisfied with nothing less than the very best in everything we do. We will continue to raise the bar for everyone. The great fun here will be for all of us to discover just how good we can really be.

Ask yourself: Why are values important to you? Probably your answer depends on how you are associated with the company. You may be an investor, a customer, a supplier, or an employee of a certain company, in which case it is entirely up to you whether you want to be associated with a company that has poor values. For example, would you want your name associated with a company like Enron? Now ask yourself how values can improve your budget process. Your company's value statement alone will not help; but if the company practices what it preaches, then it can smooth the process.

An example of a value to improve the process is *communication*. Goals should be communicated regularly to all employees. And communication should be a two-way street: employees should be able to speak openly with the management; likewise, management should be able to speak openly with the executives of the company. Another value would be to give employees *responsibility* for their job and their decisions. Employees typically do a better job if they are challenged and feel that their work is respected.

RISKS

We live with risk every day, both in our working and personal environments. For example, you must manage the risk of investing your money, whether you take risks in the stock market or place your money in a certificate of deposit. Typically, a company or an individual will increase risk to generate a larger return. The stock market presents a greater risk than a certificate of deposit, but you should anticipate a larger return over time to compensate for the extra risk.

Companies must make decisions on a daily basis that may have profound risks for the future of the company. There are risks in emerging industries, such as the presence of market and technological uncertainties, difficulties of forecasting and budgeting, and the need for large investments. Two indicators of the risk of emerging industries are the high cost of capital and the frequency of corporate failure. Therefore, it is imperative that management effectively manages risk in order to succeed. Managing risk alone does not guarantee success; but it will be very difficult to succeed without managing risk. There are four different types of risk that management must consider:

1. *Economic risk*. These risks, such as fluctuations in business activity, changes in interest rate, and purchasing power, are inherent to a company's operating environment. These are typically impossible for an organization to control, but managers must be aware of these when making business decisions.

2. *Business risk*. This is the uncertainty regarding a company's capability to earn a reasonable return on its investment in light of the revenue and cost factors, which include competition, product blend, and management aptitude. This risk is based on the strength and/or weakness of the individuals running your organization.

3. *Financial risk*. Financial risk refers to the capital structure of the organization and its capability to meet its financial demands, such as paying off claims against it. If a company cannot meet its financial obligations, then there will be many competitors looking to take advantage. Currently, for example, Adelphia Cable has filed bankruptcy and the satellite companies in Southern California have started an ad campaign that talks of Adelphia Cable's demise.

4. *Accounting risk*. This is inherent in the submission and choice of the accounting methods, which include management leeway in controlling the production of the accounting process. Recently, this has become more of a risk since many organizations are using the illegal accounting methods that have brought down many organizations, such as Enron and Global Crossings.

The following are some of the ways that companies can cope with risk:

- *Cooperate with lead users*. A *lead user* is typically the industry leader or the company that has developed new technology. Cooperating is most important during the early phases of industry development. It is vital to monitor and respond to market trends and customer necessities, to avoid mistakes in technology and performance. Companies should try to identify users whose present needs will become general market trends in the future and to develop close ties with such customers, and doing so can be essential to maintaining technological progressiveness.

- *Limit risk exposure.* Organizations should try to adopt investment procedures to minimize their exposure to risk. Many companies do not have the cash flow to overcome the downturns in the market. A good example are the dot-com companies: They spent money like there was no tomorrow, then most went out of business when the economy slowed. A way to limit risk is to partner with another company or to create an alliance with other companies when developing new products. This has become more commonplace in the twenty-first century.

- *Be flexible.* Flexibility is critical to a company's long-term success and survival. Market changes and technological advances are becoming more difficult to forecast; therefore, it is essential that organizations be able to quickly and effectively respond to these changes.

- *Assign capital risk to each business unit.* This will enable the company to see which departments/entities are increasing the shareholders' wealth and which are not. You may use a measurement called Economic Value Added (EVA) to determine the true economic profit of a department. It is calculated by taking the operating profit and subtracting an appropriate charge for the opportunity cost of capital invested in a department.

- *Analyze competitors/economy.* Companies should have competitor analysis available at all times, and it should be regularly updated. It is good business practice to always be aware of any changes in your competitors' marketing plans, products, or management that may affect your business. It also make good business sense to keep an eye on the future of the economy and to forecast the effects that the economy might have on your business.

- *Develop a corporate strategy.* A strategy that is communicated and built upon the management's strength will be beneficial to a company both in the short- and the long-term. This topic is covered later in this chapter.

STRENGTHS AND WEAKNESSES

It is very common to find companies that have difficulty determining their strengths and weaknesses. Companies are often changing their dynamics through acquisitions, new employees, new products, or new technologies. These changes can be better managed if the leaders are aware of the company's strengths and weaknesses before changing the dynamics of its organization.

Companies can use a checklist, or a consultant, to determine their strengths and weaknesses periodically and to attribute a level of importance to each category. The question that companies need to answer is: should it limit itself to those opportunities for which it has the required strengths or consider better opportunities for which it might need to acquire or develop additional strengths? Microsoft is a great example of this in regard to the X-Box. The company's strengths were in software, but it also had tremendous strengths in marketing, so it acquired a company that was creating videogame software and designed a videogame for the home. Though sales did not meet expectations, Microsoft nevertheless attempted to use a current strength on a product for which it had no experience. The point is, your organization does not have to stay away from its weaknesses or try to improve them, but it is important to know that weaknesses can be turned into strengths. If a company is always trying to fix its weaknesses, then it may spend all of its time doing this rather than capitalizing on its strengths.

There are two different types of charts that your organization can use to help determine its strengths and weaknesses. The first one includes two different types of matrixes: an *opportunity matrix* and a *threat matrix*. The opportunities are classified according to their attractiveness and their probability of success. The company's probability of success is revealed by its market and its competition. The most successful company will be able to create customer loyalty and maintain it. Any product or service that is in box 1 shows that the company should definitely go after these prospects. Companies should stay away from opportunities in box 4, and instead follow the prospects in the other two boxes (see Exhibit 8.2).

OPPORTUNITY MATRIX

Success Probability

	High	Low
High	1	2
Low	3	4

(Attractiveness)

THREAT MATRIX

Probability of Occurrence

	High	Low
High	1	2
Low	3	4

(Seriousness)

CHECKLIST FOR STRENGTH/WEAKNESS ANALYSIS

Marketing	Performance	Importance
1. Company Reputation	_____	_____
2. Market Share	_____	_____
3. Product/Service Quality	_____	_____
4. Pricing Effectiveness	_____	_____
5. Distribution Effectiveness	_____	_____
6. Promotion Effectiveness	_____	_____
7. Sales Force Effectiveness	_____	_____
8. Global Coverage	_____	_____
Finance		
1. Cost of Capital	_____	_____
2. Cash Flow/Liquidity	_____	_____
3. Financial Stability	_____	_____
Manufacturing		
1. Facilities	_____	_____
2. Economies of Scale	_____	_____
3. Capacity	_____	_____
4. Technical Skill	_____	_____
Organization		
1. Leadership	_____	_____
2. Flexible	_____	_____
3. Employees	_____	_____

EXHIBIT 8.2   Positioning Tools

Threats are classified by the probability of occurrence and in the seriousness. Companies will need to take immediate action for threats in box 1, ignore those in box 4, and evaluate the other types of threats. In conclusion, an ideal business will have many high opportunities and few major threats. A mature company will have few opportunities and few threats. A company with few opportunities and many threats will not last long, while a speculative company will be high in both categories.

The checklist is a way for companies to grade themselves on a scale in many different categories. The grading scale can be 5 for a major strength, 4 for a minor strength, 3 for neutral, 2 for a minor weakness, and a 1 for a major weakness. For importance, the scale might be 3 for high, 2 for medium, and 1 for low. You should be on the lookout for weaknesses that have a high level of importance so that it can be improved upon. Honeywell, for example, has a great program that is designed to improve the weaknesses in intercompany communications. Each department is required to rate its own strengths and weaknesses and those of the other departments with which it interacts. This is a proactive step by Honeywell, one that enables it to determine each department's weaknesses.

ENDNOTES

1. Thomas A. Stewart, "Reassessing the Corporate Values Statement," *Business 2.0* (March 13, 2002), access at *http://www.business2.com/articles/web/0,1653, 38800,00.html.*

2. Shari Caudron, "Strength in Numbers, Part Two," *Controller Magazine* (March 1996): 31.

9

IMPROVING THE
BUDGETING PROCESS

Usually, the budget process is met with trepidation and lack of interest, and often, managers will complete their budget at the last second, without any planning, even though they were given months to do so. The budgeting process also imposes a lot of stress on all participants, due to expected improvement, time constraints, and lack of tools. There are also many issues that companies need to be aware of during the process, such as political concerns and employee motivation. Executives may want the budget to meet a certain objective, whereas the managers may want to be more conservative if they are responsible for their numbers. Some statistics regarding the budgeting process are:

- Planning is likely the most reviled corporate process, consuming an astonishing 25,000 person-days annually at a typical billion-dollar company.
- On average annually, 5 months are spent on revisiting the strategic plan and 4 months on financial planning, leaving just 3 months a year when a typical company isn't actively planning.
- The annual cost of the budgeting process, in a typical Fortune 500 company, is in the $20 million-plus range.

This chapter will show how important the budgeting process should be to you and your company and how it can be used as an important tool every day. A budget is basically a plan for the business for the coming year created from the objectives, priorities, and strategies of the corporation. Today, more employees are involved in creating a budget, which implies that budgeting is a more complex operation within organizations. Though it is a much simpler task to distribute the budget to numerous employees, thanks to technology, the process becomes more complicated as well.

Budgeting involves planning and control, and should answer many questions, such as: Where does the company want to go? What does the company have to do? Can we achieve the targets that are set? How do we allocate resources? In terms of management control, managers should ask: Where are we? How does our budget compare to the actual numbers? What happened and why? What are the alternatives? Efficient decision making is essential for a company to survive, and the following pages will help you learn to make the best decisions. In addition, Exhibits 9.1 and 9.2 will give you a guideline to the budgeting process.

1. Set corporate goals.	• R&D
2. Prepare standard forms.	• Capital expenditures
3. Train employees.	5. Corporate budget—finance
4. Send the budgets out to	department and overhead
departments:	6. Consolidate budget.
• Sales budget	7. Balance sheet budget
• Production budget	8. Calculate cash flow.
Materials	9. Review consolidation and
Direct labor	request department changes.
Overhead	10. Consolidate after changes.
• Employee budget by	11. Distribute budget.
department	12. Monthly variance reports
• Marketing Expense	13. Review performances.
Sales administration	
Advertising and promotion	

EXHIBIT 9.1   Budget Process Workflow Example

ESTABLISH A TIMELINE

Managers and employees often wonder if there really is a need for a timeline. The answer is yes, as it enables the project to be much more efficient. In fact, a timeline is the first step of the planning process. Any process is incomplete if tasks are not completed in the time frame set for them.

A timeline can be as simple as a baseball schedule or as complex as a computerized manufacturing process. In a budget process, every individual must be aware of the timeline for his or her department and for the entire corporation. A manager could not possibly know when his or her budget was to be completed if the executive management did not provide a timeline for the task. Without a timeline, managers would not be able to research, plan, or execute their budgets on time; therefore, the budget would not serve much purpose since it would probably be put together at the last minute.

There are many programs that can help you design a project timeline, or it can just as easily be set up in Excel. The columns that we recommend in the design phase are: the task, the person responsible for completing the task, a start date, an end date, a completed date, hours budgeted, hours actually spent on the task, and any issues that developed along the way. If detailed logs are kept, then variance reports could be created at the end of the budget process. It is also beneficial to have an assessment meeting at the end of the budget process to determine how the process can be improved in the future.

It is also important to have an initial planning and strategy session composed of all employees involved in the process. Map responsibilities for each employee along with a timeline for each person's processes. Doing this will prevent confusion because all employees will be aware of their responsibilities, as well as those of their coworkers.

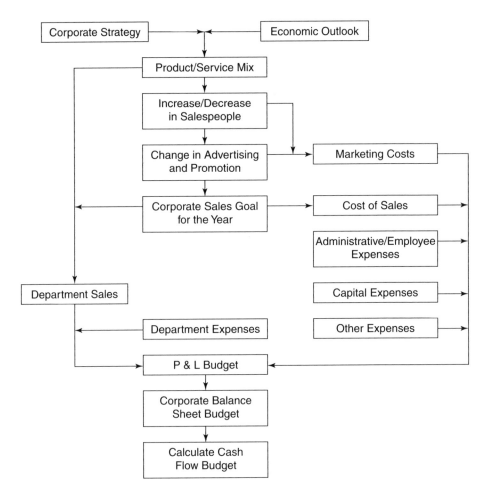

EXHIBIT 9.2   Budget Breakdown

IMPROVE DATA ENTRY

Depending on your organization, not all managers and employees will have a lot of computer experience, which can lead to data entry errors. Research the type of errors that are being entered by the users and try to determine a plan to limit these. Today, many budgeting software programs can be used to help limit the number of errors. Also consider the following for reducing these potential errors:

- Train all users on the proper way to use the software, through online demonstrations and training manuals.
- Create validation formulas within the software to ensure that realistic numbers are being entered.
- List prior-year figures so that users will have a comparable number for all entry lines.

• Use corporate goals—such as cost of sales are approximately 30 percent of revenue—to serve as guidelines for all employees.

DO FORECASTING

A budget comprises an entire year of projected amounts. For example, a revenue budget will be predicted for all 12 months of a given fiscal year. A forecast encompasses actual amounts for certain months and forecasted amounts for the rest of the year.

Note: For simplicity the rest of this section assumes that your company is on a calendar fiscal year.

If, for example, your organization has three months of actual data, then your organization can forecast the amounts for April–December based on the actual amounts in the first three months. This is typically called a *rolling forecast*. The budget should be complete and should not be touched at this point; that said, it is still important to forecast the next months based on information that was unavailable during the budget process.

Forecasts, which are as important as budgets, have a couple of key differences from them. A forecast should not be as detailed as a budget, since the forecast will be redone every month if you are doing a rolling forecast (which may be done every month, every other month, or once a quarter). Some companies will use their annual budget as a guide or template and then update it every month after the actual numbers have been updated. Other companies may have a 24-month rolling forecast, while still others have a 4- to 8-quarter rolling forecast, which means that they will forecast each quarter.

There are two primary benefits to the rolling forecast: It persuades managers to plan on a continuing basis, rather than as a static event; it enables the company to provide more reasonable numbers if there are events that the company did not plan for, such as a downturn in the economy.

There are also some negatives to using a rolling forecast. Like a budget process, managers and employees must forecast responsibly and not regard it as a chore, as it has to be completed possibly once a month. Companies may have trouble setting goals and communicating them to the employees because of the constant need to forecast; or the goals may change too often and cause confusion.

REPORT ON BUDGETS

There are numerous reports that a company can create to report on its budgets, but ultimately a budget should be used as a comparison tool. A budget is the prediction of a future year's occurrence; therefore, it is best to compare the budget to actual amounts for the current and previous years. Some of the most popular reports include:

• A 12-month budget or 12-month forecast (Exhibit 9.3)
• Income statement with variance (Exhibit 9.4)
• Balance sheet (Exhibit 9.5)

TEST COMPANY
2002 MONTHLY BUDGET SUMMARY
Currency: USD   ($1000s)

	Jan	Feb	Mar	Apr	May	Jun	Jul	Aug	Sep	Oct	Nov	Dec	Totals
REVENUES													
Product 1	510	554	540	538	531	601	605	632	621	690	701	675	7,198
Product 2	408	443	432	430	425	481	484	506	497	552	561	540	5,759
Product 3	230	249	243	242	239	270	272	284	279	311	315	304	3,238
Returns and Refunds	–38	–42	–41	–40	–40	–45	–45	–47	–47	–52	–53	–51	–540
TOTAL REVENUE	1,110	1,204	1,175	1,170	1,155	1,307	1,316	1,375	1,350	1,501	1,524	1,468	15,655
COST OF SALES													
Product 1	107	116	113	113	112	126	127	133	130	145	147	142	1,511
Product 2	135	146	143	142	140	159	160	167	164	182	185	178	1,901
Product 3	34	37	36	36	36	41	41	43	42	47	47	46	486
TOTAL COST OF SALES	276	299	292	291	288	326	328	343	336	374	379	366	3,898
PROFIT MARGIN	834	905	882	879	867	981	988	1,032	1,014	1,127	1,145	1,102	11,757
EXPENSES													
Compensation	101	101	101	101	101	104	104	104	109	111	116	111	1,264
Depreciation/Amortization	75	75	75	76	76	77	77	80	83	83	85	84	946
Utilities	45	45	45	45	45	45	45	45	45	45	45	45	540
Travel and Entertainment	57	57	60	62	62	62	63	63	70	75	65	65	761
Professional Services	13	13	13	15	15	13	13	13	15	15	15	15	168
Other Expenses	5	5	5	5	5	5	5	5	5	5	5	5	60
TOTAL EXPENSES	296	296	299	304	304	306	307	310	327	334	331	325	3,739
NET OPERATING PROFIT	538	609	583	575	563	675	681	722	687	793	814	777	8,018

EXHIBIT 9.3   Twelve-Month Budget

TEST COMPANY
INCOME STATEMENT WITH VARIANCE
Currency: USD ($000s)

	First Quarter			Second Quarter			Third Quarter			Fourth Quarter			Totals		
	2002 Budget	2001 Actual	% Var	2002 Budget	2001 Actual	% Var	2002 Budget	2001 Actual	% Var	2002 Budget	2001 Actual	% Var	2002 Budget	2001 Actual	% Var
Gross Operating Revenue															
Product 1	1,604	1,586	1.1%	1,670	1,700	-1.8%	1,858	1,800	3.2%	2,066	2,100	-1.6%	7,198	7,186	0.2%
Product 2	1,283	1,200	6.9%	1,336	1,300	2.8%	1,486	1,400	6.2%	1,653	1,650	0.2%	5,758	5,550	3.8%
Product 3	722	712	1.4%	752	762	-1.4%	836	811	3.1%	930	866	7.4%	3,239	3,151	2.8%
Returns and Refunds	-120	-140	-14.0%	-125	-150	-16.8%	-139	-160	-13.1%	-155	-185	-16.1%	-540	-635	-15.0%
Total Revenue	3,489	3,358	3.9%	3,633	3,612	0.6%	4,041	3,851	4.9%	4,494	4,431	1.4%	15,655	15,252	2.6%
Cost of Sales															
Product 1	337	340	-0.9%	351	355	-1.2%	390	375	4.0%	434	444	-2.3%	1,512	1,514	-0.2%
Product 2	423	444	-4.6%	441	435	1.4%	491	550	-10.8%	545	555	-1.7%	1,900	1,984	-4.2%
Product 3	108	111	-2.5%	113	111	1.6%	125	122	2.8%	139	140	-0.4%	486	484	0.4%
Total Cost of Sales	868	895	-3.0%	905	901	0.4%	1,006	1,047	-3.9%	1,118	1,139	-1.8%	3,898	3,982	-2.1%
Gross Profit	2,621	2,463	6.4%	2,728	2,711	0.6%	3,035	2,804	8.3%	3,376	3,292	2.5%	11,757	11,270	4.3%
Expenses															
Compensation	303	290	4.5%	306	298	2.7%	317	310	2.3%	338	322	5.0%	1,264	1,220	3.6%
Depreciation/Amortization	225	222	1.4%	229	275	-16.7%	240	250	-4.0%	252	255	-1.2%	946	1,002	-5.6%
Utilities	135	145	-6.9%	135	145	-6.9%	135	145	-6.9%	135	150	-10.0%	540	585	-7.7%
Travel and Entertainment	174	200	-13.0%	186	210	-11.4%	196	215	-8.8%	205	195	5.1%	761	820	-7.2%
Professional Services	39	25	56.0%	43	28	53.6%	41	40	2.5%	45	35	28.6%	168	128	31.3%
Other Expenses	15	18	-16.7%	15	16	-6.3%	15	14	7.1%	15	17	-11.8%	60	65	-7.7%
Total Expenses	891	900	-1.0%	914	972	-6.0%	944	974	-3.1%	990	974	1.6%	3,739	3,820	-2.1%
Net Operating Revenue	1,730	1,563	10.6%	1,814	1,739	4.3%	2,091	1,830	14.3%	2,386	2,318	2.9%	8,018	7,450	7.6%

EXHIBIT 9.4 Income Statement with Variance

TEST COMPANY
2002 BALANCE SHEET
Currency: USD

Assets

Current Assets

Cash and Equivalents	3,891
Accounts Receivable	8,962
Prepaid Expenses	555
Deferred Taxes	150
Other Current Assets	85
Total Current Assets	13,643
Fixed Assets	5,123
Intangible Assets	12,231
Deferred Financing Costs, Net	1,895
Other Assets	85
Total Assets	**32,977**

Liabilities and Members' Equity

Current Liabilities

Accounts Payable	713
Accrued Expenses	3,657
Current Portion of Long-Term Debt	135
Other Current Liabilities	179
Total Current Liabilities	4,684
Long-Term Debt	6,789
Other Long-Term Liabilities	5,678
Deferred Taxes	7,654
Total Liabilities	20,121

Members' Equity

Common Stock	2,159
Additional Paid-in Capital	5,109
Retained Earnings	–11,013
Net (Income) Loss	11,917
Total Equity	8,172
Total Liabilities and Members' Equity	**32,977**

EXHIBIT 9.5   Balance Sheet

- Exception reports (Exhibit 9.6)
- Key performance indicators (KPIs) (Exhibit 9.7)
- Sales detail budget (Exhibit 9.8)
- Three-line report (net revenue, expenses, margin, and margin percentage) (Exhibit 9.9)
- Capital expenditures (Exhibit 9.10)
- Foreign exchange variance (Exhibit 9.11)
- Headcount by department (Exhibit 9.12)

COMPLETE ANALYSIS

You must research the type of analysis that will be useful to all levels of management before starting the budget process. For example, let's assume that Tom, a manager at a large company, wants to see revenue by product and by customer. Within this data, Tom wants to know the volume purchased of each product and the price for which each will be sold. However, Tina, the budget manager, never asks Tom about his needs. She designs a revenue entry form that only has monthly revenue by customer; she does not include product or volume information. So when Tom wants to view the volume and product information after the budget is complete, the data is not available.

Often, managers do not know exactly what they need; therefore, it is best to probe them during the research process and make suggestions on certain types of data that currently are not available. It will cause many delays if managers ask for additional information in the middle of the budget process. Many reports can be created for revenue budgeting, such as sales by customer or product, variance reports to previous year, percentage of total sales, and trend analysis. It is best to plan and design these reports before the revenue budgeting begins.

Many managers continually look backward by comparing and analyzing the prior month's data. This is important if it is being used to determine future trends, but frequently it is only analyzed because it is "someone's job." Companies should also look forward to determine future trends, so that they spend time analyzing both the future and the past.

It is important to encourage finance employees to become, essentially, internal consultants. Consultants generally try to get their clients to buy into their solutions because they believe that these are the best improvements. Finance employees should be doing the same thing with their managers and with employees outside of their department. Don't argue with them; instead show them why and how you are going to make new analysis reports that will improve their jobs.

ENFORCE ACCOUNTABILITY

Accountability may be the most important aspect of budgeting, because all the hard work spent creating the budget will be for naught if the employees involved in the budget are not held accountable for their budget numbers. That said, there is some

TEST COMPANY
2002 OPERATING EXPENSE EXCEPTION—GREATER THAN 15%
Currency: USD

	Jan Budget	Feb Budget	Mar Budget	Apr Budget	May Budget	Jun Budget	Jul Budget	Aug Budget	Sep Budget	Oct Budget	Nov Budget	Dec Budget	2002 Total
Group Health/Dental Insurance													
2002 Budget	6,556	6,622	6,688	6,755	6,822	6,890	6,959	7,029	7,099	7,170	7,242	7,314	83,146
2001 Actual	5,555	5,388	5,227	5,488	5,762	5,705	5,648	5,591	5,759	5,932	6,110	6,293	68,458
Variance	18.0%	22.9%	28.0%	23.1%	18.4%	20.8%	23.2%	25.7%	23.3%	20.9%	18.5%	16.2%	21.5%
Long-Term Care Insurance													
2002 Budget	6,687	6,754	6,822	6,890	7,028	7,099	7,169	7,241	7,314	7,387	7,461	84,809	71,881
2001 Actual	5,833	5,658	5,488	5,762	6,051	5,990	5,930	5,871	6,047	6,228	6,415	6,608	
Variance	14.6%	19.4%	24.3%	19.6%	15.0%	17.3%	19.7%	22.1%	19.7%	17.4%	15.1%	12.9%	18.0%
Workers' Compensation Insurance													
2002 Budget	4,012	4,052	4,093	4,134	4,175	4,217	4,188	4,230	4,272	4,315	4,358	4,402	50,449
2001 Actual	3,383	3,282	3,183	3,342	3,509	3,474	3,736	3,699	3,810	3,924	4,042	4,163	43,546
Variance	18.6%	23.5%	28.6%	23.7%	19.0%	21.4%	12.1%	14.4%	12.1%	10.0%	7.8%	5.7%	15.9%
401(k) Employer Match													
2002 Budget	4,204	4,246	4,289	4,331	4,375	4,244	4,116	3,993	3,873	3,873	3,373	3,873	49,289
2001 Actual	4,600	4,610	4,650	4,803	4,809	4,811	4,833	4,910	5,001	5,054	5,010	4,950	58,041
Variance	-8.6%	-7.9%	-7.8%	-9.8%	-9.0%	-11.8%	-14.8%	-18.7%	-22.6%	-23.4%	-22.7%	-21.8%	-15.1%
Employee Bonuses													
2002 Budget	10,000	0	0	0	0	20,000	0	0	0	0	0	0	30,000
2001 Actual	7,500	0	0	0	0	35,000	0	0	0	0	0	0	42,500
Variance	33.3%	NA	NA	NA	NA	-42.9%	NA	NA	NA	NA	NA	NA	-29.4%

EXHIBIT 9.6 Exception Report

TEST COMPANY
KEY PERFORMANCE INDICATORS
Currency: USD

	Jan	Feb	Mar	Apr	May	Jun	Jul	Aug	Sep	Oct	Nov	Dec	Total
Salaried/Hourly Payroll Expense													
2002 Total Salaried/ Hourly Expense	45,045	44,910	45,908	45,908	46,906	47,904	47,904	48,902	48,902	49,900	49,900	50,898	472,987
2001 Total Salaried/ Hourly Expense	37,111	37,111	38,114	38,114	38,114	38,114	38,114	39,117	39,117	40,120	41,123	42,126	466,395
% Variance over Prior Year	21%	21%	20%	20%	23%	26%	26%	25%	25%	24%	21%	21%	23%
% Total Operating Expense	15%	15%	15%	15%	15%	16%	16%	16%	15%	15%	15%	16%	15%
Bad Debt													
2002 Bad Debt	4,964	4,986	5,328	5,003	5,171	4,783	4,592	4,600	5,383	5,745	5,687	5,977	74,238
% of 2002 Net Revenue	0.4%	0.4%	0.5%	0.4%	0.4%	0.4%	0.3%	0.3%	0.4%	0.4%	0.4%	0.4%	0.5%
2001 Bad Debt Expense	5,113	5,136	5,701	5,353	5,533	5,310	5,097	5,105	5,975	6,090	6,028	6,336	97,241
% of 2002 Net Revenue	0.4%	0.4%	0.5%	0.4%	0.4%	0.4%	0.3%	0.3%	0.4%	0.4%	0.4%	0.4%	0.5%
Total Operating Expenses (Includes Management Fees)													
2002	296,296	295,704	298,701	303,696	304,304	306,306	307,307	309,690	326,673	333,666	331,331	325,325	3,738,999
2001	285,926	288,607	297,265	306,183	315,369	314,738	314,109	313,480	312,853	312,228	311,603	310,980	3,683,341
% Variance over Prior Year	4%	2%	0%	–1%	–4%	–3%	–2%	–1%	4%	7%	6%	5%	2%

EXHIBIT 9.7 Key Performance Indicators (KPIs)

TEST COMPANY
SALES DETAIL—BUDGET
Currency: USD

Customer	Product	Jan	Feb	Mar	Apr	May	Jun	Jul	Aug	Sep	Oct	Nov	Dec	Total
A	1	120	120	120	120	120	120	125	125	125	125	125	125	1,470
ABC	1	11	12	13	14	15	16	17	18	19	20	21	22	198
B	1	158	168	180	175	170	225	225	240	240	240	225	220	2,466
C	1	175	180	180	185	185	190	190	195	195	200	200	205	2,280
ZZZ	1	46	74	47	44	41	50	48	54	42	105	130	103	784
A	2	85	85	85	85	85	85	90	90	90	90	90	90	1,050
B	2	150	155	155	155	160	165	165	165	170	170	170	155	1,935
C	2	100	126	130	130	130	145	145	150	150	160	160	160	1,686
XYZ	2	73	77	62	60	50	86	84	101	87	132	141	135	1,087
A	3	65	70	70	70	70	70	70	70	70	80	80	80	865
ABC	3	85	85	85	85	85	85	85	85	85	85	85	85	1,020
B	3	50	50	50	50	50	50	50	50	50	50	50	50	600
C	3	26	28	20	23	18	20	11	13	15	57	49	49	329
ZZZ	3	30	44	38	37	34	65	67	79	74	96	100	89	754
Total Revenue		1,174	1,275	1,235	1,234	1,213	1,372	1,372	1,435	1,412	1,610	1,626	1,568	16,525

EXHIBIT 9.8 Sales Detail Budget

TEST COMPANY
THREE-LINE REPORT
Currency: USD

	March, 2002			Year-to-Date		
	Actual	Budget	Variance	Actual	Budget	Variance
Product 1						
Revenue	603	540	63	1,586	1,604	(18)
Cost of Sales	106	113	(7)	340	337	3
Gross Margin	497	427	70	1,246	1,267	(21)
Gross Margin %	82.4%	79.1%		78.6%	79.0%	
Product 2						
Revenue	379	432	(53)	1,200	1,283	(83)
Cost of Sales	135	143	(8)	444	423	21
Gross Margin	244	289	(45)	756	860	(104)
Gross Margin %	64.4%	66.9%		63.0%	67.0%	
Product 3						
Revenue	231	243	(12)	712	722	(10)
Cost of Sales	29	36	(7)	111	108	3
Gross Margin	202	207	(5)	601	614	(13)
Gross Margin %	87.4%	85.2%		84.4%	85.0%	
Total						
Revenue	1,213	1,215	(2)	3,498	3,609	(111)
Cost of Sales	270	292	(22)	895	868	27
Gross Margin	943	923	20	2,603	2,741	(138)
Gross Margin %	77.7%	76.0%		74.4%	75.9%	

EXHIBIT 9.9   Three-Line Report (Net Revenue, Expenses, Margin, and Margin Percentage)

TEST COMPANY
2002 CAPITAL EXPENDITURE DETAIL
Currency: USD

Category/Asset Description	Purchase Month	Company	Cost	Life Yrs	Jan	Feb	Mar	Apr	May	Jun	Jul	Aug	Sep	Oct	Nov	Dec	Total
Furniture																	
New Furniture	1	1	10,000	7	119	119	119	119	119	119	119	119	119	119	119	119	1,429
Chairs	1	1	5,000	7	60	60	60	60	60	60	60	60	60	60	60	60	714
Chris's Condo	3	1	300,000	7	0	0	3,571	3,571	3,571	3,571	3,571	3,571	3,571	3,571	3,571	3,571	35,714
Desks	1	2	5,000	7	60	60	60	60	60	60	60	60	60	60	60	60	714
Filing Cabinet	1	2	2,500	7	30	30	30	30	30	30	30	30	30	30	30	30	357
Chairs	1	2	3,333	7	40	40	40	40	40	40	40	40	40	40	40	40	476
Bill's Hood Ornament	4	2	333,330	7	0	0	0	3,968	3,968	3,968	3,968	3,968	3,968	3,968	3,968	3,968	35,714
Bill's Very Cool Sunglasses	3	3	500,000	7	0	0	5,952	5,952	5,952	5,952	5,952	5,952	5,952	5,952	5,952	5,952	59,524
Total Furniture Depreciation					308	308	9,831	13,800	13,800	13,800	13,800	13,800	13,800	13,800	13,800	13,800	134,642
Equipment																	
Really Needed Equipment	1	10-511	55,555	5	926	926	926	926	926	926	926	926	926	926	926	926	11,111
Workstation for New FTE	3	01-330	5,000	5	0	0	83	83	83	83	83	83	83	83	83	83	833
Workstation for New FTE	9	01-330	5,000	5	0	0	0	0	0	0	0	0	83	83	83	83	333
Total Equipment Depreciation					926	926	1,009	1,009	1,009	1,009	1,009	1,009	1,093	1,093	1,093	1,093	12,278
Total Depreciation					1,233	1,233	10,841	14,809	14,809	14,809	14,809	14,809	14,892	14,892	14,892	14,892	146,920

EXHIBIT 9.10 Capital Expenditures

TEST COMPANY
FOREIGN EXCHANGE VARIANCE
Currency: USD

	Budget	Actuals	Variance	% Change	Budget		
					w/Act. Rate	Variance	% Variance
REVENUES							
Product 1	7,198	7,186	12	0.2%	6,838	−348	−4.8%
Product 2	5,758	5,550	208	3.8%	5,470	−80	−1.4%
Product 3	3,239	3,151	88	2.8%	3,077	−74	−2.3%
Returns and Refunds	−540	−635	96	−15.0%	−513	123	−19.3%
TOTAL REVENUE	15,656	15,252	404	2.6%	14,873	−379	−2.5%
COST OF SALES							
Product 1	1,512	1,514	−2	−0.2%	1,436	−78	−5.2%
Product 2	1,900	1,984	−84	−4.2%	1,805	−179	−9.0%
Product 3	486	484	2	0.4%	462	−22	−4.6%
TOTAL COST OF SALES	3,898	3,982	−84	−2.1%	3,703	−279	−7.0%
GROSS PROFIT	11,758	11,270	488	4.3%	11,170	−99	−0.9%
EXPENSES							
Compensation	1,264	1,220	44	3.6%	1,201	−19	−1.6%
Depreciation/Amortization	946	1,002	−56	−5.6%	899	−103	−10.3%
Utilities	540	585	−45	−7.7%	513	−72	−12.3%
Travel and Entertainment	761	820	−59	−7.2%	723	−97	−11.8%
Professional Services	168	128	40	31.3%	160	32	24.7%
Other Expenses	60	65	−5	−7.7%	57	−8	−12.3%
TOTAL EXPENSES	3,739	3,820	−81	−2.1%	3,552	−268	−7.0%
NET OPERATING PROFIT	8,019	7,450	569	7.6%	7,618	168	2.3%

EXHIBIT 9.11 Foreign Exchange Variance

TEST COMPANY
HEADCOUNT BY DEPARTMENT

	Jan	Feb	Mar	Apr	May	Jun	Jul	Aug	Sep	Oct	Nov	Dec	Average
Sales													
Salespeople	8.0	8.0	8.0	8.0	8.0	8.0	9.0	9.0	9.0	9.0	10.0	11.0	8.75
Administration	2.0	2.0	2.0	3.0	3.0	3.0	3.0	3.0	3.0	3.0	3.5	3.5	2.83
Total Sales	10.0	10.0	10.0	11.0	11.0	11.0	12.0	12.0	12.0	12.0	13.5	14.5	11.58
Marketing													
Managers	2.0	2.0	2.0	2.0	3.0	3.0	3.0	3.0	3.0	3.0	3.0	3.0	2.67
Supervisors	1.0	1.0	1.0	1.0	2.0	2.0	2.0	2.0	2.0	2.0	2.0	2.0	1.67
Analysts	8.0	8.0	8.0	9.5	9.5	9.5	9.5	9.5	11.0	11.0	11.0	11.0	9.63
Total Marketing	11.0	11.0	11.0	12.5	14.5	14.5	14.5	14.5	16.0	16.0	16.0	16.0	13.96
Manufacturing													
Managers	6.0	6.0	6.0	6.0	6.0	6.0	6.0	7.0	7.0	7.0	7.0	7.0	6.42
Supervisors	14.0	14.0	14.0	14.0	14.0	14.0	15.0	16.0	17.0	17.0	17.0	17.0	15.25
Workers	90.0	93.0	93.0	93.0	98.0	98.0	98.0	103.0	103.0	111.0	115.0	100.0	99.58
Total Marketing	110.0	113.0	113.0	113.0	118.0	118.0	119.0	126.0	127.0	135.0	139.0	124.0	121.25
Information Technology													
Managers	2.0	2.0	2.0	2.0	2.0	2.0	2.0	2.0	2.0	2.0	2.0	2.0	2.00
Computer Analysts	8.0	8.0	8.0	8.0	8.0	8.0	10.0	10.0	10.0	10.0	10.0	10.0	9.00
Total Information Technology	10.0	10.0	10.0	10.0	10.0	10.0	12.0	12.0	12.0	12.0	12.0	12.0	11.00
Total Headcount	141.0	144.0	144.0	146.5	153.5	153.5	157.5	164.5	167.0	175.0	180.5	166.5	157.79

EXHIBIT 9.12 Headcount by Department

danger in being overly strict in regard to accountability. For example, a manager may try to defer a cost if he or she intends to go over budget, or to hold revenue for a later period if the manager has already met the budget for the current period. Managers' reviews should include an evaluation of their budgets, which may affect their compensation if they are not meeting the targets of the organization.

Another issue is that while the budget variances may be reported on, they are not investigated. What is the point of creating variance reports if the variances are not going to be questioned and investigated? Organizations should try to create *ownership* of the budget numbers among the managers, to make them responsible for investigating and explaining the variances in their budgets. Employees and managers must understand the impact that missing budget targets can have on an organization.

SUPPORT ENABLERS

The following are examples of important enablers that contribute to the improvement of your budgeting processes.

Human Resources

When hiring employees the human resources department should strive to hire energetic and competent people who will improve the overall organization. These employees should be motivated to work on and to improve the budget. Also, human resources should ensure that the employees who are on the front line with the customers have an impact on the budget, as it is they who will have intimate knowledge of the future demand.

In Chapter 17, we offer many suggestions regarding the human resources enabler, such as coordinating with the IT department, shared responsibility between departments, and open access to data.

Training

Training, unfortunately, is an area that is often overlooked. Proper training is essential to ensure that the budget is accurate and completed in a timely manner. Training for the budget should entail:

- Giving all employees involved in the budgeting some knowledge of accounting basics
- Explaining the budget process to the necessary employees to ascertain that the budget process is consistently followed
- Training employees on the software that is being used for the budget, whether it is Excel or an ERP package
- Training more than one employee to administer the entire process in case something happens to the primary person.
- Explaining allocations to managers—they will be allocating costs, but they are rarely informed how those costs are calculated.

There are also some questions that should be answered regarding the training of your employees:

- Do the employees understand their jobs and the standards that they are expected to meet?
- Are there sufficient resources for the employees, and do they have a logical set of responsibilities?
- Do the employees understand the consequences or rewards of the outcome of their jobs?
- Are reviews regularly scheduled so that the employees get the feedback they need to do a good job?
- Do the employees actually have the necessary skills and knowledge to complete their jobs?

Establish Workflow

Workflow can be defined as "how the work gets done." Organizations typically produce their outputs through countless cross-functional work processes, such as the production process, the sales process, or the billing process. But many companies do not pay enough attention to the workflow, and an organization is only as good as its processes. Processes should meet customer needs, be effective and efficient, and ensure that the goals and measures are driven by the organization and the customers' requirements. There are three main variables in determining the effectiveness of a company's processes: *goals*, *design*, and *management*.

Goals

The "internal" customers—employees, managers, or executives—in your corporation should drive the goals because budgeting is an internal (as opposed to an external customer) process. The budgeting process should be measured both on the way it meets the internal customers' needs and for the value it ultimately adds to the external customer. Each organization should have goals for its budget process that meet the corporate vision and goals.

Design

Once the goals have been established, you should make sure that the processes are designed to meet the goals effectively. Processes should lay logical, streamlined paths to the achievement of those goals. The key functions of the process should enable the users to meet the process goals successfully. Budgets that eventually result from internal bickering, time delays, lack of ownership, and lack of knowledge effect budgets.

Management

The final variable is process management. A well-planned process that is not managed effectively will still fail. Managers should set the goals for each critical process and ensure that they are being met. The management of the budgeting process should also entail asking for employee feedback. The feedback should involve process performance, identifying process deficiencies, and resetting process goals if the employee requirements have changed. Managers must also ensure that each step in the process has enough resources, whether that includes staff, equipment, or additional money.

Technology

In today's complex times, it is virtually impossible to create an accurate and dynamic budget in Excel because spreadsheets were not designed for budgeting. The main problems that employees complain about before using a budget package are that the process takes too long, the data is inaccurate, there is a lack of control, and the system is not reliable. Fortunately, budgeting programs today can help users create more efficient and accurate budgets; and they can eliminate many duplicate spreadsheets. A budgeting program will enable you to standardize forms and reports, as well as minimize employee errors.

Before choosing budgeting software, you should spend enough time researching your company's needs. Budgeting software cannot solve your current problems automatically and, in fact may only automate your mistakes. Many companies will try to fit software to their budgeting process rather than fitting their budgeting process to the software that is best for them. Typically, companies blame technology when a project does not go well, but the failure can usually be traced to an internal problem with processes or a poor decision in the software purchase. It is best to have a software "champion" to maximize its benefits for your organization.

The following list highlights some of the advantages of using budgeting software:

- There is a controlled data entry environment with business rules and validations that will ensure consistency throughout the organization.
- Currency conversion and consolidation are staples of budgeting software.
- Multidimensional analysis of your business can be done quickly and accurately.
- User security and access control are difficult in Excel, but easy to control in a software package.
- You can maintain a history of budget versions by copying the data to a new version.

Also, a central database offers the following benefits:

- Data collection improves because it will be available immediately after entry for reporting and analysis purposes.
- There will be no need to transfer files between employees.
- Maintenance is simpler because a change to a budget input form will be immediately available to all users.
- The system will have integrity because all users will be using the same model.
- You will be able to create more analysis reports because the data will be centrally located.

Use the following checklist to ensure that the installation of a new budgeting and planning software is successful:

- Explain to all employees associated with the budget process why the budget process is being changed. Employees will more readily accept the software in the long run if they feel that they were associated with the product from day one.
- Describe how the new system will help employees do their job more efficiently and effectively by giving them more tools, which will enable them to make more informed budgeting decisions.
- Possibly pilot the software within one department or division first, then communicate the early successes to all employees. Another possibility is to start with a less complex budget, then use a step-up procedure to add complexities. Too often, organizations make the mistake of trying to implement all the new functionalities immediately into the new process. That causes employees to feel overwhelmed, and possibly blame it on the system itself.
- Wean managers off spreadsheets by explaining how the new system can improve their budgeting accuracy.
- Check the data that has been entered or uploaded into the new system for accuracy and consistency. Remember, "garbage in, garbage out" holds true for all software packages since they are simply databases. This point alone could kill the credibility of the new system, as most employees will not understand how the data goes into the system.
- Install a new mind-set within the organization. Managers and employees usually want to know what the system costs, but more attention should be paid to what the organization will save.

It is also important to determine the role technology plays in the budgeting of numbers. For example, technology can be more beneficial for determining costs than any of the other budget figures. Allocations are a large part of any organization during budgeting, and at times the calculations can be extremely confusing. It is difficult to standardize data in Excel, but budgeting software can automatically calculate the allocations in a particular order. The software will also enable you to do some what-if analyses on your current allocations methods with little effort. For example, you may want to see what the effect on costs would be if you changed the allocation method from headcount to percentage of revenue. This change might take a couple of days to do in Excel, but probably less than an hour using budgeting software.

Set Strategic Targets

Possibly the number-one error in budgeting is not preparing the corporate plan *prior* to starting the budget. Companies should link their budgets to their corporate strategy to ensure that the projected resource requirements are available to support the expected expectations of the organization. The strategy must be effectively communicated to all employees so that they know and recognize all actions that lead to an enhanced operating profit. Strategic targets—such as increasing revenue by 15 percent or cutting expenses by 4 percent over the next three years—that are set prior to the budgeting process must be communicated to the employees involved in the overall process. This information is vital to all managers if they are to create a budget that reflects the corporate strategy.

Organizations should analyze the following points after finishing their strategic targets for the budget year:

- Ensure that executives articulate and communicate the strategy.
- Ensure that the strategy makes sense in terms of external threats and opportunities, given the internal strengths and weaknesses of your organization.

Use Best Practices

The following best practices apply to the overall budget process:

- *Budget and plan for all aspects of the company.* For example, if you budget 20 percent extra sales this year, but manufacturing and marketing expenses have not been adjusted, then your budget will not be accurate for all aspects of the company; therefore, your overall budget will be incomplete and inaccurate.
- *Align operational budgets with strategic goals.* It is common to fail to define the strategic goals, especially among small businesses. Managers often try to get by day to day rather than looking at the big picture; this means you frequently will work harder instead of smarter. Set a clear strategic direction that will show where you want the business to be in three to five years and that will enable your organization to allocate time and financial resources more effectively and efficiently. The best competitive strategy can make up for countless tactical errors, but no amount of effort can offset the wrong strategy; similarly, a great plan that is not executed is the same as not having a strategic plan. There is no point in creating a plan if the organization is not going to follow it or communicate it to their employees. A strategic plan must be formulated with input from appropriate managers and then communicated to all necessary employees.
- *Make all employees responsible for their budgets.* If your employees are going to participate in the budget process, then they should be responsible for their numbers. Employees and managers are responsible and graded on their everyday jobs, and the budget should be part of what they are judged on. Managers and employees will put more analysis and thought into their budget if they are held accountable for their numbers.
- *Communicate goals, objectives, and a time frame to all employees.* If the goals and objectives are not communicated to the managers and employees, then how are the goals to be achieved? Managers and employees are the ones who are going to work daily to achieve the goals of the company, but they must understand the goals and the timeline set to achieve these goals.
- *Grant access to all relevant data.* If employees are told the corporate strategy, then they should be able to view the progress of the strategy. This entails

viewing data and reports or being given access to create their own analysis reports. Of course, certain data and analysis must be off-limits to employees, but they should be able to see data and reports that impact their jobs. It gives them a sense of pride and accomplishment when they can view relevant reports.

- *Provide responses from managers and employees.* It is important that executives listen to the managers and employees who deal with problems on an everyday basis. Many companies create budget templates without reviewing them with the people who will be entering the data. This causes many people to dislike the process, whereas their attitude would be completely different if they were given the opportunity to voice their recommendations. This will also generate buy-in from the managers and employees.

- *Budget a range of scenarios instead of a rock-solid budget number.* Some companies have very little variation in their budget from year to year, but they are the minority. Most budgets are based on numerous assumptions, and it is impossible to forecast each of these assumptions accurately. Typical assumptions are the annual raise percentage, tax rates for the corporation and the employees, and the life of capital expenditures. In addition, most companies have certain assumptions that are unique to their industry and that are more variable, such as the cost of gasoline or the inflationary rate in Turkey. What happens to a trucking company that has a strict fuel budget, then finds the price of gasoline has increased by over 30 percent across the nation? This company has no chance of meeting its budget in this case.

- *Create an analysis methodology.* Some companies have a tremendous ability to create an accurate budget in a short time period, but then have no idea how to analyze their budget during the coming year. Companies should have a set of reports and an analysis method that will enable them to analyze the company data. This method may include benchmarking data or a variance report that shows all variances over 20 percent. Numbers are just numbers if you do not have a methodology to analyze them.

- *Use budget forms consistently.* A standardized package of forms enables your company to consolidate, report, and coordinate the budget process. Commonly, certain departments or cost centers want things done differently because that is the way they have budgeted for years, but it would be beneficial to try to eliminate as many exceptions as possible. Standardize the forms for the majority or you may spend more time on the 20 percent of the departments that have exceptions than on the majority of departments.

Chapters 10 through 14 include a series of best practices for each budget process, such as revenue budgeting.

10

REVENUE BUDGETING

Budgeting revenue is the most important and necessary step in budgeting for most companies, whether small and private or large and public. But it is also typically the most difficult task because it signifies the maximum level of *uncertain forecasting*. One aspect of uncertain forecasting is the economy, which is hard to predict and can have a major effect on revenue. Many other aspects can have an effect on revenue, too, such as a natural disaster, a top customer giving its business to a competitor, or a new law enacted by the government. Revenue will be discussed in the following section topics: objectives, customer needs, chart of account considerations, drivers, top-down or bottom-up approaches, assumptions, special considerations, users, and best practices.

OBJECTIVES

Revenue is the primary driver of a company's activities. Why? Because it leads to all three main financial reports: cash flow, balance sheet, and profit and loss. The objectives of budgeting revenue are different for all parts of an organization, both internal and external. For example, a president of a company may want to make sure that revenue for the consolidated company is growing at a pace that is equal to or greater than that of competitors. In contrast, a manager might be more interested in the products that they manage; their objective is to exceed the amount that is budgeted since it may have consequences on their future compensation.

There are objectives for budgeting revenue for individuals, but you may want to know the reasons for budgeting revenue besides the company's main financial reports. An increase in revenue may signal a change in the workforce, such as to hire more salespeople. Also, revenue budgeting enables the company to plan for many costs, such as raw materials and employee compensation, since some costs are associated directly with sales. Organizations also need to determine their cash reserves for the year. The only way to accomplish this is by creating a detailed revenue budget and forecast.

The problem that most organizations face is that either objectives are not set or are haphazard before the budgeting process begins. Objectives should be communicated from the top down, and they should be explained so that everyone involved in the budget process understands each and every objective.

CUSTOMER NEEDS

Here we are referring to a customer in an internal sense, such as an employee, a manager, or an executive. Actual customers are not going to view the budget data that your organization has created for the next fiscal year. Basically, you are determining what the employees within your organization desire from the revenue budget. It should be determined how the employees and managers will use this data for the betterment of the company; employees, managers, and directors obviously will have different needs.

Note: In this section we will assume that only managers and executives will be involved in the budgeting process.

Usually, the executives are interested in the overall budget numbers, not the budgets for the individual departments or subsidiaries. Because they are more concerned with the consolidation of the budget, they may want to look at variance reports and key performance indicators (KPIs) to determine how the departments and/or subsidiaries are performing. They also need to ensure that their vision for the future is understood and is being met. Executives may also want to make some adjustments at the end of the budget, or run some what-if analyses to ensure that their revenue goals are being met in the budget.

Managers' needs are much different, as they will be doing the numbers budgeting. It would benefit them to view last year's revenue and to know the vision and goals of the management. Moreover, it is imperative that they be aware of any marketing changes, new products, additional salesforce, and new customers. Managers should be evaluated as to their accuracy of budgeting revenue; therefore, it is essential that they have the right tools to do the job, such as the company's strategic plan and workforce. These must be provided by the executives. Managers should also be aware of the information, such as revenue by product, that is most vital to the executives; this will enable them to prepare revenue data entry forms that will contain all pertinent information.

DIMENSIONS AND CHART OF ACCOUNT CONSIDERATIONS

A *dimension* is typically a segment in your chart of accounts. Examples of a dimension are entity, natural account, product, and department. With dimensions, it is important to know the type of information for which you will be reporting in the future. Additional examples of dimensions would be customer, product, or revenue type. Obviously, this will not be applicable for all companies since, for example, a retail company can't possibly keep track of all its customers. (This topic will be discussed more thoroughly in Part Three.)

DRIVERS

It is tempting to think of revenue drivers as simply price and volume sold; however, price and volume are driven by other factors both in and out of the company's control. Some of the drivers that a company can control are the maturity of its products or services, its marketing effort, and its capacity.

Mature products are much easier to forecast than a new or growing product. A product that is mature will have a gradual increase, or decrease, in growth, while a new product can have enormous growth or never get off of the ground; therefore, it is very challenging to forecast revenue for a new product. Marketing can have a huge effect on any product or service, regardless whether the product is mature or new. An exciting and effective ad campaign can influence the marketplace to value an inferior product more highly than an exceptional product. Another marketing influence might be the addition of numerous new salespeople.

Capacity is often undervalued in the budgeting process. Capacity includes manufacturing, time, ability, knowledge, and staff. Obviously, the product or service must be available, or else the product cannot be sold and the service cannot be provided. There are also revenue drivers that are external to the organization: the market, competitors, and the economy. Each product or service within a business will have a defined market. For a supermarket, it will include all families within a certain geographical distance, while the market for a business accounting software program would include all businesses of a certain size. It can be devastating for a company to misinterpret its market.

The economy is another area that all companies should prepare for. Whereas a restaurant needs to concern itself only with the local economy, a software seller will have to be concerned with the national economy. A factor in the economic environment is competition, which may be the most important driver. Competitors can change prices, tactics, products, or enhance an existing product, all of which will have an impact on the revenue generated in your organization. Your job is to determine what the impact will be.

TOP-DOWN OR BOTTOM-UP BUDGETING APPROACH

In the top-down approach to budgeting, the executives complete the budget with little or no input from managers or employees. In the bottom-up approach, the employees and managers at the department level complete the budget for their respective departments. Each department is rolled up into the consolidated budget, which is reviewed by the executives. The following list details the many factors to consider before deciding on a budget method:

- *Administration.* The time spent sending a budget to managers on a regular basis is eliminated when using the top-down method. Consolidating the budget is also eliminated because budgets will not be collected from various operating units. In sum, the number of people involved dramatically decreases in the entire budgeting process when using the top-down instead of bottom-up approach.
- *Corporate interdependencies.* A single department's activities will always affect those of another department. For example, before the sales department budgets to sell 1,000 units of a particular product, they must check with the manufacturing department to determine if it can produce that much quantity. Typically, middle

managers are more aware of the dependencies between departments than corporate managers. One positive outcome of using bottom-up budgeting is to open communication between departments during the budgeting process.

- *Employee motivation.* Using a top-down method does not inspire employees to meet the budget because the executives do not regard the employees' budget as reliable. It is essential for any organization to have the middle managers buy into the budget; otherwise, they may completely ignore the revenue projections.

- *Accuracy.* Managers who are closest to the sources of revenue, such as customers or products, may have intimate knowledge and expertise that the corporate management does not have. A top-down process may miss out on the most reliable and accurate information that is available. However, management must have the knowledge and ability to create a revenue budget when using a bottom-up approach. Managers should be graded for their actual performance against the budget recognizing that this may cause them to be very conservative in their estimates.

A bottom-up approach works best when doing revenue budgeting, since the managers will have the most intimate knowledge of the company's customers and products. Unfortunately, if a top-down approach is used, the result could be low morale. By using a top-down approach, you will not get buy-in from the managers. There should be a top-down target for overall revenue that should be communicated to the managers; and it is imperative that the executives involve the managers in revenue budgeting. In conclusion, the executives should give direction and form a strategic plan that will give the managers the knowledge and understanding they need to budget the revenue for the coming year, but they should not budget the revenue for the entire organization.

ASSUMPTIONS

Currency exchange rates for multicurrency companies can generate profits or losses that are entirely out of the control of the company. For example, a subsidiary in Thailand sells product in Thailand baht. The subsidiary budgets its revenue in baht, and the parent company in the United States converts the revenue to U.S. dollars. However, at the time the revenue is budgeted, the exchange rate is 45 baht for every U.S. dollar. Then in April, the exchange rate drops to 70 Baht for every U.S. dollar. A contract that was previously worth $1 million is now only worth $643,000. Therefore, managers or executives will need to make foreign exchange rates assumptions for each different type of currency.

One very important assumption in budgeting is the type of business. Some businesses have one or two clients that generate the majority of their annual revenue, while other businesses, such as retail, have millions of customers. A company that only has a few main customers must rely on analysis and forecasting regarding each individual customer. This requires managers to have in-depth knowledge of each customer's needs for the coming year. If however, the company has many customers, then the budget should be based on statistical analysis based on previous history and the future economy in the business sector.

Revenue is best forecast by product line. It is extremely useful to compare actual amounts against budget to determine if product lines are growing or declining. When managers have more information on individual products, they can make more accurate projections on the upcoming year.

SPECIAL CONSIDERATIONS

Deviations in revenue based on seasonality should be reflected. Retail businesses usually have their best sales period from Thanksgiving until Christmas. For some businesses, seasonal sales can represent a major percentage of their business. If your business is on a calendar year, then you may not know the results of your current peak season; therefore, it is important to inject some flexibility in the forecast. Some managers like to average revenue across the months, but this is not the best practice, as it creates problems when comparing budget versus actual amounts, and gives an incorrect view of cash flow.

When budgeting, are you aware of the marketing plan or of the number of salespeople who will be added? Do you know that your company is adding a new product line that will be given a very large marketing budget that may impact your other products? Such questions come back to strategic planning. To create an accurate budget, you must be aware of the vision of the company. Without this information your budget numbers will not be good predictors for the coming year.

USERS

The users may be employees or managers or a combination of both. Their needs mostly come down to training and eliminating human error. When using a budgeting system, you can eliminate many human errors, but to do so training is essential. We recommend that the users be given a training class, whether online, over the phone, or in person, in addition to a training manual to answer many of their questions.

In terms of revenue, the most common data entered will center on product and customer. You should try to limit the amount of data that has to be entered by the user. To do that, ask yourself questions such as: Is your revenue seasonal or consistent across the year? Your revenue budget form can be set up so that the user will enter only the annual revenue by customer or product, and the system can calculate the monthly revenue amount by a preset allocation percentage or an equal allocation. Also, you can enable users to enter the price of a product and the quantity sold, and the system will calculate the monthly or annual revenue.

You also will have to determine the type of tools that users will need to complete the revenue budget. They should know their revenue total for the current year-to-date *and* the goals for the coming year. Some companies want the current year's data as well as the prior year's data for each budgeted line item on the form. This may make the form too cluttered, but the user should be able to print the data from a report.

REVENUE–SAMPLE 1
BUSINESS UNIT 001
Currency: USD

	Jan	Feb	Mar	Apr	May	Jun	Jul	Aug	Sep	Oct	Nov	Dec	TOTAL
Product 1													
Volume	50,000	50,000	50,000	52,500	52,500	52,500	53,000	53,000	53,000	53,000	53,000	53,000	625,500
Price	10.20	11.08	10.80	10.25	10.11	11.45	11.42	11.92	11.72	13.02	13.23	12.74	11.49
Revenue	510,000	554,000	540,000	538,000	531,000	601,000	605,000	632,000	621,000	690,000	701,000	675,000	7,198,000
Product 2													
Volume	18,500	18,500	18,500	18,500	18,500	18,500	19,255	19,255	19,255	19,255	19,255	19,255	226,530
Price	22.05	23.96	23.35	23.26	22.96	25.99	25.14	26.26	25.80	28.67	29.12	28.04	25.38
Revenue	408,000	443,200	432,000	430,400	424,800	480,800	484,000	505,600	496,800	552,000	560,800	540,000	5,758,400
Product 3													
Volume	35,000	35,000	35,000	35,000	35,500	35,500	35,500	35,500	35,500	36,000	36,000	36,000	426,000
Price	6.56	7.12	6.94	6.82	6.73	7.62	7.67	8.01	7.87	8.63	8.76	8.44	7.60
Revenue	229,500	249,300	243,000	242,100	238,950	270,450	272,250	284,400	279,450	310,500	315,450	303,750	3,239,100
Gross Revenue	1,147,500	1,246,500	1,215,000	1,210,500	1,194,750	1,352,250	1,361,250	1,422,000	1,397,250	1,552,500	1,577,250	1,518,750	16,195,500
Returns %	-3.3%	-3.3%	-3.3%	-3.3%	-3.3%	-3.3%	-3.3%	-3.3%	-3.3%	-3.3%	-3.3%	-3.3%	NA
Returns and Refunds	-38,250	-41,550	-40,500	-40,350	-39,825	-45,075	-45,375	-47,400	-46,575	-51,750	-52,575	-50,625	-539,850
Net Revenue	1,109,250	1,204,950	1,174,500	1,170,150	1,154,925	1,307,175	1,315,875	1,374,600	1,350,675	1,500,750	1,524,675	1,468,125	15,655,650

EXHIBIT 10.1   Revenue Input Example

The form should be fairly simple to follow; and it would be best to avoid clutter on the form.

BEST PRACTICES

It is important to spend extra time researching revenue since it is the basis of your entire budget. Try to learn how marketing, new products, and new customers will affect the revenue budget. Also consider whether there will be any price changes by your company or your competitors, or whether any new government regulations will hamper sales. These are examples of items to consider when generating your annual budget.

For accuracy and ease of use, it is best to have the users enter a price per product along with the volume. This can be done by customer, if needed, and if possible. That said, you will not be able to budget by customer unless you have a limited number of customers. Typically, the selling price will not be the same for each customer; but if the price is the same, you can enter in a uniform price. Then the volume can be entered by customer and product. Some companies will give a recommended price and volume per department; however, the managers will usually have more intimate knowledge of this information. The program that you are using should be able to calculate the total sales based on the price and volume. Accounts such as returns and refunds can be calculated as a percentage of overall sales. The sample form in Exhibit 10.1 shows that the user will enter a volume and a price per product per month, then the form will calculate the total revenue.

11

EMPLOYEE BUDGETING

Certain companies have very elaborate techniques for employee budgeting, while other companies virtually ignore the process. But as the economy shifts to a more services-driven one, employees are becoming organizations' most valuable *and* expensive assets. Therefore, doing detailed employee budgeting will better enable you to plan for next year's availability, resource needs, and expenses.

Determining compensation for employees, whether part-time, full-time, or temporary, is controversial, and probably is the assignment managers least enjoy. One reason is that employee budgeting is fraught with contradictions. Basically, companies want to be known for paying a respectable wage; at the same time, they also want to limit the total employee expense. On the upside, however, employee budgeting is an integral part of any budget process and does not have to be as complicated as other types of budgeting.

OBJECTIVES

The objective of budgeting for employees has changed over the last few years as employees have become one of the most expensive costs for many organizations. Some companies want an estimate of their employee costs, while others want their budget employee costs to be exact. Employee budgeting includes current employee salaries, future hires, salary raises, bonuses, employee taxes, 401(k), medical insurance, and worker's compensation insurance. These constitute a large number of line items; therefore, it is imperative to get a handle on the employee costs of your organization.

Your company's objective should be to understand the impact that employee salaries and benefits have on your organization. By budgeting, you can also use what-if analyses and see how employee costs will increase or decrease based on different scenarios, such as increasing or decreasing the annual raise percentage.

CUSTOMER NEEDS

Today, companies are doing more analysis on personnel than ever before; therefore, you may start to include more detail when budgeting. Salaries, bonuses, and employee benefits can be calculated by employee and by department for reporting. New hires should be separated from current employees in the budget so that you are able to view the increase in payroll that the new hires will comprise. Also, headcount is very important today. Headcount should be done by position and department, since most executives can analyze headcount reports with this information. This type of report will enable the executives to determine whether departments are under- or overstaffed.

DIMENSIONS AND CHART OF ACCOUNT CONSIDERATIONS

The dimensions that your company chooses will be dependent on how you are going to budget your employees. If you are budgeting by individual employee, then you will need an *employee number*, at the minimum. You may also want to include a *position code*. But if you are budgeting by position code, then you will not need the employee number. This is generally used for security reasons so that no one will have access to the salary information of others.

For the chart of accounts, it would be best to have a separate account for each type of compensation and benefit. Examples include regular payroll, overtime, insurance, taxes, 401(k) contributions, and parking.

TOP-DOWN OR BOTTOM-UP APPROACH

The best practice in employee budgeting is to use a hybrid of these two methods. Upper management should make assumptions about the annual increase percentage, the month of the annual increase, the 401(k) percentage, medical and dental expenses, and tax percentages for consistency across all departments. The managers for each department should budget by individual employee after upper management determines the assumptions, as they will have a better idea whether a certain employee deserves a higher percentage increase than another employee. Management should be able to determine the bonuses, based on a departmental estimate received from the corporate offices.

DRIVERS

The main driver of employee costs is the *annual increase*. Workers in the United States typically expect a raise every year, regardless of the financial strength of the company; they also expect to see an increase regardless of the company's overall performance. But meeting this expectation goes against a company's belief that it should always try to reduce costs. Should a company always give an annual raise to every employee? An employee may not feel greater motivation to work after a raise; conversely, an employee may no longer care about performance if he or she does not receive a raise.

Some companies give multiple increases during the year, but typically, there is only one increase a year. Companies have a choice on how to communicate the annual raise to their managers. A rate can be set by the executives, which may be adjusted by individual managers with a comment as to why they are adjusting the percentage. Also, a company might communicate a minimum raise, such as a cost-of-living increase, which the individual managers can increase or leave as-is. The other choice is to give each manager complete control over the percentage increase given to employees, but with some guidelines from the executives.

A bonus is another typical employee budget driver and some companies pay out multiple bonuses throughout the year. The other drivers are hire date, termination date, medical and dental expenses, 401(k) percentages, and all taxes, such as FICA.

ASSUMPTIONS

There are many assumptions that the corporation should consider before launching the budget process. The following are the assumptions that should be included for employee budgeting:

- *Raise percentage.* There should be an annual percentage set for all employees, which can be adjusted by the managers if need be.
- *Raise month.* Typically, all raises happen in one month during the year.
- *Bonus month.* Some companies have more than one bonus month, but the month(s) should be consistent across employees.
- *Health insurance.* Typically, there is a dollar amount per employee for all full-time employees.
- *Employee taxes maximum (e.g., FICA).* This should only be budgeted in companies where employees comprise a large percentage of overall expenses.
- *Employee tax percentage (e.g., FICA).* This should be consistent across employees, and it should be determined at the corporate, not the department level.
- *401(k) maximum.* This is comparable to the employee tax maximum. It, too, should only be budgeted by companies with large employee expenses.
- *401(k) percentage.* This percentage, if any, should be determined at the corporate level.
- *Future hires' salaries.* Each company needs to determine how to calculate new-hire salaries. Basically answer: Are the managers of each department going to determine the salary of their new employees, or will human resources direct them?

SPECIAL CONSIDERATIONS

The main consideration is whether to budget by each employee or by job position (salary grade). There are advantages and disadvantages to each solution:

- *Administration.* Budgeting by employee is much more complex than by job position because of employee turnover. A job position will have an average salary, along with the number of positions to be filled within each department. Using this method, it will not matter if someone is fired because another person will probably fill the position in the near future. But when budgeting by employee, the current employee has to be terminated in the budget process and a new employee then has to be hired.

- *Confidentiality.* This is a major issue in employee budgeting because it could cause hurt feelings and be demotivating if salary amounts were discovered by employees. A job position budget has greater variability and does not have a name attributed to the salary. A salary attributed to an employee is an absolute amount, whereas an average salary attributed to three accounting managers would not have as much meaning to an employee.
- *Comparison.* Many companies want to figure out what a particular person will make in the coming year. Position budgeting may not have as much meaning to a department manager, whereas a position may have more meaning to upper managers because they will not know every employee and their job titles. One major disadvantage to position budgeting is that the salary is an average, hence may not be indicative of the actual salary of positions from year to year. Another disadvantage is that headcount reports may not be accurate. An example would be if an employee quits and the position remains unfilled for six months because a qualified employee cannot be found. In employee budgeting, the headcount would be zero for those six months, but would still count as one if you are budgeting by position.

Another special consideration is the *calculation of benefits.* There are two main techniques to calculating benefits, such as FICA and SUTA taxes, insurance, worker's compensation, and 401(k) contributions. The simple way is for the organization to determine an average rate for each of the benefits and calculate it from the total employee department cost. Additional formulas can also be entered to determine the maximum FICA and 401(k) amounts per year. The positive aspect of the simple technique is the speed of calculating benefits. A company can also conduct what-if analyses quickly, by changing a percentage and determining the difference in the benefits. The disadvantage to this method is that the costs will not be 100 percent accurate. For some companies, this is not a problem, but for many others, employee benefits comprise a large percentage of their overall costs, so they want to know exactly what the total cost will be for the coming year.

The second method should be undertaken only if employee benefits are one of the most expensive costs for your organization. Basically, each employee has to be "tagged" with a benefit percentage for each of the benefits listed. For example, John Doe will have a FICA and SUTA tax percentage and insurance amount, while Jill Doe will need a percentage for herself, too. This method will determine the overall benefit expense more accurately than the simpler method.

USERS

Managers should be the only users of employee budgeting. This information is highly confidential and should be off-limits to employees. Managers should only be required to enter a few lines of data per employee, such as raise percentage (if different from the corporate raise), bonus amount, termination date (if needed), hire date for new employees, and a salary for new employees. All other information, such as monthly salary, headcount, and benefits should be automatically calculated by the system that you are using.

BEST PRACTICES

The first task that needs to be done is for the finance department to determine the tax percentage information. Basically, this is the percentage and maximum amounts for each of the taxes that your company pays out. For example, the finance department would enter 4.5 percent for 401(k) matching, with a ceiling of $72,000 in salary, which implies that an employee will no longer receive 401(k) benefits after reaching $72,000 in salary during the year.

First we will cover the current employees. The best practice here is to have human resources send the following information to the finance department prior to budgeting:

- Employee number
- Employee name
- Position code
- Position title
- Department
- Annual salary

Some managers will want additional information, such as hire date, but this is supplemental information that is not really needed to calculate any line items. Other areas are specific to certain companies, such as overtime eligibility, 401(k) eligibility, and department charged, but we are going to concentrate here on the majority of companies. For each employee, the preceding information should be locked, but the manager should be able to enter the following information:

- *Raise percentage.* This could be a global percentage from top management, but you can still grant override access.
- *Raise month.* This is usually consistent across all employees.
- *Bonus amount or percentage.* Executive should determine the guidelines for paying bonuses.
- *Bonus month.* This should be determined by the executives.
- *Termination date.* This is useful if you hire employees under contract for a certain time period.

After all of the preceding information has been entered, the system that you are using should be able to calculate a monthly salary, the bonus, and all benefits. The salary and bonus will be calculated from the amounts entered by the manager, while the benefits will be calculated from the percentages entered by the finance department.

For new hires, there are only a couple of differences. First, there should be an entirely separate form for new employees. Though you probably won't know the name of these future employees a name text field should be included so that the manager can enter a name or some type of description as soon as it becomes available. There also must be a hire date for new employees, because their salary will not start on the first month of the fiscal year. As noted for current employees, many of the input lines are locked, but all of this information, such as title code and salary must be open for entry for new employees. All calculations will be the same for them, except that certain benefits may be eliminated, such as 401(k), since new employees may be ineligible for these benefits (see Exhibit 11.1).

SALARY INPUT FORM
BUSINESS UNIT MANAGEMENT—01-110
Currency: USD

Existing Employee	Position	Annual Salary	Raise % Default	Raise % Override	Raise Month	End Month	Jan	Feb	Mar	Apr	May	Jun	Jul	Aug	Sep	Oct	Nov	Dec	Total
Doe, John	Supervisor	55,000	7.0%		4		4,583	4,583	4,583	4,904	4,904	4,904	4,904	4,904	4,904	4,904	4,904	4,904	57,888
Doe, Jane	Analyst	50,000	7.0%		4		4,167	4,167	4,167	4,458	4,458	4,458	4,458	4,458	4,458	4,458	4,458	4,458	52,625
Smith, Joe	Sr. Manager	95,000	7.0%	3.5%	4	11	7,917	7,917	7,917	8,194	8,194	8,194	8,194	8,194	8,194	8,194	0	0	81,106
Jones, Jane	Manager	85,000	7.0%		4		7,083	7,083	7,083	7,579	7,579	7,579	7,579	7,579	7,579	7,579	7,579	7,579	89,463
Lewis, Michael	Director	110,000	7.0%		2		9,167	9,808	9,808	9,808	9,808	9,808	9,808	9,808	9,808	9,808	9,808	9,808	117,058
White, Sam	Admin. Assistant	28,000	7.0%		4		2,333	2,333	2,333	2,497	2,497	2,497	2,497	2,497	2,497	2,497	2,497	2,497	29,470
Total Existing Employees							**35,250**	**35,892**	**35,892**	**37,440**	**37,440**	**37,440**	**37,440**	**37,440**	**37,440**	**37,440**	**29,247**	**29,247**	**427,610**

Future Hires	Position	Annual Salary	Rec #	Start Month	End Month	Jan	Feb	Mar	Apr	May	Jun	Jul	Aug	Sep	Oct	Nov	Dec	Total
TBH01	Jr. Analyst	35,000	55555-55555	3		0	0	2,917	2,917	2,917	2,917	2,917	2,917	2,917	2,917	2,917	2,917	29,167
TBH02	Accountant	40,000	43434-43434	4		0	0	0	3,333	3,333	3,333	3,333	3,333	3,333	3,333	3,333	3,333	30,000
TBH03	Temp. Analyst	32,500	45678-12345	6	10	0	0	0	0	0	2,708	2,708	2,708	2,708	0	0	0	10,833
Total Future Hires						**0**	**0**	**2,917**	**6,250**	**6,250**	**8,958**	**8,958**	**8,958**	**8,958**	**6,250**	**6,250**	**6,250**	**70,000**
Total Salary						**32,250**	**35,892**	**38,808**	**43,690**	**43,690**	**46,399**	**46,399**	**46,399**	**46,399**	**43,690**	**35,497**	**35,497**	**497,610**

EXHIBIT 11.1 Salary Input Example

12

COST OF SALES AND OPERATING EXPENSES

Managers often say that cost of sales and operating expenses is just a function of the prior year's expenses or a percentage of revenue. This is a mistake, one that shows that the managers do not understand the company's costs. Managers have to understand the costs of the organization and how they will be incurred. Without this knowledge, it is virtually impossible to estimate costs for the budget year.

Cost of sales and operating expenses may seem simple, but company accounts for these costs in different ways. For example, a small retail business might group all employee payroll costs on a line item called "salaries for operating expenses," whereas a manufacturing company might want to keep track of direct expenses to determine the actual cost of making a product. In essence, your company should avoid costing "in the dark." It is vital for an organization to understand its expenses and to know how much it costs to do business, otherwise managers will not be able to estimate costs if the corporate strategies change. Thus, it is critical for managers to look at and understand all of the components that go into each cost.

OBJECTIVES

Companies must to know their cost of goods sold in order to calculate profitability. With this information, they can determine the profitability of each product, customer, and of the overall business. Companies should be able to determine how their costs are being driven by sales, and the budget process can help them do this. By knowing where all of the costs originate, the process can be improved, which may lead to lower cost of goods sold.

It is often difficult, however, to know what the costs of goods entail. Simply, it contains *all* the costs of obtaining, maintaining, and preparing goods and services for sale. For a company that makes cups, for example, the costs would include the salaries of the employees involved in making the cups, the inventory required to make the product, plus packaging and storage costs. For a service company, the costs would include training, salaries, and any tools, such as computers, that the employees would need to complete their jobs.

Expenses are much different from cost of goods sold. Many expenses, such as rent, are fixed, while others, such as travel and entertainment, are more variable.

Costs involve marketing, bad debt, professional services, rent, maintenance, telephone, and utilities. During budgeting, companies usually want to lower their costs, but they are not sure of how to accomplish this feat. It is vital for organizations to understand where their expenses are being generated, or they can get out of control in a hurry.

CUSTOMER NEEDS

The customer in this case refers to the managers and the executives. In terms of cost of sales, for consistency, you should budget in a way comparable to revenue. Thus, if revenue is budgeted by product and region, then it would be beneficial to budget similarly for cost of sales. Profitability by product is typically a very useful report for managers and executives; therefore, you should budget cost of sales by product, at the minimum.

Most companies want the managers to budget and forecast each expense line item on the profit and loss statement, whether at a summarized or an account level. An example of a summarized account would be travel and entertainment; an example at the account level would be air travel, lodging, and car travel. Beyond this, it is important to enable the managers to view extra detail for certain line items. This is typically called *line-item detail*. For example, spending $10,000 on air travel does not tell you a lot about the future budget; but, if you list each air expense, all of which total $10,000, then it may be more beneficial during and after the budget process. If, then, for example, an executive tells you to lower the air travel expense by 10 percent, you will have some detail to support the need to budget $10,000 and, possibly, to refute the decrease.

Not all accounts need line-item detail. The following are those for which companies typically use line-item detail:

- Advertising
- Professional services
- Travel and entertainment
- Industry-specific accounts

DIMENSIONS AND CHART OF ACCOUNT CONSIDERATIONS

In terms of dimensions, cost of sales is very similar to revenue. If you budget revenue by product and customer, then typically you will budget cost of sales the same way. After all, what good is budgeting revenue at this level if you can't determine what the profit margin will be by customer or product? In terms of expenses, you can use line-item detail to budget below an account number; therefore, expenses usually do not need an additional dimension. Typically, your cost of sales start with digit 5 and your expenses start with digit 6.

TOP-DOWN OR BOTTOM-UP APPROACH

You may take either a top-down or bottom-up approach to cost of sales budgeting. In the top-down approach, executives may set a certain percentage by which to calculate the cost of sales per product. If this format is used, then it is best to use a historical percentage and adjust that percentage based on the strategic plan of the company. If a bottom-up approach is used, then the managers would need to determine the costs per product, but this will only work if the managers understand how to determine the total costs of sales per product.

In a manufacturing company, the bottom-up approach is best since there will be many more costs associated with the production of each product; in a service company, however, it may be more beneficial to use a top-down approach. For expenses, a hybrid approach is best. Many expenses have consistent amounts, such as rent and utilities, so these accounts can be determined or allocated from the finance department prior to a manager or employee entering expenses. This will cut down on the number of accounts to be budgeted and ensure that there is consistency for these accounts across all departments in the budget. All other expenses should be entered by the manager in a bottom-up approach; that said, there should also be some direction from the top, such as to cut expenses by 10 percent or to ensure that expenses are not more than 30 percent of revenue.

DRIVERS

Not only is it imperative to know what the cost of sales drivers are, but it is also important to comprehend how the drivers can affect your organization, since a small change in a cost driver can have a major or minor consequence on the business. By knowing and understanding your cost drivers, you will be able to enhance your organizational performance, because you will be able to find the opportunity to improve certain cost drivers after evaluating each of them. For example, though you may have the staff to do the payroll, you may find that it is cheaper and more efficient to outsource the job. You would not be able to make this determination without knowledge of the payroll process and the costs involved.

Typically, costs are broken into three categories: *necessary production*, *processes*, and *common price levels*. Necessary production entails the cost of goods sold. Costs increase as more products are sold, services are performed, or as production becomes more complex. For a manufacturing business, costs will be driven by inventory, employees to fill the orders, and the cost of order processing. In other words, costs are driven by revenue.

Processes, the next class of cost, describe how the work gets completed. Two of the main drivers of processes are *automation* and *outsourcing*. These will enable the company to have more fixed, as opposed to variable, costs relative to volume of the products sold. The two main costs of automation are maintenance on the system being used and amortization; but labor costs would be more substantial without automation. The other driver in processes depends on whether you manufacture in-house or outsource production. Your company will have greater control of costs if it manufactures its own product, but control may come at a substantial cost to the organization. In the former decision, labor would typically be the most expensive cost, whereas this cost typically would decrease if you decide to outsource the manufacturing process. Also, your organization will be able to lower the amount of capital investment if it outsources production.

The third category of driver is the price of raw materials. This is the one category that is beyond managers' control because they cannot always control the cost of raw materials, rent, or new equipment. Consequently, it is imperative to have a handle on the other cost drivers within the organization.

ASSUMPTIONS

The costs of sales and expense assumptions will be based on how you will enable the users to budget this data. Some companies will simply calculate the cost of sales based on the volume entered by each product; therefore, the users will have less data to enter, which reduces human error. The company can make an assumption on the percentage of costs of sales per unit sold. Another option is based on how revenue is calculated. If revenue is calculated on volume, then the users can enter a dollar amount per unit purchased for each line item. For example, you can enter $1 a unit for direct employee costs and $1.25 for raw materials. Then the system should be able to calculate the total cost of sales by account.

Normally, expenses will not be based on revenue. Many of the expenses at your organization will not change dramatically, even if revenue does. Expenses, such as marketing and travel, will change based on the company's strategy for the coming year. Your company may want to spend more to promote and advertise its product, or spend additional money on travel for its salespeople. These assumptions should be determined *prior* to the budget process and be communicated to the managers.

SPECIAL CONSIDERATIONS

Companies naturally want to cut costs, but there are a few things to consider before attempting to do this. Let's say, for example, that an executive communicates that the travel costs be cut by 5 percent for all salespeople, but he or she does not give any indication as to how to achieve this. It is unrealistic to assume that you can cut 5 percent of travel costs without a decrease in revenue. In reality, the only way to cut costs is to find more efficient ways to complete tasks or to find the products that your company needs at a cheaper price.

Managers need to understand certain cost relationships when budgeting for expenses. If, for example, your company wants to cut consulting services by 10 percent in the coming year, but will still have consultants working on a project during that time frame, possibly the only way to lower costs is to hire and train an employee to do the work. But keep in mind that the new hire will then add to the employee costs. In the end, then, though the consulting fees were reduced, the overall costs were not cut by 10 percent.

USERS

Normally, though companies budget many line items, it is beneficial to the users to keep the number of cells they have to enter to a minimum. If the users have to enter 12 months of data for more than 50 expense accounts, the time it takes to budget will be considerable. Instead, because many expense accounts are consistent over time, you can offer an allocation chart that lists the percentage of expenses per month. For example, an even allocation would be 100/12, which would equal 8.5 percent; therefore, each month would receive 8.5 percent of the annual expense for that account. This way, the users would only have to enter a total dollar amount and an allocation method, thereby cutting down approximately 500 entries on 50 accounts.

BEST PRACTICES

Cost of sales should be completed in a manner similar to revenue. In general, it will be beneficial for your company, from a reporting and analysis standpoint, to budget costs of sales by product or service, not by customer. Your costs of sales should not change by customer. For example, the costs of sales for a product should be the same whether your company is building this product for company A or company B. From budgeting revenue, you will already have the volume of sales; you should then use this same volume to determine the cost of sales. All of the costs associated with generating the product or service, such as raw materials and labor, should be calculated from the volume (see Exhibit 12.1).

The expenses can be overwhelming if you expect users to enter data for all account numbers. Thus, this is not a best practice. Instead, we recommend that you budget only the most pertinent accounts. That said, it is not realistic to assume that all companies can do this; therefore, the best practice is to have the corporate finance department predetermine the budget amount for as many line items as possible. This can be accomplished through an allocation calculation or by some calculation from the previous year's data. Otherwise, you will have many users intimidated by a budget form with more than 100 items to budget for, after finishing budgeting for revenue and employees. Try to limit the amount of information that the users have to enter on the forms. Add allocation scales (even seasonal or user-defined) that will enable the users to enter an annual amount (see Exhibit 12.2).

Finally, ask questions of the senior managers. If they tell you that you must lower expenses or cost of sales by 5 percent, but you see a future trend indicating these factors will be rising, ask how you are supposed to accomplish this. Ask if they have a plan to get new suppliers, or if they are signing long-term contracts to lower the costs. You are ultimately responsible, so you have to voice your concerns.

COST OF SALES—SAMPLE
BUSINESS UNIT 001
Currency: USD

	Jan	Feb	Mar	Apr	May	Jun	Jul	Aug	Sep	Oct	Nov	Dec	TOTAL
Product 1													
Volume	50,000	50,000	50,000	52,500	52,500	52,500	53,000	53,000	53,000	53,000	53,000	53,000	625,500
Raw Material Cost	1.10	1.26	1.22	1.11	1.07	1.32	1.32	1.41	1.36	1.63	1.66	1.57	NA
Total Raw Material	55,000	63,000	61,000	58,275	56,175	69,300	69,960	74,730	72,080	86,390	87,980	83,210	837,100
Labor Cost	1.06	1.07	1.05	1.05	1.05	1.08	1.08	1.09	1.10	1.10	1.12	1.10	NA
Total Labor	53,000	53,500	52,500	55,125	55,125	56,700	57,240	57,770	58,300	58,300	59,360	58,300	675,220
Product 2													
Volume	18,500	18,500	18,500	18,500	18,500	18,500	19,255	19,255	19,255	19,255	19,255	19,255	226,530
Raw Material Cost	5.03	5.64	5.46	5.43	5.33	6.33	5.96	6.34	6.18	7.12	7.27	6.91	NA
Total Raw Material	93,055	104,340	101,010	100,455	98,605	117,105	114,760	122,077	118,996	137,096	139,984	133,052	1,380,534
Labor Cost	2.25	2.25	2.25	2.25	2.25	2.25	2.33	2.33	2.33	2.34	2.34	2.34	NA
Total Labor	41,625	41,625	41,625	41,625	41,625	41,625	44,864	44,684	44,864	45,057	45,057	45,057	519,513

Product 3													
Volume	35,000	35,000	35,000	35,500	35,500	35,500	35,500	35,500	35,500	36,000	36,000	36,000	426,000
Raw Material Cost	0.634	0.718	0.691	0.673	0.660	0.793	0.800	0.852	0.831	0.944	0.964	0.916	NA
Total Raw Material	22,175	25,145	24,200	23,890	23,418	28,143	28,413	30,235	29,493	33,975	34,718	32,963	336,765
Labor Cost	0.35	0.35	0.35	0.35	0.35	0.35	0.35	0.35	0.35	0.35	0.35	0.35	NA
Total Labor	12,250	12,250	12,250	12,425	12,425	12,425	12,425	12,425	12,425	12,600	12,600	12,600	149,100
Total Raw Material	170,230	192,485	186,210	182,620	178,198	214,548	213,132	227,042	220,568	257,461	262,681	249,225	2,554,399
Total Labor	106,875	107,375	106,375	109,175	109,175	110,750	114,529	115,059	115,589	115,957	117,017	115,957	1,343,833
Total Cost of Sales	277,105	299,860	292,585	291,795	287,373	325,298	327,661	342,101	336,158	373,417	379,698	365,181	3,898,231

EXHIBIT 12.1 Cost of Sales Example

EXPENSES—SAMPLE
BUSINESS UNIT 001
Currency: USD

	Allocations	Jan	Feb	Mar	Apr	May	Jun	Jul	Aug	Sep	Oct	Nov	Dec	TOTAL
Even	E	8.3%	8.3%	8.3%	8.3%	8.3%	8.3%	8.3%	8.3%	8.3%	8.3%	8.3%	8.3%	100.0%
Seasonal	S1	7.5%	5.0%	5.0%	5.0%	5.0%	5.0%	5.0%	5.0%	15.0%	17.5%	17.5%	7.5%	100.0%
Seasonal	S2	5.0%	5.0%	5.0%	7.5%	12.5%	15.0%	15.0%	15.0%	7.5%	5.0%	5.0%	2.5%	100.0%
User-Def	UD	5.0%	6.5%	6.5%	7.5%	8.5%	10.0%	11.5%	11.5%	11.5%	9.0%	7.5%	5.0%	100.0%

Acct#	Account Description	Allocation	Total	Jan	Feb	Mar	Apr	May	Jun	Jul	Aug	Sep	Oct	Nov	Dec	TOTAL
6000	Expense 6000	E	45,000	3,750	3,750	3,750	3,750	3,750	3,750	3,750	3,750	3,750	3,750	3,750	3,750	45,000
6100	Expense 6100	S1	35,000	2,625	1,750	1,750	1,750	1,750	1,750	1,750	1,750	5,250	6,125	6,125	2,625	35,000
6200	Expense 6200	S2	55,750	2,788	2,788	2,788	4,181	6,969	8,363	8,363	8,363	4,181	2,788	2,788	1,394	55,750
6300	Expense 6300	UD	12,750	638	829	829	956	1,084	1,275	1,466	1,466	1,466	1,148	956	638	12,750
Total Allocation Expenses				9,800	9,116	9,116	10,638	13,553	15,138	15,329	15,329	14,648	13,810	13,619	8,406	148,500

Expense Line-Item Detail

Acct#	Account Description	Allocation	Total	Jan	Feb	Mar	Apr	May	Jun	Jul	Aug	Sep	Oct	Nov	Dec	TOTAL
6400	Water Utility	E	12,500	1,042	1,042	1,042	1,042	1,042	1,042	1,042	1,042	1,042	1,042	1,042	1,042	12,500
6400	Power in Building 1	E	22,000	1,833	1,833	1,833	1,833	1,833	1,833	1,833	1,833	1,833	1,833	1,833	1,833	22,000
6400	Power in Warehouse	E	10,500	875	875	875	875	875	875	875	875	875	875	875	875	10,500
6400																
Total Expenses 6400				3,750	3,750	3,750	3,750	3,750	3,750	3,750	3,750	3,750	3,750	3,750	3,750	45,000

EXHIBIT 12.2 Expense Example

13

CAPITAL EXPENSES

Capital expenditures are not always given the attention they deserve. In fact, they should be an integral part of your budget. Depreciation and property and plant and equipment additions can then be calculated for the income statement and balance sheet, respectively. Examples of a capital expenditure include a new server, an improvement to a building, budgeting software, and manufacturing equipment.

OBJECTIVES

Companies invest in a large variety of assets, and the objective is to maximize the value of each investment. Most firms have a limited amount of money that they can allocate to capital expenditures; therefore, it is imperative that they know the rational behind future capital expenditures. Deciding which capital expenditures to make is critical, due to the large amount of money involved and the uncertainty of future market needs. Moreover, the risks are greater since these investments happen over a long period of time; for example, a new building may not be needed long term, or the new equipment may become obsolete sooner than expected. Finally, it is also imperative to know what managers will need in the future year to improve their departments.

CUSTOMER NEEDS

The customer, in this case, comprises managers and executives. The managers will need to be able to justify their capital expenditures for the coming year. They may have ideas for increasing productivity or improving product quality, and they must be given an opportunity to present these ideas. A budget form cannot possibly contain all of the information needed to make a decision on large expenditures; therefore, a manager should keep supplemental data, such as the additional savings. A manager may have a maximum amount, such as $10,000, that he or she can expense without approval from the executives.

In terms of executives, they will need detailed information in order to make a knowledgeable decision. The supplemental information that management can provide to aid upper managers includes:

- Description of project
- Goals and objectives
- Proposed annual budget over the life of the purchase

- Evaluation and justification
- Proposed timelines
- Potential savings and benefits of the purchase

DIMENSIONS AND CHART OF ACCOUNT CONSIDERATIONS

For capital expenditures, one useful piece of information is whether the expenditure was for growth or replacement purposes. This will enable the company to determine how much will be spent to grow the company and how much to maintain current processes. In order to eliminate extra dimensions, you can use line-item detail to budget for each account type. For chart of accounts, you will typically have different account numbers for each capital expenditure type, such as furniture, buildings, or software.

TOP-DOWN OR BOTTOM-UP APPROACH

Deciding how to allocate money for each capital expenditure can be a difficult process at companies where there is a limited amount of money and many proposals. In a strictly top-down approach, though the executives will declare who will get how much, the departments will still fight for each dollar. In a strictly bottom-up approach, managers will turn in the budgets, but their amounts may be greatly reduced when the available cash is realized. Thus, a hybrid method is best for capital budgeting. Executives will determine a budgeted amount for total expenditures, then determine an interim plan of where the money will be allocated prior to the budgeting process. The managers should have a good idea of which items they will need in the next year to improve their departments.

Managers should receive some direction from the executives before they start their budgets. Thereafter, the executives review the expenditures listed by management; they analyze and approve (or reject) expenditures based on their knowledge and experience. Ideally, the managers are told how the approval process works so that they can attach any supporting documents or analysis to their budgets before the executives make their final decisions.

DRIVERS

The drivers of capital budgeting are, simply, the various categories of capital budgeting:

- *New machines and equipment.* Companies will buy new equipment in order to expand business operations.
- *Replacement machines.* These purchases are made to replace outdated machines or to increase efficiency. In the latter case, there may be revenue associated with the sale of the old machines.
- *Mandatory projects.* This expenditure is usually related to government regulations, such as the requirement to install a wheelchair ramp for handicapped consumers, or to implement new procedures to get rid of hazardous materials.

- *Other capital expenditures*. These consist of various other long-term investments, such as purchasing patent rights, acquiring land, or expanding office space.

ASSUMPTIONS

For managers, there are two main assumptions in capital budgeting. The first is the *cost of the purchase*, and this is usually a cost at "time zero"; in other words, the cash is paid by the company immediately, not over time. One concern for a company is whether a manager will have the necessary knowledge to make this determination. In terms of machinery or software that will be used by the manager's department, then it would be a fair assumption that the manager has a reasonable idea of the cost. But a manager probably would not know how much it would cost to buy land or to make an improvement to the building. These types of expenditures should, therefore, be determined by those who do know, which will usually be upper management.

The other main assumption is the *life of the purchase*. If you are only doing a one-year budget, and you do not budget your balance sheet, then this is not very important. However, the life of the product will affect your balance sheet and cash flow in terms of plant, property, equipment, and depreciation for your income statement. Many companies will set a number of years for life based on the account number. For example, a software purchase may have a life of 3 years, and a new building may have a life of 35 years. This decision should be made by top-level management.

SPECIAL CONSIDERATIONS

Business conditions, government regulations, and the economy all can have an impact on capital purchases, many of which are difficult to determine in the budget year. It is very difficult, if not impossible, to forecast for unplanned capital expenditures. There-fore, companies usually set aside a certain amount of capital to spend and conserve a certain amount for these unplanned expenditures, such as a machine that breaks down.

Many terms and calculations are used by analysts to determine which capital expenditures to choose:

- *Initial costs*. These are simply the costs of starting a project or of purchasing an expensive item, such as a building. The total is the amount that will be amortized over the life of the project.
- *Incremental cash flow*. This is the difference between the cash flow prior to the project and after the project has been completed, if all else in the organization remains the same. It is important to know how much a project will increase or decrease the cash flow in an organization.
- The following is a list of capital budgeting techniques used to determine the rate of return of the capital expenditures:
  - *Average rate of return*. This is used to determine the profitability of a project. It may be the oldest and simplest technique used in business. The formula takes the average annual future net earnings from the project divided by one-half of the initial investment. The main pitfall of this technique is that the average rate of return ignores the time value of money. The time value of money

determines the present value of cash over a period of time. In other words, a dollar tomorrow is worth less than a dollar today.

- *Payback period.* This is the number of years needed to recover the initial investment. It is up to the company to determine what is an acceptable length of time for the project. The two drawbacks to this type of analysis is that it does not include the time value of money and it ignores the profitability of the project. Basically, this method only calculates how long it will take to get money back; it ignores any revenue/savings earned after that date.

- *Net present value.* This calculates whether the present value of cash flow is greater or less than the initial cost of the project. Simply, if the net present value is greater, then the project will be accepted. The advantages of net present value are that it uses cash flow in the calculation, it recognizes time value of money, and the company will increase value if it accepts projects with positive net present values. Its drawbacks are that it is based on the forecast of the future cash flows and the discount rate that is used, and it is not simple to calculate.

- *Profitability index.* This index is calculated by taking the present value of future cash flows divided by the initial investment. If the index is greater than 1, then the project will be accepted. This is comparable to the net present value and has the same benefits and drawbacks.

- *Internal rate of return.* This is a measure of the rate of profitability. By definition, the internal rate of return is the discount rate that makes the present value of cash flows equal to the initial investment. Each company will determine its own cutoff rate, which is the required rate of return per project. The cutoff rate is determined by the cost of financing for the company and the risk level of the project. This has the same advantages of the net present value, but it is easier to calculate. The main drawback is that it often gives unrealistic rates of return.

USERS

For the users, the form should be fairly simple, because the managers will typically keep additional information in another type of format. The form should have input lines for each type of capital expenditure, for example, software or buildings. On each of these lines, the user should be able to input the following: a comment regarding the purchase, a total cost, the life of the product, and the month of the purchase. The life of the product may have been set by upper management, but if not, there should be a limitation on the number of years to select. The form will then automatically calculate the depreciation for the income statement, and the cost of the product will be stored for the balance sheet.

BEST PRACTICES

For managers, capital budgeting should *not* serve as a lesson in finance; therefore, the budget should be separated into large and small capital expenditures. The large expenditures should first be prepared and approved by the corporate finance department, then approved by the executives. In short, these expenditures should not be part of the budget until they have been approved. Furthermore, these expenditures should be prepared in much greater detail because they will come under greater scrutiny. And the finance department should inform managers of the maximum amount they can budget for each expenditure.

The budget form should be kept as simple as possible for the managers. It should be divided according to the different types of expenditures. The two entries will be cost and purchase month. The life of a capital expenditure should be determined prior to the budget by the finance department. Each type of account should be assigned a lifespan. Software may be given a life of 3 years, for example, while a building may be given a life of 35 years.

The budget software form should then automatically calculate the depreciation for the duration of the budget; hence, if you are budgeting for one year (generally), then the depreciation will be calculated by straight-line depreciation for the entire year. The cost of the expenditure will then be added to the plant, property, and equipment in the balance sheet (see Exhibit 13.1).

CAPITAL EXPENDITURES—SAMPLE
BUSINESS UNIT 001
Currency: USD

Furniture Description	Purchase Month	Cost	Life (Years)	Jan	Feb	Mar	Apr	May	Jun	Jul	Aug	Sep	Oct	Nov	Dec	Total
Cubicle Furniture	3	25,000	5	0	0	417	417	417	417	417	417	417	417	417	417	4,167
Office Furniture	4	47,500	5	0	0	0	792	792	792	792	792	792	792	792	792	7,125
Training Desks	8	12,500	5	0	0	0	0	0	0	0	208	208	208	208	208	1,042
Total Furniture Description				0	0	417	1,208	1,208	1,208	1,208	1,417	1,417	1,417	1,417	1,417	12,333

Equipment Description	Purchase Month	Cost	Life (Years)	Jan	Feb	Mar	Apr	May	Jun	Jul	Aug	Sep	Oct	Nov	Dec	Total
Tractor	1	250,000	7	2,976	2,976	2,976	2,976	2,976	2,976	2,976	2,976	2,976	2,976	2,976	2,976	35,714
Garbage Truck	4	175,000	7	0	0	0	2,083	2,083	2,083	2,083	2,083	2,083	2,083	2,083	2,083	18,750
Total Equipment Depreciation				2,976	2,976	2,976	5,060	5,060	5,060	5,060	5,060	5,060	5,060	5,060	5,060	54,464

Capitalized Software Description	Purchase Month	Life (Years)	Jan	Feb	Mar	Apr	May	Jun	Jul	Aug	Sep	Oct	Nov	Dec	Total
Budgeting Software	2	3	0	3,472	3,472	3,472	3,472	3,472	3,472	3,472	3,472	3,472	3,472	3,472	38,194
Asset Management	4	3	0	0	0	2,639	2,639	2,639	2,639	2,639	2,639	2,639	2,639	2,639	23,750
Total Capitalized Software Depreciation			0	3,472	3,472	6,111	6,111	6,111	6,111	6,111	6,111	6,111	6,111	6,111	61,944
Total Description			2,976	6,448	6,865	12,379	12,379	12,379	12,379	12,587	12,587	12,587	12,587	12,587	128,742

EXHIBIT 13.1 Capital Expenditures Example

14

BALANCE SHEET AND CASH FLOW STATEMENTS

The balance sheet and cash flow statements enable you to analyze company performance. The balance sheet gives a snapshot of the firm's accounting value on a particular date, as though the firm were momentarily still. In finance, the statement of cash flow is perhaps the most important because the value of a firm is based on its capability to generate cash flow.

Commonly, companies do not budget for the cash flow and balance sheet. With today's budgeting software, these two statements are difficult to prepare based solely on the input for the income statement; therefore, it is very difficult to get an accurate reading on them. However, a budget form can be created to enter this information, but it will usually be independent of the income statement.

OBJECTIVES

The smaller the company, the more important these two statements are. A large company will typically have many more alternatives available to it to raise cash for short-term needs than a small company. A small company, however, will need to know when cash flow is going to be a problem, hence it is imperative that cash be forecasted for the coming year to know when cash will be tight. A company will have an easier time obtaining cash at a lower rate if management knows in advance that they will need money, as opposed to trying to obtain the cash at the last minute, in which case, the company may be forced to may take any loan despite the interest rate. In other words, the cash flow statement helps to pinpoint the areas of weakness in a firm's cash position and in its capability to meet its debt obligation. Also, the cash flow statement can help to conclude the quality of earnings and the amount of cash available from these earnings.

For all companies, the objectives and motivations for doing cash flow budgeting include to:

- Determine funds for transactional needs on a daily basis.
- Determine investment income in order to take advantages of opportunities.
- Ascertain adequate liquidity for corporate growth, especially if the company has credit restrictions.
- Ensure that all debt covenants are met.

You may wonder how a balance sheet is important to a small company since the primary role of such a company is to make a profit, which implies that the profit and loss statement should get more attention. The reason is that the balance sheet is a logical supplement to an operating budget and its benefits are more profound and lasting. The main objective is to plan a mix of assets, liabilities, and equity that will:

- Permit an unrestrained operation of the business with the least investment
- Maintain enough reserve strength to cushion economic recessions
- Provide an adequate return on investment
- Provide optimal financing methods
- Use debt or equity to raise additional funds

CUSTOMER NEEDS

The customer in this case is usually a finance manager in the corporate office. This is the individual who will be creating the detail and/or entering the data into a budget form. The needs of this individual are based on the detail and accuracy required for these two statements. If the customer wants highly accurate and detailed data, then it is best to have a computer system calculate these statements based on set assumptions. However, if these statements are not given much consideration, then a simple input form can be created without much detail.

DIMENSIONS AND CHART OF ACCOUNT CONSIDERATIONS

There are very few, if any, considerations for the cash flow and balance sheet. Typically, there will probably be few line-item details and you will budget at rollup accounts. An example of an account that you might want to budget with line-item details are loans on which you make periodic payments.

TOP-DOWN OR BOTTOM-UP APPROACH

There is no need to have a balance sheet or a cash flow statement budgeted by all departments and units, because these two statements are rarely looked at on a departmental level. However, you may want to calculate each account by this level; therefore, these two statements should be prepared using the top-down approach, and all assumptions should be determined by the corporate office. Only companies that review their managers by their ability to generate free cash flow or a certain return on investment should budget cash flow and balance sheet by department.

DRIVERS

The cash flow statement is broken into three activities:

1. *Cash from operating activities*. This relates net income to the way cash is generated in the operation of the company. It portrays the actual cash receipts and

payments made by the company in its normal business operations and specifies how successfully this cash is utilized.

2. *Cash from investing activities.* This allows the company to analyze the direction of the organization's plan on the plant and equipment categories and its net working capital.

3. *Cash from financing activities.* This pinpoints the firm's capacity to raise cash in financial markets and shows the ease with which it can pay debts and interest.

ASSUMPTIONS

We are going to assume that the cash flow is calculated from the balance sheet and the income statement budget; therefore, all assumptions will be solely for the balance sheet budget. Use this list of assumptions to help you complete your balance sheet and cash flow budget:

- *Accounts receivable.* Assume the average days outstanding to calculate accounts receivable per month. Typically, only retail companies do not have any accounts receivable, and most companies do not receive all of the cash from sales within 30 days. Therefore, companies will need to determine when they will receive the cash from their sales in terms of the number of days. Average days outstanding is calculated by taking the accounts receivable times 365 days divided by the sales for the year. It is imperative that this assumption be made based on historical data. Another option is to estimate what percentage of a month's sales will be collected in each subsequent month. For example, your company may receive 5 percent of sales in the current month, 55 percent in the subsequent month, 30 percent two months later, and 10 percent three months later.

- *Prepaid expenses.* Examples are rent, interest, and insurance. These are usually budgeted at a constant amount or are increased as a percentage of sales.

- *Fixed assets.* These are calculated as part of capital expenditures.

- *Other assets/liabilities.* These will vary for each company. Some examples include goodwill and deferred charges. It is difficult to cover each possibility, so usually this will be based on the previous year's data. For example, goodwill can be determined by taking the previous year's amount and increase/decrease it based on the amortization for the coming year.

- *Notes payable.* These are dependent on the credit of the company because they may include short-term notes and revolving lines of credits. Whether a bank loans your company money or offers a line of credit is based on past earnings, current market position, demand for your products and services, competition, the economy, and your company's capability to control costs. Notes payable is also dependent on *leverage*, which is based on the amount of debt that your company has. The more leverage, the more debt; and more leverage implies more risk. Therefore, you will need to consider if your company will be borrowing more or less in the future.

- *Accounts payable.* It is necessary to estimate a normal payment cycle since each vendor may have a different payment contract with your company. You can calculate an average payment period by taking the accounts payable multiplied by 365 days and divided by the annual expenses. Another option is to separate each expense into its own category and assign it an average payment period.
- *Accruals and other liabilities.* Accrued liabilities arise when costs are incurred in one period but are not paid until a later period. Employees are a good example of an accrued liability because at the end of a month the company will still owe employees part of their wages. You can budget these in three different ways: unchanged throughout the year; as a percentage of sales or total operation expenses; or as a percentage of total payroll expenses.
- *Equity.* The objective of every company is to expand profits and grow, and all companies need more equity to do this. Some companies are able to finance the growth through retained earnings, but many sell additional stock to private investors or on the public market. Your organization has a few options for increasing equity.
  - *Limit sales growth.* When demand increases to a point above your company's capability, it can raise prices or lay off salespeople until the growth level is right. This is rarely an option for most companies, however.
  - *Keep dividends low.* Investors will be happy with this as long as the stock price is rising, but it will cause problems if the competitors are giving dividends.
  - *Sell more stock.* Most successful companies use this tactic at some point.
  - *Increase financial leverage.* To borrow more will increase the risk of the company, so this choice must be investigated and reviewed.

SPECIAL CONSIDERATIONS

You first need to decide whether cash flow will be determined from the balance sheet and income statement or will be prepared separately. If you are going to calculate the cash flow, then the cash line on the balance sheet will be the plug item. In essence, it is the amount that enables the balance sheet to balance. So using this procedure you will calculate and work out all other accounts before determining the cash account. If a cash budget is prepared beforehand, then this amount is transferred to the balance sheet.

USERS

Most likely, the users will be executives. Thus, the input form should be fairly straightforward, with lines for each of the major accounts, such as cash, accounts receivable, and accounts payable. The balance sheet should be the only area on which the executives will enter numbers; the cash flow will be calculated from the income statement and the balance sheet. Or the executives can enter the assumptions and have a computer program automatically calculate the balance sheet and cash flow.

BEST PRACTICES

Ideally, the cash flow will be determined from both the balance sheet and the income statement. The *fill account*, to make the balance sheet balance, should comprise the cash and cash equivalents. Therefore, best practices will focus on the other line items on the balance sheet. It is best to do top-down for your subsidiaries/departments and at a rollup level for the accounts. For example, there is no need to budget for each different type of prepaid expense, whereas it is helpful to budget a total prepaid expense.

The first account to determine is accounts receivable. Two ways were discussed earlier for determining accounts receivable, but one is simpler: Determine the days outstanding. After determining the number of days, you will be able to calculate the amount that the company's accounts receivable will change each month.

For inventory, you can take a percentage of the subsequent month's cost of sales. Prepaid expenses should be a set amount or a percentage of sales. The fixed assets will be determined during the capital budgeting stage, described previously. Other assets are difficult to generalize, but they may be unchanged or calculated as a percentage of sales.

The first liability is generally accounts/notes payable. Typically, the accounts payable is determined from the inventory purchased. You can calculate this as you would accounts receivable. Calculate the days payable outstanding to determine the amount of payables paid out each month. Payables are typically calculated from the inventory. Notes payable may be consistent if you are only making interest payments and your company is not borrowing any more money, but that is unlikely. You will need to make an assumption about the amount to be borrowed or paid off in the coming year based on the company's growth and leverage. Accruals and other liabilities should be calculated as a percentage of total operating expenses or payroll, or it should stay unchanged throughout the year. Existing loans can be calculated from the actual amortization schedule.

The equity accounts will be based on the company's growth potential. Your company will need to determine if it is going to sell more stock, increase or decrease dividends, or increase leverage. Many assumptions have to be made for the balance sheet; however, because you have made many assumptions during the entire budget process, and if your assumptions are reasonable and based on research, then your balance sheet/cash flow will be useful.

In the future, there will be a new approach to cash flow and balance sheet budgeting when the technology that is an offshoot of the current best practices becomes available. For example, you will have categories called sales, purchases, rent, and taxes, which are used solely for your income statement accounts. Within sales, you will set up average receivable terms for 0, 30, 60, and 90 days. You will estimate what percentage will be paid each month, just like previously. The system will then automatically calculate the cash flow and balance sheet associated with the sales— cash and accounts receivable.

Exhibit 14.1 shows that sales for January are $100,000 and that payment terms are 5 percent for the first month. Therefore, cash flow increases by $5,000 and

Currency: USD

Opening Balance		Change in Cash Flow				Balance Sheet			
		Jan	Feb	Mar	Apr	Jan	Feb	Mar	Apr
Cash	50,000	5,000	66,250	102,500	138,750	55,000	121,250	223,750	362,500
Account Receivable	100,000	95,000	58,750	47,500	36,250	195,000	253,750	301,250	337,500

Income Statement

		Jan	Feb	Mar	Apr
	Sales	100,000	125,000	150,000	175,000

Payment Terms

0 Days	5%
30 Days	60%
60 Days	20%
90 Days	15%

EXHIBIT 14.1 Integrated Profit and Loss, Balance Sheet, and Cash Flow Model

accounts receivable increases by $95,000. In February, the sales are $125,000, which implies that cash will increase by $66,250 (5 percent × $125,000 + 60 percent × $100,000). The remainder will then go into accounts receivable for February. This will continue for all sales. This format will also be set up for payment terms. Rent will, however, be different because the cash may be paid out six months early or prior to each month. Taxes will be calculated based on net income, but usually will be paid out every quarter.

15

ALTERNATIVE BUDGETING APPROACHES

ZERO-BASED BUDGETING

This budgeting process was popularized during the late 1970s when President Jimmy Carter promised to use this approach to budget government spending. Basically, zero-based budgeting is comparable to starting the budgeting process from scratch every year. Hence, this method will require more intensive planning and time. All revenue and expenses are scrutinized more closely in order to create a more accurate budget. The main benefit of zero-based budgeting is that each person involved in the process will integrate all known and expected costs without bias from previous information or data. It also forces employees to work more closely together during the budget process because they must know how each function affects the other functions of the organization. Also, new ideas and business opportunities may be discovered, as they will be given the same weight as last year's ideas.

Zero-based budgeting tries to accomplish the following:

- Assess alternative processes and establish the best ways for the organization to meet these objectives.
- Associate a cost with each activity in the organization.
- Rank all activities in order of importance; and prioritize them so that resources can be allocated.
- Establish a basis for determining how well the organization meets its objectives.

There are two main advantages to using zero-based budgeting:

1. Companies tend to use the same forms, personnel, and activities without determining whether they are effective. But by using zero-based budgeting they can eliminate forms, processes, and/or employees that are not effective during the year.
2. For convenience, most companies go with what's working, regardless whether there are more efficient options. Because zero-based budgeting does not use last year as a model for each subsequent year, new technologies, methods, and materials may be discovered that will make the company more successful.

There are, however, a couple of disadvantages to zero-based budgeting as well. The most obvious one is that it is very time-consuming, as it is a completely bottom-up approach, which is redesigned annually. Hence, employees will need much more time to complete their annual budgets. Second, although budgeting depends on many assumptions, typically companies use the previous year's assumptions as a basis. In this approach, each assumption has to be determined without looking at the previous year's budget. If the assumptions are incorrect, then the budget will not be accurate and will be of little help to the organization. In sum, this process can be useful if the organization has the time and knowledge to make accurate assumptions.

ACTIVITY-BASED BUDGETING

Activity-based budgeting is an outgrowth of activity-based costing, which characterizes the "true" cost of providing a product or service (internal to the company or external to the customer) by obtaining and analyzing how workers spend their time. Activity-based costing is often thought of as a thorough approach to allocating costs that can be used to refine pricing models and improve profitability analysis.

In simple terms, activity-based budgeting is focused on the processes within the organization that are pertinent to the success of company. Therefore, instead of budgeting for the sales department, a manager will budget for the process of securing a new sale. The manager will determine the costs associated with the sale process, rather than determining the costs of the entire department.

The success of this approach is based on the effectiveness of implementation. The positive aspects of this approach, if implemented well, are that:

- You will end up with a detailed understanding of the organization's costs.
- The company will have increased control over its expenses.
- There will be an improved understanding of the company's activities and how they are linked to the costs of those activities.
- The internal discussion of all cost drivers will improve, which will enable all employees to understand the drivers.

If not implemented successfully, the negatives aspects of activity-based budgeting are as follows:

- Results may be ignored and allocated costs can be debated since the allocation methods will be very difficult to determine when using this method.
- The approach is difficult to implement and requires the company to use an activity-based costing system.
- Workers must record how they spend all of their time, a time-consuming effort, and one that employees may resist.
- The system is all based on how employees track their time; therefore, your company must be aware of "garbage in, garbage out."

BALANCED SCORECARD

A Balanced Scorecard is a method for linking the strategies of different departments within an organization, such as marketing and manufacturing, to the overall corporate strategy. David Norton and Robert Kaplan, a Harvard Business School professor, found that the standard financial measures the majority of companies were utilizing did not provide enough information to effectively manage their companies. Kaplan and Norton recommended that managers concentrate on the financial and nonfinancial metrics that truly specify how well their companies were performing.

In essence, the Balanced Scorecard approach directs decision makers to concentrate on only the information that is pertinent to making the best decisions. Simply, the managers will view less but more relevant data; therefore, the data will be more readily available and more succinct, meaning that more time can be spent evaluating, rather than accumulating, the data.

The main drawback to this approach is determining what to measure. Management must have clear goals so that quantifiable measures can be developed to analyze the strategy. The measures chosen should cover all functional areas of an organization, such as customer service satisfaction, inventory turnover, quality assurances, and return on assets. Subsequently, these measurements must be communicated to the entire organization and everyone should be focused on improving these measurements. In order to use this method effectively, the data must be accessible to all individuals approved by the organization to view improvements.

When using the Balanced Scorecard approach to budgeting, the process is less complex because it focuses only on the measures that the management has chosen. This approach also links the organization goals and strategy more closely with budget than any other budgeting process. Typically, companies have well over 200 budget line items, but this approach recommends that you budget on fewer than 40. This approach follows the 80/20 rule, which means that 20 percent of the items in a typical budget drive 80 percent of the business.

This approach also confers some very important improvements on the budgeting process. The first is the significant time savings earned because fewer items are budgeted. And fewer measures also mean employees can be reviewed more effectively on their performance; and the employees will better understand how they are being evaluated. Employees will be more effective, too, because they can focus on the main areas in the company and not be overwhelmed by an immense process and then feel they are judged unfairly.

Like all budget processes the Balanced Scorecard also has limitations. For one, it is very difficult to find the key measures that drive approximately 80 percent of the organization, so many managers will throw in too many measures. Consequently, the Balanced Scorecard slowly becomes a typical budget as more and more measures are selected. The problem occurs primarily when the wrong measures are identified, causing the company to concentrate on areas that will have little effect on the company, while ignoring the more important ones. (Many managers will also ignore the nonfinancial measures, but this is one of the main benefits of the Balanced Scorecard.)

BEYOND BUDGETING ROUND TABLE

Consortium for Advanced Manufacturing International (CAM-I), an international not-for-profit collaborative research consortium founded in 1972, concentrates on management and technical issues of common interest to a number of organizations that combine their resources to find realistic solutions to budgeting problems. The Beyond Budgeting Round Table (BBRT), one of CAM-I's major international programs, was formed in 1998 to explore why some companies had discarded the budgeting process. (Some of the companies that have sponsored the BBRT since 1998 include Ernst & Young, Anheuser-Busch, and KPMG Consulting.) Specifically, the round table participants sought to understand the alternative instruments these companies had adopted and whether these adjustments were associated with the advancement of a new financial model that is more in tune with today's business environment.

The round table members believe that using traditional budgeting is a serious handicap in today's evolving and tumultuous markets. They would like to see companies move from forecasting to real-time responsiveness and from centralized decision making to empowerment. Also, they feel that companies must respond quickly to customer needs, become flexible to change, and adopt a set of performance management procedures better aligned with organizational objectives. The key strategy is *knowledge*, rather than *financial capital*.

Today, most companies are trying to improve performance management. Some have decentralized decision making or dismantled their hierarchies, while others use different mechanisms such as the Balanced Scorecard method just described. The "Beyond Budgeting" model may include some of these different methods, but it also provides a structure for linking them together and then prioritizing future plans. Thereafter, the business will be managed in two ways: *devolution* and *management*.

Simply defined, devolution means giving the departments the autonomy to make decisions, to enable them to respond in a more timely manner, and to determine their strategy, and to manage their resources. The goals of devolution are to create as many departments as possible for maximum benefit and to encourage the departments to simulate market conditions when dealing with each other.

Of course, company managers will need to communicate the goals and the limitations of each department. Also, they will be responsible for determining the results and evaluating the departments on their success. Management will also have to promote constant improvement and collaboration.

This new focus on the budgeting process is still in development. To date, only a few companies are using this method; it is not yet a standard.

16

IMPROVING FINANCIAL REPORTING PROCESSES

In our increasingly information-driven economy, your company's ability to change course strategically and find competitive advantages depends on having the latest data on its strengths, weaknesses, and opportunities as early as possible. Therefore, it's more urgent than ever to produce knowledge that can be acted on in time to take advantage of opportunities that present themselves. Consequently companies everywhere are scrambling to find ways to accelerate the collection, then distribution of critical financial and operating data to line managers and senior executives alike. Coupled with this demand for faster availability of financial information is the demand for information from diverse sources. In addition to the monthly financials, you may also find yourself under growing pressure from your company's management to produce statistical results (also known as *metrics or key performance indicators, KPIs*) in order to measure the success of operational decisions. These requirements may include revenues and unit sales by market segment and geographic region, gross profit by product and region, or shipping costs per customer or per order.

Because of the increasing number of data sets that find their way into the financial reporting mix, the odds are high that any BPI effort will have to address the acquisition and reporting of data that originates in nonfinancial systems, as well as to find and present relationships between financial and nonfinancial measures. Fortunately, financial applications for technologies and protocols that facilitate the sharing of data between systems, such as Enterprise Application Integration (EAI) tools and XBRL (a finance-specific version of the XML language), are becoming more commonplace.

This chapter concentrates on tasks and considerations involved in the research, design, and planning aspects of reporting process improvement. Exhibit 16.1 provides an overview of reporting process improvement within the context of the research, sell, plan, design, execute paradigm introduced in Chapter 1.

ETHICAL CONCERNS

The year 2002 will be remembered in part as the year of the accounting scandal. Ethical breaches such as those that took place at Enron and WorldCom have increased the scrutiny of CEOs and CFOs, who must now certify the accuracy of the financial

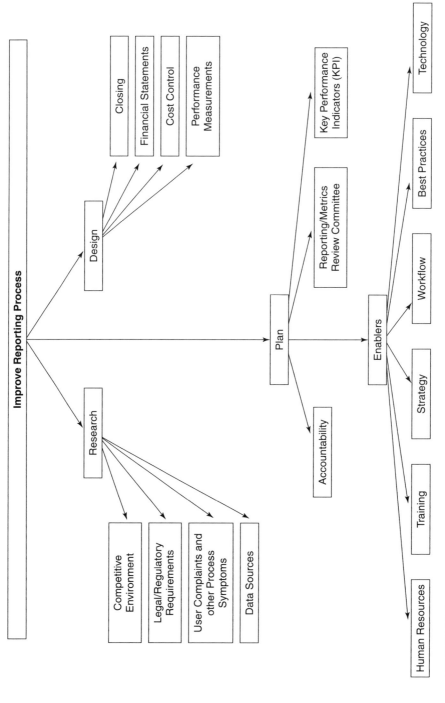

EXHIBIT 16.1 Overview: Reporting Process Improvement

statements they present to public or face possible criminal charges. This in turn puts pressure on already harried controllers, accountants, and analysts at these firms, who will ultimately be the ones to implement the new, tighter internal controls—and under even tighter reporting deadlines than ever.

The Sarbanes-Oxley Act, enacted in late 2002, represents the most sweeping accounting legislation since the Securities Acts of 1933–1934. In addition to more rigorous oversight of auditors, Sarbanes-Oxley also requires corporate officers to prove to the public that they take responsibility for the adequacy of internal controls, and that they have evaluated these controls. This requirement raises the stakes for financial business process improvement, as do accelerated deadlines for SEC filings. Changes in SEC regulations (under proposal at the time of this writing) will advance deadlines for 10Q and 10K reports. The 10Q will become due in 30 days instead of 45, while the 10K will be due at the end of 60 days instead of 90 days. The upshot of all these policy changes is that reporting processes must become faster and less convoluted. In public companies, the business process initiative must, therefore, at a minimum, meet the following goals:

- *Transparency.* This means maintaining a central repository of certified and accurate financial data, as well as a clear record of any adjustments or transformations of that data for reporting purposes. Spreadsheet models and other personal files may no longer serve adequately as an audit trail in this era of increased scrutiny.
- *Efficiency.* Shorter deadlines mean the reporting process must be streamlined; unnecessary steps have to be eliminated. And elements of that process that introduce errors or delays will have to be improved.

With accounting reform now in the forefront of the public mind, making financial process improvements will become key to winning investor confidence. In the past, BPI was primarily thought of as a means to gain a competitive advantage in the market for a company's goods and services; now it is also a means by which to attain strategic advantages in a different and equally competitive market—the market for capital.

FINANCIAL REPORTING AS A BUSINESS PROCESS

People typically think of financial reporting as an end result rather than a process. In one sense, this perception is accurate since the financial reports a company distributes internally (typically after each month-end close) summarize information recorded during the day-to-day transactional activities, which, traditionally, people tend to think of as fundamental business processes. These include inventory transactions, issuance of purchase orders, receipt and processing of invoices, and the booking of sales orders. However, the job of assembling financial statements is in itself a multiphased effort that takes "raw" data and sums, then formats and otherwise transforms these data into (hopefully) useful and actionable information. So we look at financial reporting as a kind of manufacturing process, where transactional data (from financial systems as well as other systems) is the raw material and knowledge is the ultimate end product.

Similar to any assembly-line process, financial reporting should be understood as a series of interconnected tasks or stages, in which each stage contributes a new piece of a complete financial picture. When you approach financial reporting from a process orientation, you are likely to discover that certain tasks don't contribute much real value toward the goal of producing knowledge of your company's financial and operating results. You may find that many steps in the process—including a number of the checks, reconciliations, approvals, and other administrative routines that introduce delays in the process—are being carried out by force of habit rather than to answer any critical business need. Or they may reflect outmoded policies, or a response made years ago to limitations in available technologies that have since been overcome. Constant changes in the business environment, the increasing demand for information in real time (or almost), and advances in information technology make the BPI approach essential to any evaluation of your company's financial reporting needs. Now the only question is where to begin the hunt for process improvement opportunities.

WHAT'S WRONG WITH THIS PICTURE?

Inefficient processes are marked by an excessive number of handoffs between departments or staff members, as well as iteration and rework that is due either to problems of quality or incompleteness at some stage of the process. This is especially true when there are a lot of steps that require manual adjustments, judgment calls, manual manipulations, or reconciliation of data that go into the preparation of monthly financial statements.

You may already have the general sense that all is not well in your financial reporting scenario. You may hear managers in various departments complain about how long it takes them to get regular cost center reports; or you may hear senior executives express frustration at delays in getting miscellaneous ad hoc reports for presentations they make to the board, investors, or major prospects. Trying to act on this unstructured feedback that seems to come from all directions can certainly add to the frustration. So, in this "discovery" phase of the reporting BPI project, we recommend that you begin by looking for certain symptoms. Following are some of the symptoms found to be typical of a less than optimal (if not broken) reporting process:

- *Significant delays in producing financials after a period close.* In the age of the "virtual close" 10 to 15 days is no longer acceptable in most industries. Delays of more than a week merit serious attention.
- *Numerous manual adjustment calculations repeated every month.* This is a sign that automation and/or estimates may be in order for recurring adjusting entries such as allocations, accruals, and deferrals.
- *Similar reports are used in different locations using data from different sources.* This indicates that the process has become fragmented and could benefit from more centralized control. In this chapter, we tackle the question of which finan-

cial reporting/analysis tasks should be centralized and which ones should not.

- *Lengthy access times when using reporting systems.* If you run financial statements directly from your general ledger (G/L) system, access times may become a barrier to getting and acting on financial information quickly. If users of these systems are unhappy with the time it takes to run standard or ad hoc reports, you may need to establish a plan for archiving data that are no longer needed on a regular basis. Or, you may decide to take periodic snapshots of these data and store them in a data mart for reporting purposes. In fact, the practice of data warehousing was first developed in order to cope with the burdens that frequent and complex queries can place on high-volume transaction processing systems.

- *No interim data available.* Of course this is a problem if your industry is highly volatile and requires up-to-the minute data for rapid response. In this case, you should look into implementing some form of "virtual close" (see Chapter 18).

- *Major effort (and a lot of manual steps) required to consolidate multiple entities.* This is a trickier issue if your subsidiaries operate on different G/Ls and use different charts of accounts.

- *Rekeying data from printed reports to spreadsheets.* The real downside, in addition to wasted time, is the fact that these kinds of manually generated reports are bound to have discrepancies, whether due to human error or differences in presentation, with the original data from which they were copied. Then you'll spend even more time trying to reconcile your numbers to those in, say, a spreadsheet that the marketing department is using. It's a bit like having a clock on the wall of each room in the house, all of which show different times.

- *A lot of copying, pasting, and manipulation of data from reports.* Even if the departments in your organization can get their financials in electronic format, the format and organization of the data may not allow easy interpretation and thus require further manual copying and reformatting.

- *Reporting delays due to statistical data and performance metrics.* A major effort is required to convert/consolidate data from multiple systems (e.g., G/L, payroll, CRM, etc.) in order to get statistical data onto financial reports. Part of the problem may lie in choosing the wrong metrics, or too many metrics, and may not be the fault of the source systems exclusively.

- *Difficulty or delay getting to G/L transaction detail when researching variances.* For example, rummaging through the A/P department's file cabinets whenever the origin of a specific charge against your cost center has to be pinned down.

- *Time-consuming process for distribution of reports.* Really a corollary to the first symptom in this list, part of the delay in getting month-end reports to decision makers in a large company may be the distribution of paper printouts, particularly in a highly mobile company where many front-line managers have to make decisions on the road. Finding a way to provide reports electronically, provided that the security risks are acceptable and can be managed, is usually the answer.

- *A lot of time spent fulfilling "on-off" requests from management.* Since one of the goals of BPI is to make people out in the field more self-sufficient, look for technology enablers that will let front-line managers, executives, and their staff do more self-service.

The foregoing list is not meant to be exhaustive, as each company is different and will suffer varying degrees of impact from these process "symptoms." In a smaller company, some rekeying or manual manipulation of report data may prove less of a barrier to information sharing. As with all financial processes, you will have to weigh the negative impact of a keeping a faulty reporting process against the cost of fixing it.

Hopefully, these guidelines will steer you toward specific and actionable agenda for change, rather than general complaints. Looking for these diagnostic clues should also give you an idea as to the kind of BPI work that will be necessary. If the problem is one of access times and distribution of data, then the technology enablers for these processes require the closest scrutiny. If problems result primarily from old habits (a lot of manual adjustments, rekeying of data) then the workflow enabler should probably receive the most attention. Finding the answers to these questions will help you to estimate the scope and cost of your financial reporting BPI project. If it becomes clear that the technology enablers are what need overhauling, you can expect a larger budget than for a BPI project that would concentrate primarily on workflow.

LOOKING FOR IMPROVEMENT OPPORTUNITIES

The decision to improve, or not, will of course be made in the context of other BPI opportunities you have within the finance department, as well as elsewhere in the company. We've already stated the strategic importance of faster financial reporting cycle times to most companies. A reporting BPI effort can have a high impact and, since the process involves relatively few participants, a relatively low cost and duration to implement. If it becomes clear that the financial reporting BPI will have a significant impact on decision making (and you noticed more than, say, four of the symptoms listed), then it's time to dig deeper into your financial reporting processes to find which processes need the most improvement. Before addressing specific problems in your process (and odds are, you already have a rough idea as to which ones are the cause of the problem), we suggest that you first start with a *process map* that links all activities directly related to financial reporting. We find it useful to subdivide the financial reporting process into four pieces:

1. Period close (quarter, month, year)
2. Reporting of financial position (i.e., financial statements)
3. Reporting for cost control (includes reports to cost center managers and variance analyses)
4. Reporting for performance measurement (includes relevant statistics or key performance indicators)

Of course you're not limited to four, and can choose to subdivide financial reporting to whatever degree makes sense. Throughout the remainder of this section we will base our examples on this division of reporting into four subprocesses. A process map might link these subprocesses together, as shown in Exhibit 16.2.

As you delve further into the current or as-is state of the process, the overall process map should guide you to specific subprocesses so you can in turn start mapping them, using the flowcharting conventions described in Chapter 1. We suggest mapping all processes only down to significant milestones, where the process is moved forward or work-in-progress is handed off between people and/or departments, taking special note of those steps where delays are introduced. It is best to resist the urge to draw the whole process in minute detail. The incremental work of mapping every task and data entry routine in minute detail won't necessarily contribute much value. What you'll be looking for here are those points in the process that introduce the most delays and quality problems and are therefore ideal starting points for your BPI project. Later on, you will probably find it helpful to diagram, or map, these problem areas in greater detail.

Exhibits 16.3 and 16.4 provide examples of how the reporting process might be broken down into their respective milestones. Once this is done, you can continue mapping problem areas down to specific tasks in order to determine where delays are introduced. The examples assume a less-than-perfect process so that we can show improvements later on.

We realize that, in some companies, tasks such as allocations, currency conversions, and elimination entries are accomplished by making entries in the general

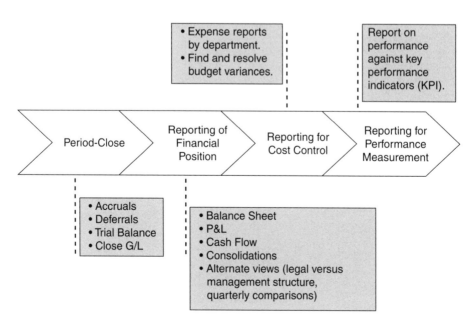

EXHIBIT 16.2   Map of Processes

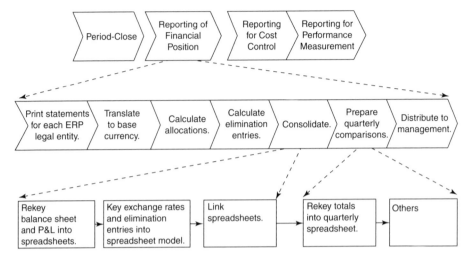

EXHIBIT 16.3   Reporting of Financial Position

ledger. In that case, you would include these steps in your map of the closing process rather than the financial statement process. In fact, you may find that there is enough overlap between closing and financial statement preparation to justify approaching them as a single process.

One you have identified the key financial reporting processes, and especially those more prone to delays and problems of data quality, it's time to frame each process in terms of the process enablers mentioned in Chapter 1.

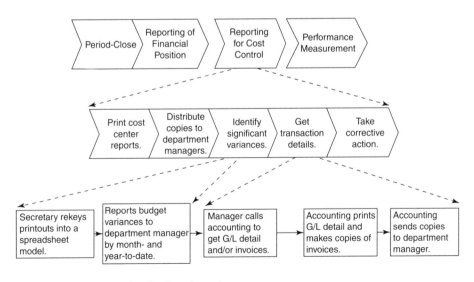

EXHIBIT 16.4   Reporting for Cost Control

EVALUATING REPORTING PROCESS ENABLERS

Now that you've seen a fairly detailed view of how the four key financial processes might take place in a typical company, where should you start looking for improvement opportunities? At this stage it might be tempting to dig into the workflow and start shifting tasks to a different sequence or to different people. But workflow is only one of the enablers you'll need to address; a more thorough approach should examine the underlying conditions that led to this faulty workflow, which may stem not so much from bad habits as from limitations in available technologies that existed when the process was designed, or from rules, procedures, and strategic initiatives drafted to suit a business environment that has since changed.

In Chapters 17, 18, and 19 we suggest the ideal characteristics of each enabler as they apply to the financial reporting process. Depending on the size of your company, your organizational structure, and your budget, some of these suggestions will be relevant and some won't. The process enablers—human resources, training, corporate strategy, best practices, technology, and workflow—comprise the linchpin of any process improvement effort. Therefore, you should assess the impact of each of these enablers on any process you are looking to improve, whether positive or negative. By improving these enablers, you improve the process. Exhibit 16.5 is an example of how you might assemble these rankings in a tabular format. Each process enabler is ranked by its negative impact (on a scale of 1 to 5, where 5 has the most impact) on the process. Those that cross a certain threshold (impact of 3 or greater in this example) are considered for improvement.

Process: Month-End Close

Enabler	Constraints/Weaknesses	Impact	Action
Human Resources/ Training	• Accounting staff not adequately trained to handle more difficult transactions such as intercompany sales. • We wind up correcting a lot of coding errors at month-end.	5	Improve
Best Practices	• We allocate 50 different accounts down to the cost center level. • Each of our 12 foreign subsidiaries runs a routine to translate its transactions to dollars prior to closing. Each sub maintains its own exchange rate table.	3	Improve
Technology	• We lack a means of collecting travel expense reports online, so we spend a few days around month-end tracking down errant expense reports. • Booking of allocations and accruals is not automated.	2	Leave as-is

EXHIBIT 16.5   Process Enabler Ranking   *(continues)*

Process: Month-End Close (Continued)

Enabler	Constraints/Weaknesses	Impact	Action
Workflow	• We have several approval steps for journal entries; if a manager is unavailable, the process is delayed. • Field offices forward invoices in batches the week before close, where they are entered into the A/P system by accounting staff at the home office.	4	Improve

Process: Reporting of Financial Position

Enabler	Constraints/Weaknesses	Impact	Action
Human Resources/ Training	• Analysts are not adequately trained on how to handle intercompany transactions. • Analysts and accountants have to turn to IT department for new reports because they are unfamiliar with the reporting software we use.	4	Improve
Best Practices	• We prepare notes and commentaries after month-close, after books are closed and we have preliminary financials.	2	Leave as-is
Technology	• We have more ERP instances than we need, and the chart of accounts is not consistent between them. • Elimination is a manual task. We have to run a report on intercompany charges, then add these up and enter the eliminating entries in a spreadsheet model.	4	Improve
Workflow	• Analysts key printed report figures into spreadsheets, then link them for consolidation. • We copy data from the standard format into spreadsheets that satisfy ad hoc views and comparisons requested by upper management.	4	Improve

Process: Reporting for Cost Control

Enabler	Constraints/Weaknesses	Impact	Action
Human Resources/ Training	• Cost center managers aren't sure how to interpret financial reports. They don't understand why certain accruals or allocations are booked to their cost center.	4	Improve
Best Practices	• Major variances are reported to managers two weeks after close, when the standard report package is sent out. There is no interim checking of variances by finance staff.	3	Improve

EXHIBIT 16.5   *Continued*

Process: Reporting for Cost Control (Continued)

Enabler	Constraints/Weaknesses	Impact	Action
Technology	• We have no means of automating access to G/L for cost center managers. They call finance whenever they have questions on specific variances. • We have to refer any requests for ad hoc variance analysis reports to IT. We then have to test these to make sure they reconcile.	3	Improve
Workflow	• The process of printing and distributing operating statements for cost centers is time-consuming. • Managers (or their assistants) have to rekey the figures from these printouts into spreadsheets if they want to do any kind of analyses.	4	Improve

Process: Reporting for Performance Measurement

Enabler	Constraints/Weaknesses	Impact	Action
Human Resources/ Training	• Responsibility for reporting key metrics is not shared among departments. Even though HR keeps track of headcount in its system, Finance duplicates the process for its own reports. The same happens with sales forecasts.	3	Improve
Best Practices	• We don't have agreement on the key metrics that matter throughout the company. Each department compiles and reports the statistics that matter to it. • There is no linkage between the measures that we report and company strategy, and they seem to have little value in predicting future outcomes. Instead, managers use them to explain why they are over- or under-budget.	5	Improve
Technology	• We rely on spreadsheets for reporting on key indicators such as market share, number of new accounts, and cash-conversion cycle. • There is no one system that collects, compiles, and reports these figures so that interested managers have access to them.	4	Improve
Workflow	• The task of reporting new and lost accounts by sales territory requires sign-off from several sales managers. • We have to query two systems and make a number of calculations in order arrive at standard product costs.	2	Leave as-is

EXHIBIT 16.5   *Continued*

17

HUMAN RESOURCES, TRAINING, STRATEGY, AND WORKFLOW

HUMAN RESOURCES

Ultimately, the success of any process improvement agenda depends on a trained, capable, and motivated staff. The following are suggestions on how to make the most of the people who support the financial reporting process:

- *Organize around financial processes.* For companies with larger accounting staffs, it may make sense to set up cross-functional accounting teams since many finance functions are interrelated.[1] By organizing the people around financial processes, they gain a broader perspective on their individual role in these processes, and have a better idea to whom they should refer problems. The integration of functions within teams also allows for fewer departmental barriers in getting quality issues resolved. A team approach of this kind should involve cross-training team members on each other's tasks. This has the benefit of helping team members see their work in the context of a larger workflow, as well as enabling the team to compensate when members go on vacation or medical leave.

- *Centralize the financial analyst job function.* Consider ways to centralize the analyst function while decentralizing the tasks typically given to financial analysts. Tasks such as formatting data for reports, charts, and graphs, or choosing fonts for financial presentations are best left to department managers and their staffs. Offering a standard set of front-end reporting tools capable of combining quantitative and graphical presentations facilitates this self-service approach (see Chapter 19) and allows the analysts to concentrate on more valuable tasks, such as looking at significant variances and trends and providing advice on these trends to management. Making financial analysis a *shared service* (versus a task each business unit does for itself) will enable you to emphasize and report on standard goals and measures of success and to apply them across divisional boundaries.

- *Coordinate with the IT department.* Your reporting BPI project is going be a systems project, by and large. Whether this will entail the enhancement of existing systems or acquisition of new ones, IT will have to be involved in every step of the project. Perhaps the best way to ensure that this happens is, again, to cross-train. By cross-training more technically oriented finance staff in database and report-writing applications, you become less reliant on the IT department every time subtle changes are required in the content or layout of financial reports. A more ideal arrangement is to allow sharing of staff between these departments, since increasingly the lines between finance and information technology job functions are blurred as both departments share the mandate of getting useful information onto the desktops of decision makers throughout the organization.

- *Share reporting responsibilities between functional departments.* Resources tend to be wasted on duplicated efforts that take place due to departmental barriers. Unless top executives assign accountability for a reporting process that spans multiple departments, this will continue to happen. For example, one area that can pose problems is counting the number of people who work for a company. Usually, human resources counts them. But since finance doesn't trust human resources, finance winds up counting them as well. This kind of duplication occurs not only with personnel data, but also to some degree with sales estimates and other key performance metrics, and frequently leads to discrepancies and misinformation. Nonfinancial departments should be consulted, included, and held accountable for the reporting of nonfinancial numbers.

- *Require open access to pertinent financial data.* This means giving front-line managers direct access to the information they need to do their jobs. But we want to emphasize the word "pertinent," because we're not advocating that you throw open the doors to the back office. In many organizations, the attitude persists that control of information is power. When finance evolves to view itself as an information service, not an information guardian, it can achieve process gains by pushing a lot of low-level decision making and variance analysis to the front lines, where it belongs. This requires not only a change in mind-set but a willingness to invest in infrastructure (or the deployment of resources the company already has) that will speed the delivery of information.

- *Provide incentives for good transactional data.* If your data is bad to begin with, new software won't necessarily correct the problem. The people who input G/L data aren't always given incentives to keep the data "clean." Errors such as coding of duplicate entries, entries without the appropriate offsets, or entries to the wrong account are often tolerated with the understanding that the month-end closing process will sort these problems out. Instead, why not consider avoiding discrepancies at the source, by providing training in problem areas and instituting a measurement program that reports quality feedback every month and rewards financial process teams with recognition and bonuses for reaching improvement targets. These targets might include reductions in data entry errors, as well as reductions in the closing times for the general ledger and subledgers.

- *Establish a communication strategy.* If new software and processes are going to take hold, you should establish the means and a plan to communicate the uses and benefits of new systems. This might include a dedicated intranet site, classroom training, or online learning resources for end users. Your communication campaign should explain how to navigate the new system and provide regular notifications to the user community when new data are available (after period closes, for example).

- *Designate a financial reporting committee.* Your organization has many stakeholders in the reporting process. Input from line managers, senior executives, and cost center managers is critical to understanding whether your process improvements are hitting their mark. In fact, interviews and discussions with this group may determine which initiatives are funded and adopted and which will be skipped for now. We suggest that you formalize this feedback loop by organizing a committee that represents key beneficiaries of the process throughout the company. This will include not all but at least a representative panel of information consumers, including managers of divisions, product lines, the executive committee, and department or cost center managers. This group should comprise a metrics committee (which can be a subset of the group) that will determine the nonfinancial measures that must be included in the reporting mix. The cross-functional nature of any metrics-gathering program makes this an ideal source of specifications for that project.

TRAINING

Several job functions may be affected by process changes, so be sure to budget time and money for retraining as process improvements are implemented. Those affected may include not only "producers" but also "consumers" of financial information. As we mentioned under human resources, try to facilitate self-service access to any data required for decision making from the front lines.

Department/Cost Center Managers

Are managers trained to use financial systems and reports, or are reports just thrown in their laps with no explanation? One opportunity here, especially if you are investing in new technology enablers, is to train managers on tasks such as spotting and controlling variances (even how to get ledger detail if this is available online), rather than leaving these tasks solely to the analysts.

Accounting Staff

If the period close is a source of delays, you might want to consider more frequent and standardized training on transactional systems, such as the G/L and subledgers, in order to cut down on data entry errors. A lot of the delays that emerge in the consolidation and preparation of financial reports originate in transactional systems, where postings can easily be made to the wrong accounts. Although systems can be customized with "business rules" that prevent input errors, many G/L tasks require judgment calls on the part of the staff accountant or clerk who has to determine how an entry should be booked. Providing structured training and documentation on more troublesome procedures such as intercompany transactions, accruals, and entries to reverse errors can go a long way to improving the reporting process. If you deal with tangible merchandise, your training initiative might include practices for isolating and reporting on those high-cost and high-volume inventory items that require more frequent cycle counting.

Analysts

Whether responsibility for financial analysis devolves to the corporate controller (as is often the case in smaller companies) or has a dedicated staff of a dozen people, analysts will need training on database systems and report-writing applications that will inevitably support your BPI efforts companywide. Once they understand how to use reporting applications to link data from various source system databases, such as the general ledger, customer relationship management (CRM), or manufacturing systems, they can take a lot of the burden off of your IT department. Analysts tend to have a better understanding of the business and can therefore concentrate on those technical reporting requirements that are most essential to management decision making.

Since a company's financial analysts are often the ones charged with the task of producing consolidated statements, they will need training on postclose consolidating entries, such as currency translation adjustments and eliminations. By formulating a clear policy on the calculation and booking of these kinds of entries, and by training both G/L accountants and analysts to work together on the entire process, including the booking of intercompany transactions and elimination entries, a lot of errors can be avoided.

STRATEGY

Your reporting process should support the company's strategy. Whether this strategy is to acquire new customers and market share, or to retrench and cut costs, the reporting process will determine whether management has the information they need to make the strategy happen. Consider the following principles as you look for ways to bring your reporting process into harmony with your organization's strategic aims:

Review Reporting Requirements Often

Regularly review reporting routines to determine what is useful (and what is not) to strategic decision making. Your current monthly reporting run may include a number of trend reports or other specialized views that developed as ad hoc or one-off requests that applied to a particular project, but no longer have any current use. The exercise of improving reporting speed will force you to examine any nonvalue-adding activity anyway. Once you have formed a financial reporting review committee, this will become the group that meets to review reporting routines and determine what supports strategy and what does not.

Agree on Key Metrics

Alignment of financial and reporting systems with the company's strategy requires not only fast delivery, but delivery of the *right* metrics. By "metrics" we mean measure, whether financial or otherwise, of a company's operational outcomes. Metrics may include statistical figures such as volume sales, headcount, or number of first-time customers. Many companies combine both financial and nonfinancial metrics to generate ratios that provide indicators of the financial impact of certain events, such as costs per new hire or acquisition costs per new customer. Companies that have done the best job in identifying the key metrics that drive their business are the ones most likely to base decisions on predictors of future performance rather than markers of past performance.

Determining which metrics are needed and the method of acquisition and/or calculation of metric data can only come through a process of discussion and agreement. The team that meets to decide these questions will be cross-functional, consisting of members of diverse departments like operations, logistics, marketing, and engineering. One major barrier to faster reporting processes is the time spent handling a barrage of ad hoc requests that come from senior management looking for special information, usually for a one-time presentation or to resolve an isolated variance. By agreeing on the key metrics that measure a company's health and the strength of its future, the review team cuts down on one-offs of this kind and focuses on a set of indicators and the consistent, timely readouts from these indicators. Many prospective metrics are tracked by various departments for their own use, even though other departments might also benefit from adopting similar metrics. In some cases, the same statistic is tracked in departments but is described and applied differently. As common metrics are discovered, it's important to develop a common terminology to describe these metrics that will become standard across departments or divisions. While this list may change over time, it should be subject to a regular review process that evaluates it against overall strategy. Questions you should ask of your reporting metrics: Do they measure our success at achieving a strategy? Will they suggest a course of action?

Your choice of metrics will depend largely on your industry. An airline, for example, will have an interest in load factors (the percentage of seats occupied), on-time arrivals, lost bags per X number of passengers, flight cancellation rates, and formal complaints per X number of passengers. Strategy will also determine which metrics you choose to monitor. Companies in growth mode, that are concerned primarily with market share, will naturally concentrate on customer measures, including the number of sales to new customers, retention rates, and customer acquisition costs. While the financial impact of such measures may not be known at the beginning of an initiative to track them, a perceived logical relationship might justify the effort of determining the existence and degree of financial impact. Depending on the degree of diversification of your company, the number of metrics you choose to monitor may range from 5 to 25. For each of the most important metrics, you may want to appoint a manager in charge of determining how the data for his or her assigned metrics will be collected. In some cases, of course, the same manager will be responsible for several metrics. Managers of corporate functions such as human resources, plant operations, engineering, and sales, as well as the administrators of the information systems that support these departments, will typically take on this metrics manager role. In some cases, this role may be shared among two or more managers if inputs from multiple systems/departments are needed for a given metric, or in cases where some oversight is needed to lessen the temptation for individual managers to "adjust" the numbers in their own favor (see Exhibit 17.1).

The reporting/metrics team should determine the frequency of metrics as part of its plan. Less frequent reporting (monthly or quarterly) may suffice for companies that have lower business volatility—for example, mature businesses with low margins, such as major retailers, supermarkets, monopolies, and government agencies. Companies that are more susceptible to changing market conditions will need to evaluate metrics more frequently, even daily.

Find a Context for Metrics

A metrics program can support a number of common strategic improvement initiatives, such as activity-based costing (ABC) or Economic Value-Added (EVA). Some

	VP Sales	Controller	Production Manager	Personnel Director	Shipping Manager	VP Marketing
Won/lost deals	X					
Customer satisfaction						X
Rate of Return (ROI, EVA, etc.)		X				
Cash conversion cycle		X				
FTEs by department				X		
Training days per employee				X		
Average days to fill order					X	
Industry benchmarks		X				X
Cost variance by product		X	X			

EXHIBIT 17.1   Metrics Responsibility Chart

examples of performance measurement approaches that can provide a framework for metrics are:

- *Activity-based costing.* Activity-based costing is an accounting method that assigns costs to activities rather than to departments. This enables resource and overhead costs to be more accurately assigned to the products and the services that utilize them. In order to accurately associate costs with products or services, the ABC approach establishes a cost for significant activities based on their use of resources. Resources include labor, equipment, and materials; activities include any business process that consumes these resources. When the cost of any activity is determined, it can be applied to a *cost object*, such as a product or service, based on use of activities. Knowledge of activity or process costs should enable better pricing, outsourcing, and capital spending decisions. An ABC initiative will create a demand for metrics that reveal resource drivers such as cycle times or labor hours spent on such tasks as order fulfillment, resolution of product quality problems, and other key business processes.

- *Economic Value-Added.* EVA, which was popularized by the consulting firm Stern Stewart, uses an estimated cost of capital as a means of evaluating investment opportunities and business performance. EVA is the net operating profit less a charge for the opportunity cost of the capital invested to get that profit. This cost of capital is typically a weighted average of interest rates on funds the company borrows and the rate of return expected by shareholders. Value-added approaches might make sense for companies that have weaker financial structures, low sales-to-asset ratios, and excess levels of working capital. Companies adopting EVA or similar evaluation methods (such as internal rate of return, or IRR) will establish a metrics program for measuring operating profits at various levels in the company, as well as cost of capital calculations. The difficulty of EVA, apart from arriving at a true cost of capital, is figuring out how to measure the capital. Some EVA pundits and consultants include key business processes as part of a firm's capital. Since traditional accounting systems tend to expense salaries, software development, training, and other recurring costs of carrying out business processes, the true capital invested in any project, product, or department may not be well understood. Measuring process costs and capitalizing them will likely be central to an EVA metrics program.

- *Balanced Scorecard* (BSC). This approach was introduced by Robert Kaplan and David Norton in the early 1990s. According to Kaplan and Norton, the BSC was developed as an answer to the pitfalls of managing on a purely financial basis:

  > We introduced the Balanced Scorecard to provide a new framework for describing value-creating strategies that link intangible and tangible assets. The scorecard does not attempt to "value" an organization's intangible assets, but it does measure these assets in units other than currency. The Balanced Scorecard describes how intangible assets get mobilized and combined with intangible and tangible assets to create differentiating customer-value propositions and superior financial outcomes."[2]

The main premise of BSC is that financial measures report past outcomes but do not adequately explain the drivers of future performance. Thus, traditional reporting practices often fail to inform managers, in quantitative terms, of the impact that investments in intangible assets like proprietary knowledge or an innovative business model can have on a company's financial returns. The metrics that make up a Balanced Scorecard will therefore include measures of the strength and growth of nonmonetary assets such as process excellence, customer loyalty, and employee competencies.

A BSC typically includes 15 to 20 measures. You might link each of these to corporate strategy by using a cause-effect statement to describe each metric. For example, X increase in on-time order fulfillment leads to Y increase in repeat business. Or, X increase in service rep training leads to Y increase in customer satisfaction ratings. The idea being that the thing increased (or reduced) has an impact on the achievement of an organizational objective such as revenue growth or cost reductions. So wherever possible, try to express the relationship in quantitative terms. Apart from its usefulness as a predictor of future income, the value of tracking a given metric also depends on how clearly it cascades down to various levels of the organization, so that it can be used as a basis of evaluations and incentives for executives, middle managers, and employees.

The Balanced Scorecard is often the performance measurement approach of choice for companies wanting to effect a major strategy change or concentrate on revenue growth. The BSC approach emphasizes a decentralized organization, in which the scorecard becomes the basis for evaluating employees at all levels, not just executives. The scorecard provides a framework for measuring performance from four perspectives: *financial* (ROI, ROE, and cash flow), *customer* (customer additions, customer satisfaction rates, etc.), *internal* (primarily business process factors such as number of defects and cycle time), and *learning/growth* (quantity of employee training, certifications, etc.). The BSC therefore combines traditional measures of financial performance with more predictive, operational measures that apply to a company's business model and internal processes. Some common BSC items include:

- Customer satisfaction ratings
- Number of days per account activation
- Customer loss or retention rates
- Cash conversion cycle time
- Business process cycle times (such as filling orders, processing invoices, etc.)
- Operating expense per unit of sale
- Segment/market share
- Rate of return (ROI, ROC, ROE)
- Performance in any of the preceding against industry benchmarks

Of course, the contents of the scorecard may vary between industries, between divisions of a company, and over time. Most BSC consultants will emphasize that scorecard measures should cascade throughout the organization. Measures of performance at the executive level should in turn be linked to measures that apply to directors and department managers all the way down to individual employees.

WORKFLOW

Reporting processes tend to be highly iterative. Typically there are several rounds of adjustments, allocations, and eliminating entries before statements and management reports are finally released to a more general audience. The objective of workflow improvement is to remove some of these iterations and rework tasks from the monthly closing and reporting process, while allowing managers enough flexibility to look at their financial results from multiple vantage points in order to identify meaningful trends, seasonality, and cause-effect relationships.

Once you have charted your process in detail, evaluate each task within the process using the following criteria:

- *Does it add value?* A new piece of the financial reporting picture should be contributed by each step. If not, then consider why that step is being done. It may be that it is a holdover from old systems.
- *Is the task adequately automated?* Look for ways to replace clerical tasks with straight-through processing, especially those tasks that move data from one system to another.
- *Are too many people involved in the task?* Look at the workflow overall. As a rule, the less often data and documents change hands on the way to a final product, the more efficient your reporting process will be. Mapping your reporting process will probably reveal that delays are introduced when work changes hands.
- *Are tasks done in parallel?* A lot of the sequencing of tasks is by tradition. Probably your best opportunity to change this is at month-end close. The precedence of A/P over fixed assets probably can't be helped due to the dependency of one on information established by the other. But, as you look at the overall process map for reporting, you are bound to find some tasks that can be done in parallel.
- *Is there an audit trail to prior phases in the process?* This is especially unnecessary where your data must undergo a series of manipulations or transformations (e.g., converting data from diverse G/Ls into a common chart of accounts) before they are consolidated and presented. If errors are discovered, they should be traceable to the step in the process that produced the error. For example, after each step in a conversion process, a trial balance or checksum report may be produced to ensure that no data is lost or that signs or amounts have not been mishandled.

You should find ways to either remove or improve tasks that don't meet these criteria. Consider removing those tasks that contribute little or no value to the end product. For all other steps in the workflow, try to apply other process enablers, such as training or technology, to those that could be made more efficient or less error-prone. Again, much of the inefficiency in the reporting process arises from problems of data quality. By offering better training to those involved in the "feeder" systems, as well as enhancing the technologies that support the reporting process, your workflow improvements become almost inevitable.

ENDNOTES

1. Shari Caudron "Strength in Numbers, Part Two," *Controller Magazine* (March 1996): 31.
2. Robert S. Kaplan and David P. Norton, "Transforming the Balanced Scorecard from Performance Measurement to Strategic Management: Part I," *Accounting Horizons* (March 2001): 87–104.

18

BEST PRACTICES

The financial reporting BPI project provides an ideal opportunity to implement a best practices initiative, since a change in practices will involve changes to policies and procedures that will in turn have an impact on process workflows. That said, it's important to state that we consider best practices to be just one of an interrelated set of business process enablers; hence, any new best practice initiative should be considered in the context of its impact on the other enablers. You'll have to evaluate whether the current human resources, training, and technology enablers are adequate to support any best practices under consideration.

Sources of ideas for best practices abound. Apart from a growing literature on the subject (especially dealing with period-end closes), consultancies such as the Hackett Group in Akron, Ohio, and Best Practices Benchmarking Consulting LLC in Research Triangle Park, North Carolina, offer specialized services in this area. The major accounting firms offer various benchmarking and best practices services as well. In this chapter we offer a synopsis of a few financial reporting best practices, based on our own experiences with clients, that we feel are worth passing on.

CLOSING

If it takes more than a week after the period close to get financials, your closing process merits scrutiny, and there are obvious reasons for considering best practices in this area. Improvements in closing will speed the delivery of critical information to decision makers in your company, and the time you save in closing gives managers that much more time to spot opportunities and steer clear of problems. As mentioned earlier, recent changes in SEC deadlines for submission of 10K and 10Q financials have created an additional impetus for public companies to close their books faster.

Difficulties with the period-end close are likely to pose your biggest obstacle to reporting process improvement. For this reason, a growing number of consultants and management gurus are writing on this topic. The term *virtual close*, first coined by executives at Motorola and Cisco Systems, has gained wide acceptance. It refers to the ability to close the books within hours of period-end. These companies have leveraged their competency in information technologies in order to automate and carry out closing processes incrementally, throughout the month, leaving less cleanup work at month-end. Both firms boast of being able to close their books and produce financials in one day.

While this impressive feat may lie beyond your company's ability and needs for the time being, there are a number of virtual close principles that can help you shave days off your closing process:

- *Reduce the number of ERP instances.* Packages such as SAP and Peoplesoft allow multiple instances, or installations, that use their own chart of accounts and store information in separate databases. Reducing the number of instances may make the process of monitoring data quality, closing the books, and consolidating results after period closes much easier. Often, these distinct instances were set up only to accommodate differences in coding semantics rather than differences in how business units actually operate.

- *Standardize the chart of accounts across your organization.* Even if you have multiple general ledgers, using a common set of accounts will at least eliminate painstaking conversions when consolidating (see Chapter 21 on redesigning the chart of accounts for design principles you can use in this project).

- *Update subledgers and post to the general ledger throughout the period.* Part of the virtual close concept is that closing become an ongoing activity rather than a period-end crisis. As part of your closing calendar, establish routines to review, correct, and update accounting modules such as payroll, accounts payable, and accounts receivable throughout the month.

- *Use automation to post subledger transactions and journal entries often.* Typically this is accomplished using stored database queries that identified approved, unposted journal, and subledger entries. In some cases, we find that journal entries are first collected in external files (such as a spreadsheet), sent for approval, and then rekeyed into the accounting system. Again, finding ways to collect these data and record approvals in a single system will make the process faster.

- *Take advantage of technologies that enable frequent entries to journals and subledgers.* These include Web-based applications that will allow remote or traveling employees to input expense reports, billable time, or sales orders from wherever they are.

- *Use automation to calculate and book entries for allocations and accruals.* Most ERP systems have these capabilities built in. If your G/L system doesn't, it is still possible to develop scheduled procedures that make these changes directly in the database where the G/L transactions are stored. If you use a financial consolidation application, you may be better off managing allocation there versus correcting the general ledger.

- *Calculate allocation bases prior to close.* You can base allocation percentages on averages from prior periods, or drop percentage allocations altogether in favor of fixed amounts that are derived from the budgeted amounts (be sure that the budget for these items is predictable and stable, based on experience). A third alternative is to allocate based on the prior month's amounts, and use estimates in month 12.

- *Post and reconcile intercompany transactions throughout the period.* Instead of waiting until period-end, make posting and balancing of intercompany transactions part of the regular routine. This may be handled either in the general ledger or an external consolidation application.

- *Reduce the number of period-end adjustments.* This includes allocations, recurring journal entries, and intercompany charges that occur at all levels of the organization. Instead, try to reserve these activities for the top two or three levels of the company consolidation structure. Accounting departments often devote too much time and effort to the minute details of allocations between cost centers, departments, or business units. It also helps to leave overhead allocations out of the budget target on which management bonuses are based, since this is the reason people insist on making allocation schemes so complex in the first place. You might also establish materiality rules for adjusting entries, and eliminate those that don't cross this threshold.

- *Use frequent Flash reports throughout the period.* By determining a standard of portfolio of interim reports and queries on data in the G/L and subledgers, you can make near-real-time decisions on variances or take action to correct journal entry errors. Such reports might focus on a series of accounts where booking errors are most common. Daily reporting encourages a tighter, more systematic month-end reporting process because it suggests additional controls and checks that can be placed on the GL and subledgers where the data originate.

- *Use weekly or daily cycle counting of inventories that target high-use and high-volume items (those most likely to cause variances when miscounted).* Most ERP, manufacturing, or industrial automation packages that have inventory features contain reports that allow users to identify, list, and update stock levels for these kinds of items.

- *Hold provision meetings in advance of the period-end.* One of the benefits of technology enablers such as database query tools is that information on variances can be found in advance. Reviews of provisions and judgment reserves, as well as statement commentaries, can now be performed prior to month-end.

- *Conduct a process review after each close.* This will enable you to identify deviations from best practices, as well as safeguards to prevent them.

REPORTING

Perhaps the most significant step to take toward process improvement is to implement an information system that manages financial reporting and consolidations centrally. Such a system might be part of an *analytics platform*, which often consists of a suite of applications that include OLAP analysis as well as budgeting and forecasting modules. An analytics platform will typically act as a financial data warehouse, external to your accounting or ERP system, that houses summarized G/L balances as well as the logic that enables the consolidation of legal entities, elimination of intercompany transactions, allocations, minority-interest calculations, and currency translation. These suggestions for improving the reporting process assume that you have either implemented such a system or have plans to do so.

We divide the task of financial reporting into three categories: *reporting of financial position, reporting for cost control,* and *reporting for performance measurement.*

Reporting of Financial Position

By "reporting of financial position" we mean the standard complement of financial statements that a company issues after each period-close, including balance sheets, income statements, and statements of cash flows. The following practices are recommended to optimize the speed and accuracy of the process that generates your key financial reports.

- *Establish a centralized repository for reporting hierarchies and consolidation rules.* Use a reporting/consolidation system to maintain the multiple rollup structures of accounts, legal entities, business units, products, and other financial or statistical reporting entities. In addition to the traditional legal reporting structure, most organizations are also understood in terms of markets, products, and customers. A reporting system should capture information and allow consolidation of financial results at these levels; it should also accommodate multiple rollup structures to support presentations of results for both internal views and external reports for bankers and investors (such as reports by segment). Since the reporting structure will change over time to suit the evolution of key drivers such as markets, products, and customers, the reporting system must have the flexibility to reflect these changes. Mergers and acquisitions create issues of cross-ownership that can complicate intercompany transactions and delay the closing process. A reporting system can address these concerns by incorporating consolidation rules, such as percentage ownership, into the rollup structure so that computation of minority interest becomes an automated task rather than a painstaking calculator exercise.

- *Automate eliminations of intracompany transactions.* Intracompany transactions don't always have clear governing controls. Automating these processes can therefore increase accuracy in such error-prone tasks as matching intercompany transactions with their offsets. Reporting applications can also calculate elimination entries and allocations, but in general you should try to record these at a high level, instead of doing so at the department or cost center level. Where possible, try to incorporate intercompany logic and offsets within the G/L package. A journal entry screen, for example, might be modified to enforce the entry of a corresponding company code for transactions that occur between two legal entities. When these transactions are summarized and consolidated later on, it is much easier to identify those transactions that should be eliminated. Some reporting systems will allow you to incorporate logic that removes charges between two companies that consolidate to a common parent company. For example, a sale between company A and company C might be excluded automatically from the consolidated revenue figure whenever the P&L is run for the parent of A and C. This should reduce the demand for postclosing entries and offsets after a period close (see Exhibit 18.1).

- *Automate currency conversion.* A reporting system should give you the ability to maintain foreign exchange rates in a single table. This will facilitate reporting of subsidiaries in local currencies, as well as of the parent company. It will also enable you to standardize the exchange rates used for reporting purposes instead of leaving the task of currency translation up to subsidiaries that submit financials periodically. The system would then carry out currency conversion as reports are generated, using the currency that the end user selects. The system should also accommodate the tracking of multiple exchange rates for different types of accounts (e.g., balance sheet versus income statement) in order to accommodate Financial Accounting Standards Board (FASB) guidelines for reporting foreign exchange gains and losses.

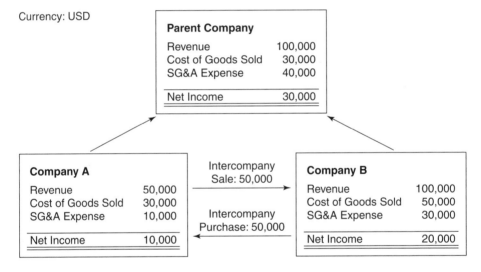

Currency: USD

Parent Company

Revenue	100,000
Cost of Goods Sold	30,000
SG&A Expense	40,000
Net Income	30,000

Company A

Revenue	50,000
Cost of Goods Sold	30,000
SG&A Expense	10,000
Net Income	10,000

Intercompany Sale: 50,000

Intercompany Purchase: 50,000

Company B

Revenue	100,000
Cost of Goods Sold	50,000
SG&A Expense	30,000
Net Income	20,000

Transaction Detail

Company	Counterpart	Account	Amount
A	B	4000 Revenue	50,000
A		5000 Cost of Goods Sold	30,000
A		6000 Selling Expense	10,000
B		4000 Revenue	100,000
B	A	5000 Cost of Goods Sold	50,000
B		6000 Selling Expense	30,000

Since companies A and B consolidate to the same parent, any transactions occurring between these two entities can be excluded when the parent is reported. The system automatically removes the shaded transactions in the table from parent company totals without booking additional eliminating entries or any need for a third elimination company. Matching reports might also be run as a check to ensure that each intercompany transaction has a matching opposite transaction of the same amount.

EXHIBIT 18.1   Automatic Eliminations

- *Facilitate frequent preliminary reporting.* As just mentioned, interim reports facilitate real-time decision making. In the early stages, there may be problems with the data, especially since you may be accessing G/L information prior to the booking of material accruals. Interim reporting needn't rely exclusively on the G/L; in fact, you might opt to draw directly on the "feeder" systems in some cases. Start with more summary level views that can be used for management decision making, such as sales order statistics and receivables aging. Again, the decision on what and when to report should depend on feedback from your reporting committee as part of the ongoing review of reporting requirements.
- *Develop notes and commentaries in advance.* By adopting these concepts of the virtual close, you can begin drafting notes and commentaries to financial statements that are forward-looking and address future actions to be taken in response to current variances. Starting this process in advance of the month-end close will give you more time to develop a meaningful commentary and prevent this last-minute activity from holding up the release of financials to internal users as well as the public.

Reporting for Cost Control

Reports for cost control, especially variance reports, will have a larger audience than the standard package of financials, therefore the method of distribution becomes more of an issue. In addition to the foregoing guidelines for financial reports, we make the following best practice recommendations for cost center-level reports:

- *Develop a plan for electronic distribution of reports via e-mail and the web.* Cost center reporting is where the self-service approach becomes especially important. Many organizations today still rely on paper printouts to accomplish this task. The result (in addition to wasted paper) is that ad hoc analyses are cumbersome and require rekeying into a spreadsheet. If your reporting application has e-mail capabilities, you might consider using these as the primary means of distribution of your standard report package. Cost center managers might receive this package as a file attachment, such as a spreadsheet or .pdf file in their in-box every month. For example, a financial package for cost center managers might include:
  - Month, year-to-date, and annual trend expense reports
  - Variances
  - Payroll
  - Capital equipment purchases and depreciation

  A spreadsheet attachment has the advantages of allowing end users to do their own analyses with these data. While many corporate finance and IT departments are looking to banish the spreadsheet (and with good reason), the spreadsheet can still serve its intended purpose as a presentation and analysis tool. By giving users data in a standard, comprehensive format that they can, in turn, embed in other presentations will relieve the number of requests of your finance and IT departments for one-off reports that cater to specialized presentations or views. This is the *push* method of distributing reports—whereby data is distributed automatically directly to interested users . You can also use the *pull* approach, by posting reports on an intranet site where users will enter an ID and password to see all reports that pertain to them. In this case, it is up to the users to decide which reports or ad hoc analyses they need to see. A Web distribution approach should give users the option of selecting, downloading, and/or printing individual reports as well as the full package of relevant financials.

- *Automate access to G/L detail.* Your Web-based distribution strategy should also include *drill-down* capabilities. Although for the moment these may lie beyond the capabilities of many packaged reporting applications, there is a growing trend in the financial applications industry to make general ledger details available online. The concept of drilling down refers to the ability to progress from a summary financial view to a more detailed one by selecting any of the data elements in a report. For example, if you are viewing a report that shows financial results by quarter, you might drill down by selecting the first quarter, and thus view results for January, February, and March. The same principle is possible with account balances in an expense report. The idea here is that a user who notices a substantial variance in, say, relocation costs or travel and entertainment, might choose to expand that account to see all of the charges that hit that account during the past month. In effect, this drill-down selection will trigger another report that shows general ledger detail for a selected account. Such a capability can save significant time in tracking down variances and routing inquires to the accounting staff whenever a manager is trying to research monthly variances. Thus, managers can browse through their financials, see major variances, and drill down to the detail behind specific variances as needed. This will increase the efficiency of inquiries that go back to the accounting staff and ensure that inquiries are accompanied by complete information. A manager sending an inquiry regarding a specific charge will in this case be able to include a specific posting ID as well as the date and dollar amount of the charge. The reporting application might even include an e-mail option that copies details of the transaction in question into the body of an e-mail message to the general ledger department (see Exhibit 18.2).

- *Highlight major exceptions.* Cost center reports should focus on exceptions and trends. Include in your monthly package a report that highlights line items that deviate beyond an accepted tolerance. Rather than report the same 1,000 account lines every month in the same cost center reports, provide detail first on those line items that show a variance of, say, more than 5 percent from the norm.

Reporting for Performance Management

Performance management reporting will include the portfolio of KPIs, or scorecard, that your reporting committee has established as measurements of the financial health and success of the enterprise. This was covered in more detail in Chapter 17, but the following practices are recommended in implementing a metrics program as part of the overall reporting process:

Innovative Applicances, Inc.
Operating Statement — Coffee Maker Manufacturing (Dept. 4059)
As of July 2xxx
Currency: USD

Acct	Description	Current Month			Year-to-Date		
		Actual	Budget	Variance	Actual	Budget	Variance
5301	Direct Labor	7,726	6,667	16%	82,210	80,000	3%
5302	Sick Pay	100	83	20%	700	1,000	-30%
5303	Vacation Pay	351	250	40%	2,457	3,000	-18%
5304	Holiday Pay	344	417	-17%	4,200	5,000	-16%
5305	Indirect Labor	1,630	1,333	22%	15,500	16,000	-3%
5306	Overtime Premium	1,301	1,000	30%	11,471	12,000	-4%
5307	Corporate Benefits	3,000	3,750	-20%	41,024	45,000	-9%
Labor Subtotal		**14,452**	**13,500**	**7%**	**157,562**	**162,000**	**9%**
5412	Maintenance—Equipment	400	250	60%	2,600	3,000	-13%
5415	Rent—Building	577	250	131%	2,863	3,000	-5%

User clicks hyperlink to see G/L Detail

General Ledger Detail
1001-4059-5301 Direct Labor

Period	Source	Reference #	Date	Description	Debit	Credit	Balance
6	AA	REVSL	6/2/2002	Accrual - Reversal	-	514	(514)
6	AA	M2923	6/3/2002	Salary Accrual	6,000		5,486
6	AP	M2924	6/4/2002	Temp - Overtime	410	-	5,897
6	AP	M2925	6/15/2002	Temp - Overtime	205	-	6,102
6	AP	M2926	6/16/2002	Temp - Overtime	362	-	6,463
6	AP	M2927	6/16/2002	Roberts Staffing	514	-	6,977
6	AP	M2928	6/16/2002	Roberts Staffing	749	-	7,726
Total Direct Labor					**8,239**	**514**	**7,726**

EXHIBIT 18.2   Accessing G/L Detail Online

- *Establish standards for combining data from nonfinancial sources* (such as CRM and Payroll). Different systems may rely on different coding conventions of vendor codes, customer, codes, or geography. Your efforts to compile and combine metrics based on data from diverse systems may require that you standardize these codes across systems, where possible. Where standardization isn't feasible, your company's reporting committee should at least agree on an 'official' translation for equivalents in different systems.

- *Meet regularly to review KPIs.* As mentioned earlier in Chapter 17, any metrics program will benefit from putting a team in place to identify and review the metrics that are tracked in your reporting process. Ideally, the team will consist of long-time employees who know the systems and data being captured and are more intimately familiar with the business; but the team should also include rising stars, who will bring outside expertise and a fresh perspective. This team should meet regularly to review the effectiveness of the KPIs on the list. Your KPI list may resemble a restaurant menu: popular items will stay on the menu, less desirable ones will be taken off and substituted with new KPIs. The idea is to continue the search for useful business intelligence in your data.

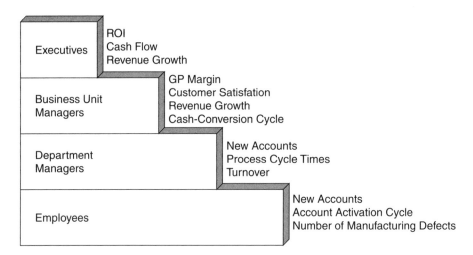

EXHIBIT 18.3   KPI Hierarchy Example

- *Establish a hierarchy for KPIs.* A company with diverse business units or divisions may find it necessary to use different KPIs for different operating units. However, it is useful to find linkages between these KPIs and the overall strategy. KPIs may cascade throughout the company (see Exhibit 18.3).
- *Report KPIs often.* Since your nonfinancial metrics will combine results from nonfinancial sources, reporting KPIs needn't follow the same closing schedule as financials. Availability of metric data should follow a schedule driven by management needs rather than by traditional reporting cycles.
- *Separate KPIs from financials, if necessary.* Especially in the early stages of a metrics program, you may be better off separating the reporting of metrics from financials. Some metrics, such as sales revenue by territory, may take time to calculate due to an extensive need for judgment calls, exceptions, and management approval. While this is not the ideal scenario, the nature of some statistical measure may require this.
- *Present KPIs in a graphical format.* Charts, graphs, and histograms make it easier to view trends and relationships. KPIs have also been represented as a speedometer (to show rates of growth) or as color-coded maps (to show sales volume by geography). However, this degree of sophistication may be a bit overboard for most companies. The important thing is to find a method of presentation that conveys changes, trends, and the composition of financial data in the clearest possible terms.

19

TECHNOLOGY

The technological aspect of the BPI reporting project should include a standard set of front-end tools that can combine quantitative, graphical, and narrative information. These should permit flexible, ad hoc analyses that reduce the time the finance staff spends on low value-added work. You may find that every time the CFO has to make a presentation to the board, half the finance department winds up scrambling around trying to collect and rekey data from P&L statements into PowerPoint slides, or obsessing over font colors and sizes. A common reporting platform will deliver the basic data sets in a readable format that can, in turn, be embedded directly into popular office applications such as spreadsheets or presentation slides. However, the technical end of your BPI project is likely to concentrate on the behind-the-scenes applications, such as relational and OLAP databases, as well as the applications and routines these databases will use to receive and summarize data from transactional systems.

An assessment of the BPI technology enablers begins with an inventory of operational and financial systems, such as subledgers and CRM systems, which will serve as key data sources. This will require that you find and map relevant data from these systems to a common reporting structure, using a common terminology. There are four technology enablers that are essential for reporting BPI, which are described in the following subsections.

ANALYTICS APPLICATIONS AND THE FINANCIAL DATA WAREHOUSE

As of this writing, the market for financial analytics software is highly competitive, so you are likely to find a number of viable alternatives in the marketplace. The system you choose should allow integrations to multiple general ledgers, as well as sources of operational data such as payroll, CRM, and subledgers. In many organizations that lack a centralized reporting application, the logic and layout behind financial reports resides on separate files, such as spreadsheets and personal database applications (such as Microsoft Access or FoxPro), and can be scattered throughout the organization. You can improve the reporting process by establishing a standard rollup structure and naming conventions for accounts, product, and cost centers that facilitate a rapid consolidation of financial data. Whether you buy an off-the-shelf application or develop one internally, establishing an analytics platform where core financial reporting tasks can be carried out centrally will enable you to make dramatic improvements in reporting efficiency and accomplish several process improvements:

- Do away with spreadsheets and flat-file databases (such as Access or FoxPro) except as presentation and analysis tools.
- Carry out consolidation tasks for the whole organization.
- Calculate and store key figures, such as KPIs or Balanced Scorecard.
- Compare financial and statistical results across business units or divisions.
- Reduce disagreement on performance measures, as well as the manual effort involved in calculating and recording them.
- Enforce standardization of data and the use of a common language throughout the organization. For example, make sure that the identifier used for Federal Express in one division (whether it is a customer, a vendor, or both) is the same used for Federal Express in a different division.
- Give users a single source that makes the task of finding, combining, and slicing and dicing financial or statistical data less cumbersome.

Analytics applications allow users to summarize, analyze, and present data from a shared database (or collection of databases) which is, essentially, a financial data warehouse. You (or your application vendor) will probably decide to use a combination of relational and OLAP databases as the physical structures of the data warehouse. The relational and OLAP models represent very different approaches to database design, and the nontechnical reader may find a brief overview of differences between these two models worthwhile.

The relational database model seeks to reduce data redundancy as much as possible. This is why online transaction processing (OLTP) applications such as CRM, general ledgers, and subledgers use the relational model. Less redundancy within database tables means greater speed when writing new records to the database. If you plan to use an analytics application for data entry (in order to collect and consolidate budgets), it will probably conform to the relational model to some extent.

The task of organizing the data in the relational database model, also known as *normalization*, seeks to eliminate redundant data by separating related sets of *attributes* into separate tables (where an attribute corresponds to a column in a table). Thus, in designing a relational sales order database, you would separate customer records and sales order records into distinct tables to avoid repeating customer attributes such as customer ID, name, address, and so on for each sales order.

Of course, normalization isn't without its consequences. The term *performance hit* is common in database parlance, and refers to the increase in access times that accompanies any splitting of data into different logical tables. This happens because the task of joining data from two separate tables adds to the complexity of a query. In other words, when you run reports on a relational database, your query against that database has to undo the work of normalization. While normalization is good for storing data to a database, it has an adverse impact on query performance.

The online analytical processing (OLAP) model is geared toward summarizing and reporting transactional data as fast as possible. Since they are intended only for reporting purposes, OLAP databases are deliberately *denormalized* so that there is less need to join multiple tables in order to assemble a meaningful view of the data. Another essential feature of OLAP databases is *aggregation*. This is a means of precalculating results for more commonly used queries—especially high-level summaries—in order to improve access times. OLAP databases and OLAP browsers are designed to facilitate the rapid development of ad hoc reports that show a quantitative measure (e.g., revenue or unit sales) along two or more dimensions (e.g., time, business unit, product, or geography).

Corporate environments where reporting needs constantly change can benefit from OLAP, to help meet the growing demand for self-service among the data consumers within these organizations. Again, we emphasize that your consolidation system may employ both relational and OLAP database platforms to accomplish different tasks, according to your budgeting, reporting, and analysis requirements. While a few OLAP database platforms have *write-back* capabilities that allow users to update numbers manually in an OLAP cube, they generally aren't adequate for all but the most basic budgeting requirements.

As of this writing, several of the leading database brands, such as Microsoft SQL Server and Oracle, offer OLAP integrations to their relational database management system (RDBMS) applications. A relational database therefore can act as a staging area for a series of OLAP cubes that serve specific reporting needs. For example, your consolidation database may store all the rollup structures and elimination entries needed for balance sheets, P&Ls, and cash flow statements. This database might in turn feed data to a balance sheet cube, an income statement cube, and a cash flow cube.

Adding OLAP capabilities enables the following process improvements:

- Allows direct integrations to popular spreadsheet applications, which means less rekeying
- Enables users to generate detailed views on their own, rather than waiting on IT or finance departments to spec out and design more detailed reports.
- Serves as an excellent tool for understanding variances, especially if drill-through to transaction detail is permitted (see Chapter 18).
- Helps users to better understand the relationship of organizational structures such as divisions and product lines to the numbers, and to see the evolution of these relationships over time.

Most reporting needs that aren't part of the half-dozen or so standard financial reports (such as the balance sheet, income statement, and various operating statements) can be answered with an OLAP solution. OLAP relieves the burden on overtaxed IT departments and gives data consumers more freedom of choice. It also lightens the burden on finance and IT departments by reducing the number of financial reports those staffs need to maintain and check for accuracy—they may still have to do regular quality assurance on, say, one or two OLAP cubes versus 100 or 200 reports, but this is progress! Finally, it gives greater freedom to end users by letting them set up specialized views that accommodate their departments reporting needs, save these views, and use them again in the future until circumstances change (see Exhibit 19.1).

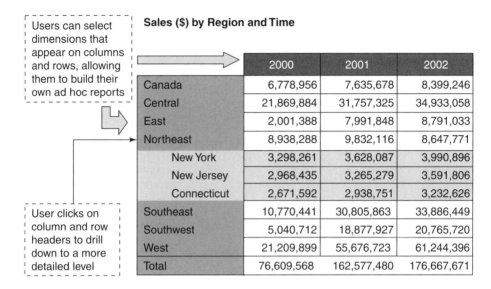

EXHIBIT 19.1   Sample OLAP Report

To summarize, the rule of thumb is to start with a single, somewhat normalized data warehouse where detailed and integrated (i.e., from multiple sources) corporate financial data will be stored. This data warehouse will serve a broad range of financial reporting needs, will have no bias toward any one report or user, and will represent the ultimate authority on financial results. The data warehouse can in turn be used to feed any number of data marts that are optimized for specific views of that data, such as balance sheet and P&L reports. Data marts are more likely to conform to the OLAP model and should be tailored to the reporting needs of specific departments, product lines, or divisions.

EXTRACT, TRANSFORM, AND LOAD: COMBINING DATA FROM DIVERSE SYSTEMS

Automating the task of extracting, formatting, and cleansing data from diverse systems throughout the company is essential to improving the reporting process, especially if process improvement for you entails the addition of new nonfinancial metrics into the reporting mix. Even if your reporting requirements are entirely financial, the prospect of a merger or acquisition with another organization that uses different financial systems may make this a crucial consideration as you seek to consolidate financial data from different accounting packages.

Extraction, transformation, and loading (ETL) is a generic term in the software industry that refers to any of a variety of products or methods that enable the transportation of data from one system or database to another. The terms *extract* and *load* are straightforward, and refer to the tasks of copying data from a source system into a destination system. However, since the systems or databases in question are likely to use differing coding and formatting conventions for their data, an intermediate step between the *extraction* and the *load* is normally required. Thus, the term *transformation* in this context refers to the series of logical rules or tests to which data are subjected as they are moved from source to destination. These rules will ensure that the data meet your reporting requirements. During transformation, all necessary corrections to data that don't meet these requirements are applied.

More than any other aspect of process improvement, ETL will require close and continual cooperation between the finance and IT departments. The IT department will of course have the necessary expertise to write the routines and develop applications to extract, transform, and load data from source systems into your financial consolidation system. Since integration efforts are probably underway for applications being used elsewhere in the company, your IT department probably already has one or more tools at its disposal that can accommodate your integration requirements. You will want to take an inventory of available ETL tools prior to starting this project. As of this writing, most commercial database vendors provide methods of reading and importing data from external sources.

It is useful to subdivide the task of implementing ETL into three phases:

1. Evaluating your data.
2. Defining data transformation rules.
3. Select software.

Evaluating Your Data

Start by assessing the condition and accessibility of your source data. At this stage, you pose three questions: What data do I need? Where (e.g., in which systems or files) are these data located? How good are these data? The first two questions should be understood from your meetings with your metrics team, as well as interviews with those who will be the consumers of information from your reporting processes. Hence, your evaluation will concentrate primarily on the third question.

The data evaluation will yield a collection of information about source systems and their content that will facilitate the correct use of data, in the proper context. Targets of data evaluation may include internal systems, such as the general ledger, CRM and manufacturing, as well as external files and databases that may contain market research, customer satisfaction data, or industry-specific statistics. This systematic analysis should be done before attempting to extract data from any source system, files, or database. These sources will comprise data structures such as files, tables, and fields. Once the data structures within a source system have been identified, your data evaluation should cover all of the following topics for each data structure that you plan to use:

- *Content.* What the data actually mean from a business point of view (e.g., product codes, customer codes, demographic codes, etc.)
- *Format.* Examples of format are text versus numeric, size limitations, special characters allowed, and so on.
- *Quality.* Consistency, completeness and correctness

- *Structure*. Relationships to other data tables and fields
- *BPI-specific uses*. Mapping of values from the source system to corresponding values in the analytics/reporting system

Start the evaluation with whatever information is provided about the data in external sources. These will include documentation that may have been provided by application vendors, as well as manuals written by employees or external consultants who helped implement the systems from which you want to gather data. You may also need to follow up by interviewing those most familiar with the design and maintenance of your source systems. This collection of external sources about a system's contents is typically known as *metadata*, or data about data.

Be aware, however, these external sources may prove to be of limited value, since ultimately the real data may have deteriorated from the specifications set forth months or years ago. Minor system fixes and modifications may have gone undocumented, and information about relationships between values held in different tables or fields are often not well explained. And, over time, users may have begun to use free text fields for different purposes. So the ultimate authority on the condition of your data is the data itself. Unlocking this information may require hours or even days of querying database tables in a source system, using the metadata you have already gathered as a guide, to look for undocumented relationships between database tables and fields, as well as inconsistencies.

Defining Data Transformation Rules

The transformation step in the ETL process does the job of quality assurance, making sure that the data going into your reporting/analytics system are accurate and fit for use. The evaluation stage will no doubt leave you with some hints as to the nature and extent of quality problems in the source data. If problems are widespread, you should probably opt at this point to clean and correct the data in your source systems before going any further.

Even after defects are dealt with in the historical data, errors may continue to creep in, so you'll need to monitor the process for bad data. Errors that go undetected may skew aggregate values when the data are summed for reporting purposes. Thus, you will probably want to include a reconciliation step after each significant transformation task (such as code conversions and summation of numeric values). In BPI dogma, normally we caution against an excess of checking and reconciliation steps, but when automated and placed at strategic checkpoints throughout the process such reconciliation steps can save time and effort over leaving reconciliations for the end. The task of "tying out" becomes more time-consuming after the data have been summed, when it becomes trickier to trace mismatches between source and destination systems back to their origin. The transformation step should monitor data as it passes through specific checkpoints in the process, filter out invalid data, and forward nonconforming data through the proper channels for corrections.

The definition of transformation rules starts with an evaluation of users' needs, then proceeds to the translation of the needs into logical rules and procedures that can be put in place at the system level:

1. *Define standards of content, format, and completeness according to user needs.* In the evaluation stage, you assessed the current quality of transactional data. Now you are in a position to set expectations for future data quality, as well as establish the rules that will be followed in the transformation of data. The team should agree on minimum standards that ensure that the data are complete, accurate, and useful to those who will base management decisions on these data. These standards should specify essential content, optional content, tolerance levels for errors and inconsistencies, and formatting.

2. *Translate standards into logical transformation rules.* Here are some examples of logical rules you might use to implement the content and formatting standards you've set for your data. Your ETL application will apply one or more of these rules to the data that pass from your source system(s) to your reporting/analytics system:

   - *Value limitations.* Some fields should only contain values from a specific range or list. This is usually necessary for fields that contain dates, account codes, currency codes, or product codes.

   - *Consistency.* Which fields in each record must be filled out in order for records to be consistent and comparable? For example, whenever field A is filled out, must field B also be filled out?

   - *Completeness.* Which fields in a record must be filled out in order for that record to provide adequate information to the user?

   - *Formatting.* Should a field contain text, or numeric value? Do you need to add special characters such as quotes, commas, or dashes to make the data more readable to the user?

   - *Reconciliation.* Do aggregate balances in the destination system agree with aggregate balances in the source system?

3. *Establish procedures to handle errors and exceptions.* Once transformation rules have been defined, the financial BPI team should agree on and document procedures for testing compliance to these rules and fixing errors. The team should also distinguish the types of errors that can be resolved at the system level from those that may require human intervention, and determine methods of routing different types of errors to the appropriate destination.

Choosing the Right Software

Probably you already do a number of ETL tasks on your own. These tasks may include: copying data from a Microsoft Excel spreadsheet to a Microsoft Access database; running a series of queries in the Access database to clean the data and make sure they use a standard set of account numbers, date formats, department codes, and so on; and then export the data to another Excel file, where you might format the data to look like a proper P&L statement. While this approach works well for small operations, it doesn't scale well and doesn't lend itself to transparency or a well-understood process. And it takes time away from value-added tasks and spends it on data conversion tasks, which can be easily automated. At this stage, you should have enough information to guide you in selecting the application(s) you will use for data transformation. The ideal scenario is to keep the whole process in a single application that can:

- Store the programming logic for all data transformation and quality rules.
- Connect to and retrieve data from all the sources you intend to use, including relational databases (Oracle, SQL Sever, DB2, etc.), spreadsheets, text files, and older legacy systems such as mainframes.
- Graphically represent the mapping of fields in source systems to fields in the destination system.
- Manage the workflow, or sequencing of data transformation tasks.
- Track errors, resolve errors, and send notification of errors.
- Scale to handle increasing volumes of data.

As mentioned earlier, database vendors typically bundle some form of data extraction/import tool along with their relational database that can accomplish most, if not all, of the tasks just listed. A variety of stand alone products also are on the market that can accomplish these tasks from a single user interface (see Exhibit 19.2). (For a listing of ETL products and vendors, refer to the buyer's guide in Chapter 29.)

USING XBRL FOR EXTERNAL REPORTING

As mentioned in Chapter 5, the Extensive Business Reporting Language (XBRL) is becoming more commonplace as a means of publishing financial data for external users. XBRL relies on a taxonomy, or a vocabulary, of standard labels for each line item in a financial statement. This taxonomy can go down to whatever level of detail is appropriate to your reporting and analysis processes. Using a standard taxonomy, statements and other financial documents become portable within and outside the company and can be exported to other systems regardless of font styles, coding conventions, or column and row sequences. When viewed with a Web browser, an XBRL document can look like any other financial statement. The XBRL tags will be invisible, but they will be recognizable to XBRL-enabled applications so that data for an XBRL file can be loaded with minimal effort.

XBRL is intended primarily for reporting financials to the public, in a format that users can easily load into their own financial applications for analysis and comparison. For example, XBRL will make it a lot easier for securities analysts or bankers to download financials from the Internet directly into a modeling application, instead of rekeying the data. XBRL might hold the same promise for companies looking to

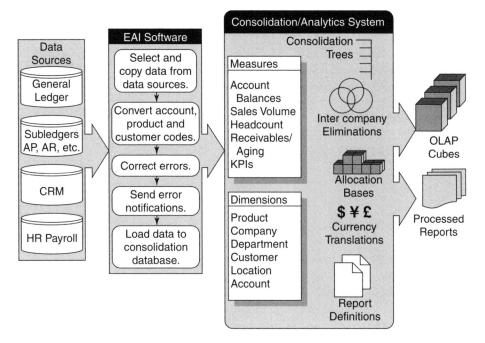

EXHIBIT 19.2   Consolidation System Diagram

synchronize the formatting of data originating from diverse G/L packages within their own organization that have to be consolidated centrally. This might make sense if both the parent and subsidiaries charts of accounts change frequently, making it easier to synchronize to a common XBRL taxonomy; or where the parent has less then 100 percent ownership, and thus control over what the subsidiary does is limited.

INTRANETS, EXTRANETS, AND BROWSERS: USING THE WEB TO DISTRIBUTE OPERATING AND FINANCIAL DATA

Whether you decide on a push or a pull method for report distribution, a dedicated intranet site should be established for reporting applications. The site should serve as the point of entry to reporting and budgeting applications, as well as to the online library where updates and instructions on financial systems can be found. Evolutions in the Web capabilities of most commercial reporting and OLAP applications are making the company intranet the ideal means of providing access to end users, while spending minimal effort on installation and maintenance. The Web interface in these applications typically provides a scaled-down version for end users, who can enter the system, using a password, to see reports and ad hoc queries with data pertaining to their own department or function. System administrators and report

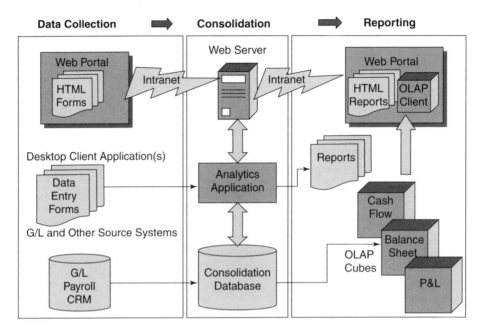

EXHIBIT 19.3 Web-Based Analytics Application

developers will probably continue to access reporting application through a "thick" client that is installed on their PCs.

As more information becomes accessible online, take extra care to ensure that your reporting applications have adequate security measures in place to restrict access to data to the appropriate users (see Exhibit 19.3).

20

BPI MAKEOVER

Once you have researched reporting processes, evaluated process enablers, and determined where and what kind of improvements to make, you're ready to take a look at how the new process will work. This usually means charting the whole process again, taking into account savings in time and personnel resources you expect to achieve.

In this chapter, we'll revisit the example process described in Chapter 16. To that end, we assume the following improvements have been made in relevant process enablers:

- *Human Resources*. You have:
  - Trained finance staff on analytics applications.
  - Conducted an ongoing series of training sessions for accounting staff on those types of G/L and subledger transactions that have been identified to be the most problematic during period close.
  - Presented a two-hour seminar to department managers on their operating statements and accounts payable and general ledger procedures that affect their cost centers.
- *Technology*. You have:
  - Implemented an analytics application that now automates a number of the reporting and consolidation tasks that were previously done manually.
  - Integrated the reporting system with G/L and A/P accounting system modules to allow managers to browse their departments' financial transaction detail online.
- *Best Practices*. You have documented procedures for allocations, eliminations, currency translations (and translation adjustments), and consolidations, as well as a clear audit trail within the reporting system for each of these steps. Controller now receives Flash reports throughout the months so that significant budget variances can be spotted and corrected before period close. This shaved two days off the financial review period.
- *Workflow*. You have targeted steps that introduced the most significant delays and errors. These determined the choice of technology and training initiatives in which to invest.

To represent this future state graphically, you can follow the same workflow charting conventions that you used to frame the as-is process. Exhibits 20.1 and 20.2 are examples of how processes might change as the result of a BPI initiative. Before and after examples are put side by side (these examples are slightly simplified in order to meet space constraints).

SUMMARY

You can improve business processes by strengthening the enablers that make these processes possible. During the research and planning phases of your reporting BPI project, concentrate on your company's people, training, strategy, best practices, and information technology infrastructure to the extent that these factors have a direct impact on reporting processes and tasks. Charting the workflow of your reporting processes is a useful exercise that can help you determine where these enablers fail

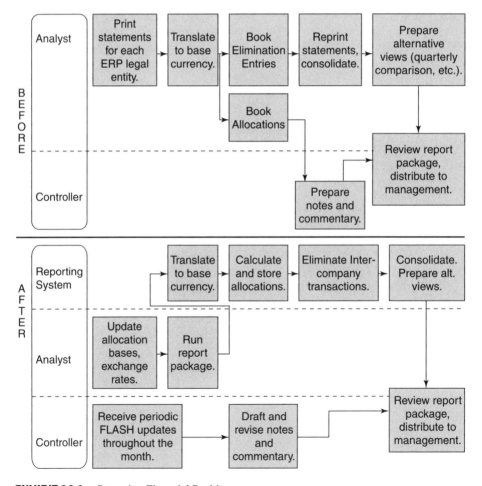

EXHIBIT 20.1   Reporting Financial Position

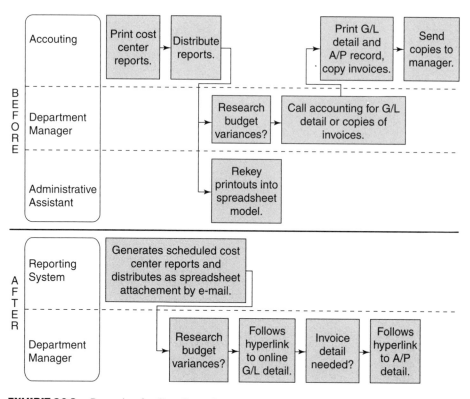

EXHIBIT 20.2   Reporting for Cost Control

to live up to their full potential. By identifying weak points in the process—those tasks where errors and delays are introduced—you can identify the enablers involved in those tasks and start thinking about ways to enhance them.

Always weigh the payoff as you rank potential reporting BPI initiatives. Every company has a threshold beyond which incremental improvements will take on costs that outweigh the value of increased efficiency. What is the advantage of reducing your closing cycle to one day? Is it worth the effort and cost of achieving that goal? It may be relatively easy to reduce the closing cycle from 14 days to 5 days, but the work, training, and system enhancements required to get from that point to a two-day close may not offer sufficient payback. Where this threshold lies depends on your organization's needs and innate competencies. Ask: What information do we need and when do we need it? What information technologies do we know well, and how can we take advantage of that knowledge? High-tech companies such as Cisco and Motorola tend to have a higher comfort level with automation and are therefore better equipped to achieve a one-day close. The push for lasting and continual process improvement must be balanced with what is realistic and necessary to achieve the operating results you are looking for. Remember that the goal of process improvement is to get maximum value from the work performed by people and systems, not to beat specific and arbitrary deadlines.

PART THREE

DESIGNING THE ULTIMATE CHART OF ACCOUNTS

21

CHART OF ACCOUNTS REDESIGN

Simply defined, a chart of accounts (COA) is a system used to organize financial accounts in the general ledger. It is a listing of all the financial accounts of an entity that classifies transactions in an orderly and systematic manner. It should be designed to capture the information needed to track financial results and to make decisions based on that purpose. It ultimately serves as the backbone of the financial accounting system, as well as that of the financial reporting system. Only information recorded with an account code from the chart of accounts will be recorded in the financial records, and from there in financial reports. Most important, the COA provides the framework for determining the information presented to management and to other users of the financial statements.

The financial accounts contained in the COA may consist of one segment or many segments. When several segments are used to create a financial account, this is commonly referred to as an *account string*. If only one segment is used, this will be the *natural account number*. This segment is the core segment of all account strings and will exist in all account numbers. The natural account number is used to record the effects of transactions on the primary financial accounts in the general ledger, for example, cash, accounts receivable, revenue, expenses, and so on.

In addition to the natural account number, an account string may consist of items such as department, product, location, entity, and so on. In more advanced accounting systems, the number of fields used and the length of each field are user-defined. The size of the business, the number of entities contained in the consolidated reporting entity, the number of products, and the types of information to be tracked will ultimately determine the number of account segments contained in the account string.

PURPOSE

The purpose of the COA is to serve as a means of recording financial transactions and of reporting on the information recorded in the financial system. A well-designed COA can facilitate accurate bookkeeping and reporting. In contrast, a poorly designed one will cause many problems, because information needed to create standard reports may not be readily available and significant amounts of time and effort may be required to do routine activities. Thus, the COA should lay the foundation in the accounting system from which management obtains the information necessary to meet regulatory reporting requirements and internal and management reporting requirements. With little or no manual manipulation of the data, management should be able to quickly and easily obtain the past and current financial status of the business, as well as the information needed to project the future performance of the business.

WHEN TO REDESIGN

Almost inevitably, at some point, an organization's COA will need to be redesigned or revised. Perhaps information needed to evaluate the performance of the business can no longer be easily gathered, or the operations have changed enough so that routine transactions cannot be easily entered into the general ledger. Depending on the circumstances, it may be easier to take a "ground-up" approach to redesigning the COA; that is, start from scratch with a completely new COA, such as when implementing a new accounting or ERP system. However, when taking this approach, many things must be considered, such as how to map the historical data recorded with the current COA to the new COA. (This will be discussed later in this chapter.) Additionally, you must make sure that you have the appropriate systems and personnel to properly implement the new COA.

Circumstances that warrant redesigning the COA, or at least considering doing so, include:

- *Reporting*:
  - The current COA does not provide the information necessary for the current reporting requirements.
  - Significant manual manipulation of the data using a program such as Excel is required to produce standard financial statements and reports.
  - Much time and effort is required to consolidate information across the enterprise.
  - Information is not readily available to analysts for decision-making purposes.
  - The reporting focus changes, for example, changing from a geographic focus to a business unit focus.
- *Accounting*:
  - The current COA is unable to properly record routine transactions.
  - Significant amounts of data necessary to produce financial statements are maintained outside of the accounting system (e.g., many offline reporting or data collection systems).
  - Accountants frequently have difficulty determining which account numbers to use for transactions.
  - Budget data is captured differently from the actual transactional data.
  - The account segments and descriptions are used inconsistently throughout the organization.
  - The COA segments are no longer used for their original intended purpose(s).
  - Duplicate segment descriptions (two or more values having the same description) are common throughout the entity.

- *Corporate Structure*:
  - Organizational structure changes occur, through restructurings, acquisitions, or divestures.
  - A major operational structure change occurs (e.g., services and/or products are introduced or discontinued).
  - The manner by which the business and employee performances are measured is incongruent with the way the information is tracked in the accounting system.
  - New systems have been put into place.

One of the most common reasons for developing a new chart of accounts is due to the purchase of new accounting software, which could be as simple as a new general ledger package or as complex as the installation of a full enterprise resource planning (ERP) system. Usually, an ERP implementation will involve the integration of many previously unconnected and/or disparate systems; as a result, installation of ERP software will almost always require the creation of a new COA. Furthermore, the ERP system will generally provide the capability to capture much more data than previously.

Regardless of why the COA is being revised, revising the chart of accounts should not be viewed as a simple task. Changing the COA will affect much more than just the general ledger, so everyone who will be affected should have some input to the final decision-making process.

22

CREATING A NEW COA

GENERAL DESIGN CONSIDERATIONS

Obviously, you should not undertake the task of revising or redesigning your chart of accounts if nothing is wrong with it. Therefore, it is extremely important to identify the current weaknesses in your COA to make sure they are not transferred into the new chart of accounts. And do not make the mistake of believing that all problems will be fixed by creating a new chart of accounts. It is essential to isolate the problems caused by an insufficient chart of accounts from problems caused by poor and inefficient operating procedures.

Before deciding what to include in your new chart of accounts, answer the following questions:

- *Reporting*:
  - Which reports need to be prepared for external reporting purposes?
  - Which reports need to be prepared for internal/management reporting purposes?
  - What financial decisions, evaluations, and assessments are made based upon financial statements and reports?
  - What level of detail is required in your reporting?
  - Have all regulatory and statutory reporting requirements been considered?
- *Accounting*:
  - What are the weaknesses that you wish to fix in your current system?
  - What information do you need to obtain from the accounting system?
  - What are the system capabilities for capturing financial and statistical information?
  - How flexible must the accounting and reporting system be?
  - Who will be the users of the accounting and reporting systems?
  - Who will be affected by the implementation of the new system (consider all functions in the organization, not just accounting)?
  - Have all regulatory and statutory accounting requirements been considered?
  - How easily can users be trained to use the new chart of accounts?
  - How difficult will it be to map the current chart of accounts to the new chart of accounts?

- *Corporate structure*:
  - What will the business look like in the future?
  - How much time is available to make this change?
  - Are the current weaknesses in your system due entirely to the chart of accounts, or are there policies and procedures that need to be addressed as well?
  - What resources are available for this type of project: time, personnel, and so on?
  - Who are the people desiring this change?

The best way to begin designing a chart of accounts is to first define your reporting requirements and your company structure. Initially, construct the COA structure around your GAAP reporting requirements, followed by your management reporting requirements. Make sure to consider all reports, including those that satisfy external requirements as well as those that help you with internal management and decision making,

The most important item to consider when designing the chart of accounts is the type of information you want the system to provide. Your ability to quickly obtain meaningful information and easily produce financial reports and statements is completely dependent upon how well your chart of accounts is designed. If you are creating a new chart of accounts, as opposed to restructuring an old one, this may be a bit more difficult. When you are redesigning a chart of accounts, you at least have an idea of what is missing from the current system or what improvements you would like to make.

Ensure that you are cognizant of all the regulatory requirements to which you must adhere and of any regulatory reports that you must produce. Agencies setting such requirements include the Financial Accounting Standards Board (FASB), the Government Accounting Standards Board (GASB), the National Association of College and University Business Officers (NACUBO), the Federal Energy Regulatory Commission (FERC), banks that require periodic financial information, and others. Based on your industry, confirm that the COA enables you to meet these reporting requirements. Also consider tax reporting needs and any state and local reporting requirements, which may vary from entity to entity, depending upon the city, county, state and/or country of operation.

After identifying your reporting requirements, identify the types of structures that your organization has and make sure that the COA can be used for all of these structures. For example, sales managers may need to view sales information and profitability on a geographical basis, whereas another manager may need to view the same information on a departmental basis. Moreover, the legal and regulatory reporting structure may be different from that used for internal reporting purposes. A well-designed COA will allow you to capture and report information under any of these structures.

It is also imperative that you fully understand the capabilities of your accounting and reporting systems. If you are in the process of shopping for such a system, it is vital that your requirements be finalized and well defined *prior* to beginning your search. If not, you could easily be persuaded to invest in a system that is unable to solve your problems. Document your exact requirements, then have software vendors demonstrate how their accounting and reporting systems will meet your needs.

If you are not replacing your current system, consider investing in the services of a consultant who knows the full capabilities of your system. You may be overlooking some useful functionality; or you may be unaware that an easy modification of your system could quickly resolve some of the issues that you are trying to fix by redesigning your chart of accounts. A consultant will know the most efficient way to use your system to meet your needs, and will likely have experience dealing with other customers facing the same problems as you. As with purchasing a new system, make sure you know what your requirements are, or what you want to fix, before bringing in a consultant. A consultant is most effective when you can clearly identify your objectives.

If you decide to modify your existing system, be wary of making too many customizations or modifications. Too often, customizations can turn into lengthy and costly changes that may have unintended effects on other modules in the system, particularly if you are using many third-party modules. Moreover, sometimes modifications cannot be transferred when the software is upgraded or a new version is released. Therefore, before you modify your system get answers to the following questions:

- What will the modification accomplish?
- Has this type of modification been done for other clients?
- What portions of the system will be affected by these changes?
- How will third-party modules interact with these modifications?
- How long will it take to make these changes?
- Will these modifications need to be redone with the next software release, and who will be responsible for paying, if that is the case?
- What type of recourse will you have if the modifications do not work as intended?

One effect that can easily be overlooked is how the COA changes will impact the end users, particularly when the changes are driven from the corporate level, as opposed to a regional or operating entity level. Often, the chart of accounts is being changed to meet the needs of corporate users; nevertheless, all the end users must be considered, from the individual entity managers to the bookkeepers who enter the daily transactions. Frequently, the current system meets the needs of the individual users at the entity level, and they will not understand why it is being changed. The inefficiencies of the current system will have to be explained to them, along with the overall corporate goals, so that they can understand the reasons behind the change. During this process, you should also solicit important input and suggestions from them. Then use this input to help update your organization's accounting policies and procedures as part of your chart of accounts design project. A chart of accounts can only capture the information that is entered into the general ledger; it cannot determine what type of information or how to input it to the general ledger. These are policies and procedures that must be determined prior to going live with your new chart of accounts.

A good rule of thumb to follow when creating a new chart of accounts is to make the chart as simple as possible, yet flexible enough to permit simple revisions as your reporting requirements change over time. It is best to plan only for likely changes, not every potential change, or else you may end up with a much more complex COA than you will ever need.

SEGMENT AND VALUE CONSIDERATIONS

When considering a new chart of accounts, two extremely important factors must be considered first: *structure* and *codes*.

Structure

One of the first decisions to make when designing the chart of accounts is how many dimensions you want to be able to use for reporting purposes. This number directly impacts how many segments will be included in the account string. Naturally, there are trade-offs between having too many or too few. If there are too few, the transactions in the general ledger may not be recorded at the level of detail required for meaningful reporting and analysis; if there are too many, the bookkeeping process may become too cumbersome, causing the accuracy of the recorded transactions to suffer.

Determining the structure of the new chart of accounts includes deciding on the number and types of fields, or segments, in the chart of accounts; the order in which they appear in the account number; the relationships and dependencies among them; any validation requirements; and the format of the individual fields, for example, length, numeric or alpha values, uppercase or lowercase, and so on.

Codes

The individual codes, or values, contained within each segment of the account are the actual codes that comprise the various natural accounts, cost centers, products, and so on, contained in the chart of accounts structure. Determining the individual codes contained within each segment of the account string requires deciding on the length of each particular segment and the complexity of the numbering logic to be contained within each segment.

It is not a good idea to use a combination of alpha and numeric values in your segments, as doing so may make it difficult to properly order and sort your account numbers. It may also slow down the keying of transactions into the accounting system. (One exception is when an entity identifier is used in your account string purely for reporting purposes. Because this value is of such a different type from the others, it may make sense to have this field contain alpha values, while all others contain numeric values. That said, if you then input this value as part of the routine transaction processing, using an alpha value is not recommended, as this may slow down the input process.)

DESIGN FACTORS

Keeping in mind the previous discussion, consider the six factors described in the following subsections when designing the structure and contents of the new chart of accounts.

Dimensions

Dimensions, or granularity, define the information to capture. Depending on the nature of the business, companies are usually interested in analyzing their data along the following dimensions: product, activity, department or cost center, geography, legal entity, project, and, occasionally, customer. The specification for the chart of accounts must include all the data elements that will form part of the new structure, together with an explanation of the rules to follow for recording the information.

The deciding factor on how many and what type of dimensions to include in the chart of accounts will be the degree of detail that the company wishes to build into its transactional systems. It is tempting to include all dimensions on which the operations of the business can be analyzed, but there is a cost associated with having too many elements: Doing so increases the time required to process and input the data, as well as the possibility of error. Consider the cost-benefit trade-off to determine if a particular element should be contained within the chart of accounts.

Conversely, there may also be a cost associated with having too few segments. The structure of the chart of accounts should clearly reflect the current business processes and accommodate any potential or planned future organizational changes. Each measured dimension of the business should be created as a separate segment. Combining dimensions into a single segment complicates the processing and calculation of consolidations, eliminations, and allocations. It also complicates the creation and maintenance of validation and security rules and reporting.

More important is that segments used to represent more than one reporting dimension limit the use of standard default values and complicate reporting by making the data more difficult to isolate. For example, if you will be tracking information by product, it is much more efficient to create a product segment that you can use with just a few natural revenue and expense accounts, rather than creating specific revenue and expense accounts for each product that you want to track.

As seen in Exhibit 22.1, if you incorporate the product dimension into your natural account segment, you will likely:

- Create more accounts than if you were to have a separate product segment.
- Lose the ability to standardize that part of the segment across all natural accounts (in the exhibit, 30 represents Product 3 for Sales, yet 50 represents Product 3 for Cost of Sales).
- Increase the number of natural accounts required to report on a particular segment.

Exhibits 22.1 and 22.2 show that it is much more efficient to incorporate a separate segment to your chart of accounts for the various dimensions you wish to report on. Fewer accounts are needed for accounting and reporting purposes, hence it is easier to standardize, as well as add, product codes since they are independent of the values of the other segments; furthermore, they are not impacted by the creation of other natural accounts, and it will be easier to create reports when the details of only one product are desired.

Description	Natural Account	Product
Sales Revenue—Product 1	40010	N/A
Sales Revenue—Product 2	40020	N/A
Sales Revenue—Product 3	40030	N/A
Cost of Sales—Product 1	50010	N/A
Cost of Sales—Product 2	50020	N/A
Cost of Sales—Product 3*	50050*	N/A
Number of unique account values	6	N/A
Accounts needed to report total sales revenues	3 **(40010, 40020, 40030)**	N/A

* Due to other existing accounts, Cost of Sales—Product 3 cannot be created to end in 30 series to be consistent with sales revenue.

EXHIBIT 22.1   Account String with No Product Code Segment

Description	Natural Account	Product
Sales Revenue—Product 1	40000	10
Sales Revenue—Product 2	40000	20
Sales Revenue—Product 3	40000	30
Cost of Sales—Product 1	50000	10
Cost of Sales—Product 2	50000	20
Cost of Sales—Product 3	50000	30
Number of unique account values	2	3
Accounts needed to report total sales revenues	1 **(40000)**	0

EXHIBIT 22.2   Account String with Product Code Segment

That said, make sure that you create segments only for those dimensions that are useful in measuring the operations and results of your business. The more data elements you have, the greater the possibility of misclassification. The right balance needs to be struck between the demands of analysts for better classified data and the internal capability of the transactional processes to capture such detail.

Don't fall into the trap of trying to make the general ledger your full accounting system, to take over for the subsidiary ledgers or other modules that are suited for specific purposes. Use your accounts receivable and accounts payable ledgers wisely; don't put more detail into the general ledger than necessary. Again, know the capabilities of your reporting system. If you will be recording information that has to be reported on a regular basis in a subsidiary ledger or a submodule, make sure that you will be able to report this information easily. Otherwise, it may need to be contained in the general ledger.

If you are considering adding certain segments because "you might use them one day," omit them. By the time that day actually comes, the reason for reporting the information probably will have changed. It is much wiser to reserve a segment for future reporting needs than to try to identify and incorporate all possible future requirements.

Organizational Capability to Capture Information

The temptation always exists to include all possible dimensions in the chart of accounts structure; but as just stated, usually this is not a good idea. By doing so, you run the risk of including dimensions that are difficult to capture, resulting in chart of accounts segments that either are not used or are misused. Many decisions related to the chart of accounts are difficult to change and are practically irreversible in an ERP context, so it is very important to consider the capability of the organization to record, report, and analyze the data captured in the chart of accounts in a meaningful manner.

You should define the details of the procedures that will enable the capture of the information in the chart of accounts prior to creating a segment there. For example, although it may be desirable to know profitability by customer, it may be extremely difficult to accurately capture and record the costs on a customer-by-customer basis if this information is not available in a timely manner. Just because a particular segment exists does not automatically mean that you will be able to accurately report on that segment. To do so, you must also have the proper procedures in place.

Furthermore, even if the systems exist to capture the data, you must take into account who will be entering this information and how much time it will take to do so. If one of the reasons you are redesigning your chart of accounts is to reduce the time required to process transactions, but your new COA requires spending *more* determining how to code transactions, you are exacerbating the problem. And don't forget to take into account the people who will be doing the journal postings: some may not have the skills necessary to identify differences in transactions that initially may appear very similar.

Legal Entity Structure

The chart of accounts must meet the basic requirement to provide all financial information by legal entity, as opposed to other ways that management may group and organize operations. This ensures that information will be captured along the dimension required to fulfill legal, tax, and statutory reporting purposes. This entity must be a balancing segment, that is, a self-balancing trial balance/chart of accounts that can be pulled by legal entity. (Note, however: This may not be a requirement for a business division where balance sheet elements, such as fixed assets and debt, are not shared, and where separate information is required only for the profit and loss accounts.)

Ease of Maintenance

When designing the chart of accounts, make it robust enough to serve the needs of the organization for many years. The design must function beyond the current quarter-end or the current year-end. At the minimum, have a vision for the finance function that goes at least two to four years out. Speak to those most knowledgeable about the future operations and plans for the company so that any significant changes that may take place in the future can be handled by this new chart of accounts.

You also should provide a logical framework for the account structure, yet at the same time make it easy to add account numbers to the chart of accounts. A simple logic whereby the first one or two digits of a segment have some meaning or relationship built into them can be very helpful; anything beyond that usually becomes quite hard to maintain. It is almost impossible to predict where the majority of the new account numbers will be added, so limit the degree of intelligent numbering that is used when creating the actual account numbers, because too-complex a nomenclature can actually complicate items such as allocations and reporting. And do not attempt to create hierarchies within the actual account sequencing; all modern reporting programs can create reporting hierarchies using trees, so you do not need to do this in the COA. Attempting to do so will cause you to either create large gaps between account numbers, which may cause you to generate more account numbers than really necessary, or make maintenance very cumbersome.

Process Enablers

These include ABC, Balanced Scorecard, Project Accounting, and others. Be mindful of the metrics and processes that currently or are anticipated to become important in the coming months and years. The potential use of enablers such as activity-based costing, product and customer profitability, departmental and entity autonomy, project-based management, and data warehousing, to name a few, must be considered so that the information needed to support these systems and processes can be easily obtained from the general ledger.

Cost of Complexity

Usually, a trade-off is required between the flexibility of the system and its capability to meet everyone's needs and its ease of use. If you create a COA that meets the needs of everyone who will use it, it will likely be overly complex and quite difficult to maintain. Probably, extra time will be required to properly classify and enter transactional data; more sophisticated staff will be needed to administer the system; more time will be required to create and maintain the data validation rules, to train the account staff, and to do reviews and reclassifications, validity checks, and so on. Though it seems ideal to have a system that can do everything, the costs of such a system usually far outweigh the benefits. How much complexity your organization can handle must be answered objectively based upon your current and future accounting and reporting needs and the capabilities of your personnel.

OTHER CONSIDERATIONS

When designing a chart of accounts, it is very easy to just focus on the particular segments and values that make up the actual chart of accounts. However, you must take a more holistic approach when creating the chart of accounts. Some other items to consider are:

- *Do not sacrifice the needs of one business or entity for the needs of another.* It's not feasible to please all parties involved 100 percent, but the system must meet the primary requirements of each entity. Obviously, designing a chart of accounts for an operation with centralized operations will be quite different from doing so for one with locations throughout the world.

- *Understand the causes of the weaknesses in the chart of accounts that you are redesigning.* Identify those problems that are caused by the accounting system, the reporting software, the reporting requirements, the personnel involved, the way the business is structured, as well as the accounting procedures and policies. Identify those problems that can be resolved by a new chart of accounts and those that cannot. Be realistic and honest about the sources of the problems. If the accounting policies and procedures are the root cause, a redesign of the COA probably will not resolve the problems you are having. Furthermore, if the reporting system you are using is at fault, a new COA will have the same problems as the old one. Make sure that the root of the problem is indeed the COA before embarking on a project to change it; otherwise, a lot of time, money, and effort will be spent without any tangible results.

- *Take a holistic approach to designing.* Though it may seem so at times, the divisions and departments of your business entity do not exist in isolation. Make sure to meet the needs of the entire organization, not just a select few. Balance the needs of the users requiring detailed transactional information with those that require only summarized monthly financial information; balance the needs of those inputting the information to the system with those reading the outputs from the system. It is a delicate balancing act, but it must be done to have a successful project.

- *Remove "shadow systems" and automate existing manual processes.* Eliminate those systems and activities that take place because the current system is unable to process the information as needed. Make one of the goals of your chart of accounts project to eliminate or reduce some of the following activities occurring outside of the system:

- Downloading transactions or the trial balance into Excel to sort or classify them as needed
- Performing allocations outside of the system
- Calculating elimination entries
- Calculating partial ownership entries
- Incorporating statistical information that is housed outside of the general ledger

Identify manual processes and determine if they can be either eliminated or automated with new software, new processes, and/or a review of the actual reasons for performing these activities in the first place. Financial information systems that meet the needs of the most particular and sophisticated users of such information reduce the incentives to develop and support shadow systems. This will save time in the closing process, provide more accuracy and timeliness to the data, and allow personnel to spend time on more important tasks.

FEATURES OF A BASIC CHART OF ACCOUNTS

The COA for all entities—regardless of their size, number of locations and departments, and the complexity of their accounting and functional operations—all share some basic common features. The natural account, for one, is a core component of all COAs. The following subsections address the characteristics of most COAs.

Natural Account Segment

At the most basic level, an organization's chart of accounts will have at least one segment, the natural account segment, which is what the majority of people think of when they hear "account number." This segment is used as the primary financial accounting classification for accounting and budgetary activity. The values in this segment are normally classified into the traditional accounting elements, assets, liabilities, and so on. The natural account must represent the lowest level at which an organization wishes to collect and report its financial information.

To provide additional information to the natural account description, some organizations use subaccounts in their chart of accounts. These break down into greater detail a particular account, such as insurance expense. For example, you may have insurance as the main natural account, then use subaccounts to break this into property insurance, workers' comp, and various other insurance categories. If you find that only a few accounts will need this level of detail, consider incorporating these codes into the chart of accounts, rather than using a segment for these values.

A subaccount can also be used to break down an account into multiple smaller units for better tracking of detailed budgets and expenses. The subaccounts may be used in any manner that benefits the reviewer of the account transactions. Each subaccount is unique to an account, but the same subaccount code may be used on multiple accounts.

When designing your chart of accounts, you want to be able to create natural breaks in the numbering sequence to differentiate the major natural types of accounts. Generally, this will follow the major categories that you report in your financial statements and will follow the order in which the items are presented in the balance sheet and then in the income statement. The following categories are typically differentiated from one another by starting the natural account number with a different number:

- Assets
- Liabilities
- Equity
- Revenue
- Expenses
- Taxes
- Statistical accounts

Statistical Accounts

Statistical accounts are contained in the natural account segment, but are different from the typical natural accounts. They are nonfinancial accounts used to track items such as headcount, square footage, and other items that are used for informational and/or allocation purposes. It is best to begin the account numbers for these items with a different number from the financial accounts, such as a 0 or a 9, to minimize the possibility of accidentally using these accounts to record financial transactions.

Furthermore, many accounting systems allow the user to identify particular accounts as statistical accounts so that these items are excluded from daily transactional processing. Also, once an account number has been designated as a statistical account, most systems allow the user to record one-sided entries to it, since amounts are not usually recorded to these accounts using balanced entries.

Department/Entity Segment

For organizations with multiple departments or legal entities, a department and/or entity segment will also be used to provide the level of detail needed to track the financial performance of the various departments. Additionally, if the organization is composed of multiple legal entities, each entity will need its own set of books for various legal and tax reporting aspects.

With a department segment, an organization can track the operations of different departments without having to create new natural accounts for each department. For example, by using different department segments, only one payroll expense account will need to be created since the department segment will identify to which department the expense belongs. Of course, there may be accounts that are applicable to only one or a few departments based upon the specific purposes of those activities.

Whenever there is a department segment, make sure that the various departments can be identified for departmental reporting purposes by using the department segment, not the natural account segment. Set strict guidelines as to how the various segments in the chart of accounts are used. And note that having different department segments will make it easy to compare the performance of the departments in financial reports.

An entity segment differs from a department segment in that it is used to track the activity of different legal entities, whereas a department segment is used to track different activities within the same legal entity. Sometimes one general ledger database will hold the accounting records for multiple entities; in this case, it is imperative to use a separate entity identifier, otherwise, there will be no way to determine to which entity a transaction applies.

Typically, each entity will have a separate database, in which case, it may not be necessary to use a segment to identify the entity since the records will be physically segregated in different databases. However, it will be necessary to determine the functionality of the reporting software that will be used for creating the financial reports, specifically how it will differentiate the transactions of one entity from another. Also, even though the records will be physically separate, if the results of the entities are to be consolidated, there must be some way of identifying the individual entities in the consolidation. To effectively accomplish this, the reporting software may need to use some sort of entity identifier in the account number. The point is, just because each entity has a separate database, doesn't mean an entity identifier is not necessary.

IDEAL NUMBER AND USE OF SEGMENTS

The ideal number of segments to use in your chart of accounts will be determined by your organizational structure, your reporting requirements, and your accounting system. The ideal number of segments is best determined by the people most familiar with the accounting and reporting requirements in your organization. There are recommendations and guidelines for various types of industries, but ultimately, the decision must be made based on the specific needs and requirements of the individual organization. The one exception is in highly regulated industries, such as a utility or a municipality, where specific account number guidelines must be followed.

To determine the number of segments, you also need to review your reporting requirements and the dimensions that are used to create these reports. If all reports are created using only the natural accounts and departments, there is no need to create an account string that would have more than two or three segments (although you may want to add an additional segment to represent entity). You may also want to reserve an inactive segment in case you are planning to report on a dimension not yet used, such as product; but only do so if that is likely to happen.

Each segment should have a specific purpose that can be used throughout the organization. If only one department or location will be using a specific segment, probably it is better to modify an existing segment for that particular use than to create a separate segment that will go unused by the majority of the people. Furthermore, each segment should provide information not captured by the other segments, or facilitate more efficient reporting. Each segment should have a specific purpose.

Some questions to ask when deciding whether to expand the natural account or to create a new segment are:

- Will the new segment values always be used with the same single natural account or will there be many combinations? For example, if product A will only be used with Account X, it may be more efficient to create a new natural account value than create a new segment.
- Will the use of a new segment significantly decrease the number of new natural accounts that need to be created?
- Will the creation of a new segment facilitate more efficient reporting?
- Will the new segment be used throughout the entire organization or by only a few people?
- Can the accounting system support the addition of a new segment?
- Will the creation of this segment cause confusion for the accounting clerks?

However, some items, such as projects, are best if they are not created as a segment in the account string. Using projects as an example, it is usually not necessary to track specific projects in the general ledger; rather, subledgers, such as a project accounting system, are used to do this. Project information is usually so detailed and of such a temporary nature that the general ledger is typically not the ideal place to track projects. Additionally, having a project segment in the chart of accounts will result in having many accounts that are no longer valid once the project is completed. This will lead to account number bloat in your general ledger and will also increase the likelihood of bookkeeping errors. If you are considering creating an account segment that will have values that will only be used for a temporary period of time, such as an employee, customer, or vendor, make sure that you explore the use of subsidiary modules.

IDEAL LENGTH OF SEGMENTS

To determine the ideal length of each segment, first determine the number of possible values that will be contained in the segment. And if there will be different categories of values contained in the segment (e.g., assets, liabilities, etc.), from those in the natural account segment, first determine what those categories will be and how many values will be in each category.

When determining the number of codes or values for each segment, it is best to completely ignore any number sequence and concentrate on the values to be used. Once you have determined the number of values for that the particular segment, you can then begin to figure out how long each segment should be. It's a good idea always to add one digit more than the number of values you will have, unless your accounting system restricts you or the length of the segment will seem overly long. For example, if you determine that you will have 15 individual product values, probably you will want to make the segment three digits long. This will allow you to add additional values as needed and to have enough room in the segment to build in a minimal amount of logic.

23

COA DEVELOPMENT PLAN

When developing a new chart of accounts, it's a good idea to take a very structured approach to ensure that all important items are addressed. Consider the following items when creating the chart of accounts:

- Determine why the COA has to be changed/revised.
- Set realistic expectations of the benefits of a new COA:
  - Do not underestimate the amount of time required to implement the COA once the final account numbers have been determined.
  - Do not expect a new COA to solve all the problems in the accounting and reporting processes.
- Establish performance metrics used to gauge the success of the project.
- Define all your reporting requirements for external users of the financial statements and internal management.
- Specify all desired reports.

It is extremely important to specify why the COA needs to be changed or revised and to keep this in mind the entire time you are going through this exercise. If the goal is to reduce the time required for month-end close or to simplify the reporting process, make sure that every proposed change to the COA will satisfy this goal. Some of the common reasons for changing or revising a chart of accounts are:

- Developing simple reports has become overly complex.
- Allocations, consolidations, and eliminations are too time-consuming.
- The company is acquiring an entity that has a different chart of accounts.
- The company is implementing new accounting software.
- There is a new management focus.
- There are new reporting requirements.
- A decision has been made to migrate all entities in an organization to a standard chart of accounts.

It's also important to set realistic expectations regarding the benefits that a new COA will confer. A new COA by itself will not magically solve the problems with your closing and reporting processes. Therefore, along with the new COA, you must establish new policies and procedures to fully realize the benefits of the new COA.

Rarely is the COA the only component in the accounting process that needs improvement. In fact, redesigning the chart of accounts and creating new account numbers is just the beginning of the process, so do not underestimate the amount of time and effort required. Budget enough time for implementation, data conversion, necessary policies and procedures revisions, and training. A hastily implemented COA will not bring about the desired results. One item often overlooked is the time required to convert the data from the old to the new. Do not make this mistake.

DEVELOPMENT PROCESS

This process can be divided into eight steps, described in the following subsections.

Determine Reporting Requirements

Before you can properly begin designing the COA, you need to determine all your reporting requirements for both internal management purposes and for the users of the external financial statements. It is vital that you obtain copies of all reports that will need to be produced by the accounting/reporting system. Furthermore, it is important to know all the inputs that are required to produce these statements as well as who the users of these statements are. This information will provide the framework you will use for designing the COA.

To fully benefit from the COA redesign, it is important to identify all reports that people would like to have but currently cannot get, whether due to deficiencies in the reporting system or because these reports are overly complex or are just too time-consuming to create on a regular basis. To that end, first request copies of the reports that people use, then learn what is required to produce them, how difficult it is to do so, and how important they are. Additionally, interview managers and others who use, but do not create, reports.

If you request only the reports that are currently being used, and fail to ask about others people would like to have, you may miss opportunities for improvement. For example, reporting on product profitability, or at least revenue by product, may not currently be done because it is difficult to do so. Moreover, the need for this report may be known only to the end users, not the people who actually create reports.

And don't forget to involve individuals from the tax and legal departments, to confirm that the changes being implemented meet their needs. You want the new COA to make reporting easier for everyone, not just a select group of individuals, and often, the tax reporting needs are quite different from those of the accounting department, due to the various activities that have to be captured, as well as the entities that are used for tax, legal, and financial reporting purposes.

Determine Reporting Focus

The reporting focus, from both a financial and a tax and legal viewpoint, will have the most significant impact on how the chart of accounts is structured. As already explained, do not combine too many dimensions into one segment. To avoid this pitfall, you have to know what your measured dimensions are. For most of your statutory reporting, this will be along the entity, department, and natural account dimensions; for management reporting purposes, this will likely encompass products, locations, and possibly even projects, though project accounting is best done through use of a project accounting module.

Possible dimensions along which you may want to report include:

- Entity
- Natural account
- Department
- Product
- Geography
- Location
- Statistical/nonfinancial data
- Series/episode/issue
- Station

Determine Offline Activities That Can Be Automated

Often, one of the advantages to be realized with a new chart of accounts is the automation of various offline reporting activities, or the elimination of so-called shadow activities, as discussed earlier. Some of these may be due to the limitations of your accounting and reporting software, while others may be due to the location of the information required to produce the reports.

Commonly, the end users of the reports will have limited knowledge as to how the reports they use are produced. Therefore it is important that the individuals who produce the reports be involved in the discussions regarding the chart of accounts. You do not want any of the limitations of the old system, of which only a few people may be aware, to built into the new system. Hence, it is very important to identify any sources of data outside of the general ledger that are being utilized. You may discover that different departments are obtaining similar data from different sources; as a result, the amounts being reported are not consistent from one group to another. Once people become aware of the difficulty in obtaining the data for some reports, new sources may be discovered; or the need for that particular report may be reevaluated.

During this exercise, it is a good idea to determine whether the data can be captured in the chart of accounts or if slight modifications to the requested data can reduce the amount of time and effort required to produce the desired information.

Common offline activities include:

- Journal entries
- Statistical calculations
- Allocations
- Elimination entries

- Intercompany reconciliations
- Routine ad hoc reporting

Determine Number of Segments

The number of segments is dependent on the dimensions that are required for reporting. Although it is desirable to use a separate segment for each measured dimension, if the majority of the transactions will use a default value for that segment, it may be better to just incorporate that into an existing segment. Make sure, though, that the dimension that you will use to host these values will not have to be reported on independently. For example, if you were to use the same segment to represent product and geographic location, it would quickly become extremely cumbersome to begin recording sales by geographic location since you would need to create a product-location value in this particular segment for every possible product-location combination. In this case, you will be listing the same location multiple times. By keeping these in separate segments, however, you would only need to populate the location segment with one value for each location, and to create one value for each unique location that you need to report.

Factors that will have an impact on the number of segments in your chart of accounts are:

- Accounting software considerations
- Types of reporting
- Complexity of determining where to record items
- Training
- Policies and procedures

Determine the Necessary Length for Each Segment

The length of each segment depends on the number of values for that particular segment. Generally you will want to include an additional digit to provide for any unanticipated growth in the segment. This will also make it possible to provide for some basic intelligence to be built into the number. For example, if you know that there may be 50 values for a particular segment, make this segment three digits long.

Also, it is better to "backfill" the number with zeros than to begin the value with zeroes. Why? Because if you need to export your account list and open it in a program such as Excel, you may lose the leading zeroes and will have to spend time reformatting the values. Also, keep in mind that whatever digit location you begin your primary sequence with will become your primary indicator; therefore, you will decrease your ability to provide some type of logical numbering if you do not start with the first digit of the number. For example, if you begin your account number with 00100, the third digit becomes your primary indicator and the first two digits are meaningless in terms of logic; but, if you begin the account numbering with 10000, you still have one or two extra digits that you can use for some type of logical indicator.

Establish Level of Detail

One pitfall to avoid is trying to capture all information in your general ledger with your chart of accounts. This is tempting to do, because it makes it easy to access the data, and you will not be dependent on any subsystems. But this is not the most effective way of recording transactions in your general ledger. Use the subledgers as much as possible, particularly for your accounts payable and accounts receivable. This allows you to capture all invoice and purchase order information without the general ledger.

Whenever you find yourself creating account values that cannot be applied throughout the entire organization, or that will only be valid for a discrete period of time, stop, and recognize they should be contained in a subledger. For example, do not create separate account codes for each customer or vendor, or you will soon find you have created a maintenance nightmare. Likewise, do not enter individual employee names in the COA, or incorporate a high level of intelligent numbering into the COA.

You do, of course, want enough detail to make it possible to quickly prepare the reports needed by the external users of the financial statements and by internal management. But whenever you find yourself creating myriad values for a particular item in your COA, that is a good indication that too much detail is being provided in the COA. Instead, investigate using a subledger to maintain this information.

And don't forget to consider the ability of your bookkeepers and accountants to manage a complex number of variables. If you have a small or inexperienced accounting staff, and you are making significant changes to the accounting system, make sure that they will not be overwhelmed by these changes. Also, consider the time and expense of training personnel on the new chart of accounts. Fortunately, reduced complexity often pays off by making it easier to enter data into the accounting system and to prepare reports using this data.

Consider Intercompany Requirements

Intercompany reconciliations can be very difficult for some companies. But as accounting systems become more advanced, and as more companies move to centralized servers for their accounting applications, it is easier to incorporate intercompany matching. Instead of creating a natural account for each type of intercompany transaction, you can use a segment to indicate the related party. This will speed up reporting, as well as consolidations, since you have a field on which you can easily query.

The use of the intercompany segment will allow you to easily match transactions from one entity with another. For example, by using the intercompany transaction code, the originating entity can indicate the receiving entity. This will make it possible to easily create reports that list the receiving entity as the originating entity and to determine if the same amounts have been recorded by both entities. Then you can use just one account, such as intercompany receivables, and match that up with an intercompany code, thereby eliminating the need to create intercompany receivable accounts for each entity.

Know the Capabilities of the Software

Of course, the entire time you are creating your chart of accounts you must keep in mind the capabilities of your accounting and reporting software, and possibly your budgeting software as well. The goal is to have as little manual intervention of the data between your accounting system, your budgeting system, and your reporting system. When all systems can share and use the same chart of accounts, it makes the monthly closing and reporting process much simpler.

Learn the full capabilities of the software. If you are planning on purchasing new software, make sure to do this *before* beginning the chart of accounts redesign exercise or you may discover that some things you wanted in your chart of accounts are not possible, or, conversely, that the software has capabilities that would have made your chart of accounts simpler to design.

It may also be a good idea to have a systems expert on hand to ensure that you are designing your COA in the most efficient manner. Most accounting systems, for example, limit the number and length of segments. You will need to know what these limitations are. Also, find out if your software allows you to temporarily inactivate, or reserve, a segment for future use. It is also helpful to know which systems will be used for your budgeting and reporting packages.

No doubt you will need to be able to produce reports that present actual versus budget comparisons. To do so, you have to know where the budget data will reside; if it will not be in your general ledger, find out any limitations your budgeting software has for using the chart of accounts in your accounting system. Be sure to choose a package that can handle all of the segments along which you budget. Furthermore, if you use a specific consolidations and reporting software package, make sure that it can capture the information you need along all important dimensions. And if you find that your general ledger contains more reporting segments than the reporting/consolidations software can handle, you must know this prior to the purchase of the software. Ask the software vendors about their products' capability to handle your specific chart of accounts. If you purchase the budgeting software that is separate from your accounting software prior to designing your COA, you may find yourself regretting that you did not purchase a more robust budgeting system than you did.

INTERNATIONAL CONSIDERATIONS

If your company has operations in several countries, you may need to keep a separate set of books for each location. Be prepared to compensate for the following items:

- Different accounting methods
- Different treatment for routine activities such as depreciation and amortization

- Use of statutory charts of accounts (in France, for example, it is mandated that all accounts with a first digit from 1 to 5 are balance sheet accounts and accounts with a first digit from 6 to 7 are profit and loss accounts)

It is vital to research the requirements of the countries in which your company operates before making any final changes to the chart of accounts. Be sure to address any items and capabilities that have to be incorporated to your chart of accounts. Seek the advice of people knowledgeable in the requirements of the countries in which you operate.

Operating in a foreign country may also necessitate keeping two books of record: one for the local reporting authorities and one for the consolidated entity. You will need to maintain some type of mapping table to make sure that the two sets of records can be reconciled to one another. Furthermore, in many countries, taxable income is determined by the financial records, a concept quite different from that of the United States. As a result, you may need to create accounts that enable you to record any adjusting entries required to report to local authorities versus the consolidated financial statements.

SAMPLE COA PROJECT PLAN

Whenever you embark upon a COA redesign project, it is imperative to develop a comprehensive project plan prior to beginning any actual work. Make sure to consider and plan for the effects of the project on the system and its users, as well as anyone else that may be affected by the COA redesign.

The following is a sample project plan that you can use as starting point for your own COA project:

1. Determine the objectives of the chart of accounts
   - Consolidates multiple organizations/entities/departments into a centralized reporting structure
   - Allows all entities to use the same chart of accounts
   - Accommodates internal budgetary control and reporting requirements
   - Enhances departmental reporting abilities
   - Accepts data from legacy systems
   - Maintains historical and year-to-date information
   - Allows the accounting and financial systems to be used as effective analysis tools
   - Maximizes software's potential
2. Hold meetings to develop and define these needs. Involve representatives from the departments, functional areas, and preparers of the financial reports.
3. Identify all shadow systems currently in place. Determine if these systems can be replaced by revising the chart of accounts.

4. Develop design proposal:
   - Determine type and number of segments required
   - Determine length of each segment value
5. Review proposal with users.
6. Incorporate feedback and finalize design.
7. Develop account numbering.
8. Map legacy chart of accounts to new chart of accounts.
9. Develop related processes.
10. Train users on new accounting system policies and procedures and chart of accounts.

RECOMMENDATIONS AND OTHER CONSIDERATIONS

When redesigning the COA, use these guidelines to increase the effectiveness, and decrease the length, of the design process:

- Educate all people involved as to why the old system does not work and a new system is needed.
- Ensure that the COA includes the categories of revenues and expenses necessary to report the profitability of specific departments and activities that are important to management.
- Review reporting requirements at the beginning, during, and end of project.
- Ensure that the COA categories allow financial information to be linked to the performance and business goals on which employees and businesses are measured.
- Keep the COA flexible.
- Keep the use of segments consistent.
- Determine the effects that the COA redesign will have on all other systems.
- Determine and plan how to transition from the existing to the new COA.
- Determine how to map data from the old to the new system.
- Maintain consistency among systems.
- Educate all users to benefits of the new system.
- Don't underestimate the time and effort required to properly revise the chart of accounts.
- Avoid having related general ledger accounts; instead of having several general ledger accounts receivable accounts, set up one broad general ledger accounts receivable account and create various types of accounts receivable in the subsidiary ledger.
- Simplify subsidiary ledger reconciliation to the general ledger data file.

- Use subsidiary modules to complement the general ledger, such as a project accounting module. These modules condense data in the general ledger by reducing the number of accounts and the volume of transactions. These modules are designed for a specific purpose, so they generally process the data faster and are better suited for recording these types of transactions.

SUMMARY

Be mindful that there is no such thing as a right or perfect chart of accounts. There are always alternatives available that are equally effective. Any chart of accounts can be seen as suboptimum when looked at from a different perspective. The point is to view the chart of accounts as a key component of the mechanism that helps the organization learn more about its internal dynamics. Foresight, coupled with business wisdom, are necessary to strike the right balance to arrive at the "best fit" for each company.

And, remember, it is impossible to satisfy everyone 100 percent, so do not make that your goal or you will set yourself up to fail. If, instead, you keep in mind the reporting requirements, the capabilities of your organization and personnel, and the capabilities of your software and reporting systems, as well as the future direction of your organization, you will succeed in developing a chart of accounts that meets the needs of your organization.

PART FOUR

INTERVIEWS

24

ROBERT BLAKE, MICROSOFT CORPORATION

NAME: Robert Blake

TITLE: Program Manger for XBRL at Microsoft, Member of XBRL
            International Steering Committee

COMPANY: Microsoft Corporation

XBRL promises to change the way companies communicate business information. Robert Blake, one of the key people in this area, was interviewed to gain some perspective on this new standard:

Are there currently any initiatives to use XBRL for internal reporting?

Right now, companies use XBRL primarily for external reporting, such as 10Q and 10K reports. That said, there are opportunities for internal use of XBRL, and we are trying to raise the level awareness among business people of XBRL's versatility. XBRL is about any kind of reporting for any size company—regardless of whether the target audience is internal or external.

Can you give me some examples of how XBRL has improved reporting efficiency?

Bank of America used XBRL to reduce its average loan processing period from two days to two hours. By standardizing its requirements of financial from potential borrows to XBRL, Bank of America is able to collect and interpret financial data more quickly, using its own software that reads XBRL documents.

Is it common for companies to use XBRL to consolidate financial data from different subsidiaries and systems?

While most people currently use XBRL to provide financial results to bankers and investors, XBRL certainly can be applied within an organization, especially for pro forma statements, wherein data may be drawn from different accounting systems. The real value of XBRL internally is that it allows you to put your financial data in a consistent and universally understandable format. For companies growing by acquisition, this can prove a valuable means to quickly integrate financial between newly merged companies.

The XBRL literature talks about taxonomies, which provide the structure a company can use to render financial data into XBRL format. Where can people find examples of XBRL taxonomies, which they can in turn modify and apply in their own enterprise?

A sample XBRL taxonomy can be found on the steering committee Web site, *www.xbrl.org*. Microsoft has also published a white paper on its own XBRL specification.

25

DEAN SORENSEN, BYWATER MANAGEMENT CONSULTING

NAME: Dean Sorensen
TITLE: Principal
COMPANY: Bywater Management Consulting

Dean Sorensen specializes in assisting organizations to establish alignment around executing strategies that create profitable growth. A central component of this focus involves a unique and innovative use of business performance intelligence software to establish more dynamic management systems that promote more marketlike behavior, while encouraging people to think and act more like business owners.

Mr. Sorensen has 14 years of management consulting experience, spanning all functional areas, across numerous industries and roles, including strategy, management systems, process reengineering, and change management. He is also a chartered accountant in Canada, having spent eight years in public accounting, where he advised organizations in all areas of financial management.

Bywater Management Consulting is an international consulting firm dedicated to helping companies achieve their ambitions. With over 20 years of worldwide experience, its seasoned consultants have performed more than 1,000 assignments in several areas, including enterprise transformation, process improvement, acquisition and partnering assistance, private equity financing, growth strategy development, strategy execution, and management systems.

Dean Sorensen answered these questions to provide you with additional ideas and perspectives for your BPI project. Not only does he offer relevant insight based on a long professional career as a renowned management consultant, but even more interesting, he has a number of original concepts that should be valuable for any financial manager:

What are your views on the current state of management systems?

Management systems are the economic models, frameworks, tools, and processes that enable organizations to define, adapt, and deploy strategy. For many organizations, they are often ill suited to meet the needs of today's competitive environment, often being described as cumbersome, inefficient, and ineffective—particularly budgeting. In fact, budgeting, as it has been traditionally used, often exacerbates the problem because it can lead people to make decisions that are inconsistent with the strategy, while undermining performance.

For many organizations, ineffective management systems are one of the root causes behind an issue that is gaining increasing attention of executives—an inability to effectively execute strategy. Organizations have made significant investments in technology (e.g., ERP and CRM) in response to changes in the competitive landscape, often brought about by Internet-based technologies. However, these investments often fail to deliver significant value. This "execution problem" is often a big problem for executives, becoming one of the key reasons for CEO dismissals.

You recently completed research on business performance intelligence software. What did you find?

A new generation of business performance intelligence software (BPIS) is emerging that integrates leading performance management practices, including active financial planning, Balanced Scorecard, activity-based costing and economic profit into more dynamic management systems. BPIS vendors are beginning to recognize that this is the key for delivering significant value to clients, while separating themselves from their competitors. In this context, two key changes are seen:

1. The ability to plan, measure costs, and manage performance around an organization's outputs, enabling organizations to integrate finance with operations, and strategy with tactics.
2. A more seamless management process, enabling organizations to continuously collect, interpret, and drive action based on a collective understanding of ever-changing market conditions and financial objectives.

To some, the implications of these changes might not be immediately obvious. However, their impact on organizations can be profound. They provide the basis to fundamentally transform management systems into powerful tools that equip organizations to cope with the complexities of today's economy.

What capabilities does business performance intelligence software provide that organizations lack today?

Business performance intelligence software provides one capability that organizations lack: the ability to optimize value for customers, while doing likewise for shareholders. Achieving this objective entails maintaining a delicate balance between objectives that generally conflict with one another. This trade-off between customer and shareholder value affects virtually every aspect of the activities and outcomes that comprise organizational performance. Therefore, performance can only be optimized when they are actively and explicitly managed throughout an organization. The only way to do so is by managing the conflicting cost and service objectives associated with every output. Since most organizations do not manage performance in this manner, they, by definition, are not optimizing performance.

As a result of your experience and research, you've developed an approach called a Value Market. How does it leverage the capabilities of BPIS to optimize organization performance?

Providing organizations with the ability to manage outputs and trade-offs is central to a performance management approach called a Value Market. It is a mechanism that promotes more marketlike behavior within organizations by creating a network in which internal buyers and sellers can interact to exchange services that create value for customers, at a cost that creates profitable growth and long-term value for shareholders. This approach enables the creation of profitable growth by:

- Driving strategic alignment by communicating objectives horizontally across functional and organizational boundaries in a manner that people on the front lines can execute
- Allowing strategies and cost structures to more naturally self-correct to changing market conditions
- Promoting a collective sense of responsibility for meeting customer needs, providing the basis to reduce cycle times
- Providing the basis to effectively empower employees by:
  - Using outputs as the basis for delegating authority
  - Establishing accountability for managing the conflicting objectives (i.e., trade-offs) associated with each of these outputs

One of the key benefits lies in its ability to transform the management process, and in so doing, the organization as whole.

You have indicated that creating a "business owner mentality" is a central ingredient of the Value Market approach. How does it provide the basis to transform the management process and the organization as a whole?

At the heart of this transformation lies a fundamental change in how organizations engage employees in managing the business. When people are accountable for managing outputs and the trade-offs between conflicting cost and service objectives, something "magical" happens. They start to think and act differently—more like business owners. No longer can one objective be met at the expense of another. They start looking for the right balance that will optimize performance, not just from a functional perspective, but from an organizational one as well. And when problems arise, these trade-offs provide the right context for making decisions.

Much attention is being paid to the budgeting process because it is viewed as a non-value-added activity that actually detracts from creating value. You have defined a process called Value Triangulation as a means to address this. Could you elaborate on it?

The changes already noted extend into the planning and budgeting process as well. Value Markets provide the basis to change the tone of the management process. Budgets become more of a funding mechanism rather than a control device. Planning and budgeting becomes less about controlling resource allocation and more about coordinating it. Between organization units, it forms the basis for establishing service levels in light of cost constraints. Between management levels, planning assumptions become explicit, rather than buried in the desk drawers of departmental managers.

The foundation for this change is a mechanism called Value Triangulation, a process that simultaneously establishes objectives for the conflicting cost and service objectives associated with every output. Rather than dictating spending limits, the process becomes one of establishing a mutual understanding about what can be achieved in light of these trade-offs, since increasing service also increases costs.

Why is a Value Market approach important for organizations?

The Value Market approach provides the means to address many of the management challenges that organizations face today, including:

- Increasing flexibility and responsiveness, without exposing the organization to undue risk.
- Fostering innovation, while creating an environment that enables it to attract and retain top talent.
- Attracting and retaining loyal customers, while maintaining profitable product and customer portfolios.
- Reducing overhead costs, while simultaneously delivering exceptional service and value. In this context, it is an essential ingredient for creating profitable growth from customer-focused strategies.

How does the Value Market contribute to entrenching the finance function in the role of a business partner and value creator?

The Value Market approach, and the technologies enabling it, present tremendous opportunities for organizations to create value and strategic advantage. However, for many, realizing this value will be challenging, for it introduces three key changes:

1. It is predicated on open and continuous dialogue between functions, as well as greater interaction between finance and operations.
2. Performance issues will be easily exposed, leaving "no place to hide."
3. Many traditional finance roles will no longer be required, as activities will either cease to exist or will be assumed by "operations."

These changes will likely present obstacles that will need to be overcome, which will require leadership. And since CFOs are typically leading efforts to establishing BPIS, this role will likely "fall into their laps." For some CFOs, this type of role will be one with which they are familiar, having already moved their finance functions to more of a business partner model. But for others, it will be out of their comfort zone. And in this sense, it will be the impetus to start their thinking about the future of the finance function in their organization.

26

BILL ELLENBACK, SOFTWARE USER

NAME: Bill Ellenback

TITLE: Accounting System Administrator

Tell a little about yourself and your company (industry, services, structure, number of employees, revenue, and so on).

I've been a finance professional for nine years. Prior to my current position, I was the lead divisional accountant for a wholesale distributor of construction and infrastructure material. While in this role, I became involved in a project whose stated goal was to take the company's 30-plus operational point-of-sale systems and consolidate them down to four or five. I was responsible for the accounting setup of the new systems, as well as the process of exporting the data and importing it to our standalone general ledger.

In my current position I am responsible for the day-to-day operations of our worldwide accounting system. The system currently includes seven different accounting databases and our budgeting and consolidation tool. We are using the latter to consolidate not only our actual data from the accounting systems, but our worldwide budget and forecast data as well. I'm also involved in improving our current processes and implementing new systems to deliver our data to both financial and management users.

Prior to the budget, does your company have a planned strategy for the budget year? Is this communicated when the budget is to begin? What is the budget used for?

Our company has a planned strategy for the budget year based upon our overall perception of the business environment and the expectations of our parent company; a memo is produced outlining our goals and objectives for the budget. This memo is discussed and distributed to all upper-level executives.

We schedule a number of preliminary meetings with upper-level executives to try to determine organizational or other changes that will impact the budget process. We do, however, seem to reorganize during the process every year even though these meetings take place. Some instructions and guidelines are developed during these meetings that are communicated to our department managers, such as proposed capital projects and new hires. These instructions are communicated to the management staff with memos, with budget system training sessions, and with a budget user guide.

When the process begins, our managers are responsible for entering data directly into the budget for their department via the Web for U.S. users and directly into the budgeting software with assistance from finance for our overseas users. By having our managers enter their budget directly into the system, rather than having the budget created for them, promotes their buy-in to the process. We also send out a budget calendar outlining our internal deadlines and when the internal reviews will take place.

The managers then review their submissions with their superiors and with the finance department to correct errors and ensure that the budget conforms to policy and instructions. Consolidated divisional rollups are reviewed and evaluated with divisional presidents, and changes are pushed back down. For example, the budgeted revenue doesn't support the new hires proposed. These reviews are also focused on getting each business unit to contribute enough to meet growth goals as formulated by our parent company. The end result of our budget process should be to adequately reflect where we believe our business will be during the budget year, while at the same time meeting the required criteria of our parent company. I guess you could say the output of our process is both a budget and a goal. The final budget is also used as our first forecast of the budget year.

How long does your budgeting period last? Is it planned to last that long? Do you have any suggestions to speed it up in the future?

Our process begins in mid-August and is typically completed in late October. We do continue to rework the budget based on the parent company's criteria and internal requirements until the fiscal year-end. We will also change the budget during the budget year if there are changes sufficient enough to warrant a recut. A major reorganization occurred for us in May and we recut the budget as if it occurred in January. We moved actual, budget, and forecast figures based on this reorganization. This is done only if it is a major change. We don't update budgets on a monthly basis for department transfers, but this will be done in the forecast process.

We sped up the process recently by greatly reducing the time required to consolidate our budget. We budget in six different currencies with divisional rollups being produced in four different currencies. Our submission to corporate is in U.S. dollars. The implementation of our new process allows each divisional unit to budget and report in its home currency. The home currencies as entered are converted to a U.S. dollar-based budget that is required by our top-level executives and parent company. The report formats developed in our new process are used by all divisions and can be executed in any currency for a department, divisional unit, or consolidation.

We also try to speed the process by getting management to make as many decisions about the business as possible before the budget begins.

Do you create a timeline prior to the budget? Do you think it helps you or that it would help you?

We create a budget calendar that is distributed to the finance departments in each country responsible for completing its respective international budget. This calendar is also sent to upper-level management so they are aware of what is required to meet the deadlines for presentation of the budget to our parent company.

We build some time in the calendar that would normally be used in our consolidation process for those units that do not complete their budget by the deadline. Our new system allows us to consolidate, review, and enter data concurrently without impacting other users. We only stop the process for the allocation processing and the printing of reports for review.

Are you using a software program that has lessened the number of data entry errors? If not, are you planning on buying one soon?

We use a software program, and it has reduced the number of entry errors. One of the best things we did awhile back was to create a global natural chart of accounts that is used consistently by our finance groups worldwide. For example, account 1200 in the United States is the same as account 1200 in Singapore. We created our chart at 1000 and ended it at 9000. We designated account ranges for captions (A/R accounts are available from 1200 to 1300). This allows some flexibility, as each worldwide unit can segregate activity in an account due for its internal requirements or government statute. Our account 1205 pertains to a specific type of receivable that must be tracked separately by Australia.

Because we use a consistent set of accounts, we are all using a single budget model. This has greatly eliminated confusion as to where to budget a particular item. Each finance group meets with their local managers to clear up questions as to where to budget a particular item. We also review data during the entry process and have managers change their postings based on our review.

Do you have a rolling forecast?

No, but it has been discussed at a low level.

Do you report on your budgets? If so, what type of reports do you use most often?

The following are our most popular reports:

- Trended Yearly Budget versus Full-Year/Prior-Year Forecast (with Variance)
- Full-Year Budget versus Full-Year/Prior-Year Forecast (with Variance)
- Trended Revenue by Month by Confirmed or Unconfirmed Status
- Quarterly Budget versus Prior-Year Quarterly Forecast (with Quarterly Variance)
- Capital Budget Detail (Total) with Trended Budgeted Depreciation
- Salary by Month by Individual
- Contractor by Month by Individual
- Revenue by Product
- Revenue by Client
- Capital Budget Purchases Summary by Month (Trended)

Does your company perform variance analysis when comparing the budget to the actual amounts? Are the employees held accountable for their numbers, and do they need to put together comments as to why they had a variance?

One factor in our company's incentive (bonus) package is dependent upon performance versus budget. Our primary variance analysis is performed on a monthly basis when we do the current forecast versus prior forecast review. Each finance group is responsible for performing this analysis when a variance exceeds a designated percentage. This is completed for the current month actual versus prior-year month forecast and current full-year forecast versus prior full-year forecast. Our full-year forecast is made up of actual amounts through the most recent closed month and future forecast months.

Our forecasts act like monthly business plans. Decisions are made during the forecast process and compared against those actually posted during closing. Decisions concerning capital purchases, new hires, cutbacks, and so on are all made during the forecasting process.

Do you use any other type of analysis or analysis tool after the budgeting process?

We build a number of supporting schedules based on our final budget. We use only our budgeting and reporting tool and Excel as our analysis tools.

Do you train your users on the budget process? Do you explain the strategy at that time? Do you see any area that you can improve?

We hold two training sessions and issue user guides for the budget system and process. A number of guidelines and limits are set and published as part of the budget user guide. For example, capital purchases must be a minimum of $1,000; and staff must be prepared to defend any proposed new hires.

Are there any areas that technology will enable you to complete the budget process more efficiently in the future?

Any technology that will help us enter our data more efficiently into our budget model would be helpful. We enter, calculate and allocate a tremendous amount of data that is necessary based on our reporting requirements.

Do the people who budget have access to relevant history in order to complete their budgets?

We distribute a "run-rate" report in our general ledger report writer that calculates a full-year expense rate based on actual amounts through July.

When our management users finalize their budget (at deadline), we copy this data to a budget version called B2–Management Submission from our original budget version B1. Our finance users make changes to our B1 Working Budget based on a review of errors, guidelines, and required changes from upper management. This allows us to keep a record of a manager's original submission to compare against the final version that has been approved by finance and upper management.

What are some of the largest obstacles to completing the budget process?

We've asked our users for a tremendous amount of data to complete the budget process, and entering this data in our system is a time-intensive process. We've eliminated many of our obstacles through the use of technology to solve our consolidation issues. Our biggest obstacles to finalizing the budget are due to changes instituted during the process that hadn't been discussed prior to the process beginning. These would include changes in the organizational structure or allocation processing.

In each of the following areas, comment whether you budget for these and how you could improve the information or the process:

- *Revenue*. We budget revenue by natural account number, client, and product. Our revenue entry sheets are also segregated by Confirmed and Unconfirmed status. Confirmed revenue is that which is guaranteed by contract in a budget year. Unconfirmed revenue contains amounts that we believe will be signed to a contract, or "stretch" amounts used to reach required levels.

- *Employee*. We upload employees by department, which includes an annual salary from our divisional payroll systems. We apply a raise amount and the month that the employee will receive the raise per employee to complete our salary budgeting. We also calculate our headcount based on the input of the users. Calculation of related payroll taxes and incentive amounts are calculated based on the amounts entered by department.

- *Cost of sales*. We do not budget cost of sales.

- *Expenses*. Managers enter their proposed expenses by department. These expenses are removed if necessary during the finance and management review.

- *Capital expenditures*. Managers enter proposed capital purchases for their department. These expenses are removed if necessary during the finance and management review.

- *Balance sheet and cash flow*. We complete a balance sheet and cash flow budget in Excel when our income statement budget is final. We do this in Excel rather than in our budgeting tool because we have fewer than 10 balance sheets to budget and we can model more easily in Excel than with a database software.

PART FIVE

SOFTWARE TOOLS
AND RESOURCES

27

SELECTING ANALYTICS SOFTWARE

Selecting analytics (budgeting, reporting and analysis) software is similar to the purchasing process for other accounting and financial software packages. However, because analytics software is typically less complex than an accounting or enterprise resource planning (ERP) solution, the selection process should be shorter and require fewer people. It is complicated somewhat, though, by the fact that there are a wide variety of budgeting, reporting, and analysis tools available (see Chapter 29), some which will fit your company's needs better than others.

Although the selection process need not be scientific, companies make better choices and save time and frustration when they take an organized approach to their software acquisition process. Before you begin, make sure you involve people from both the user side and IT. The database management (installation, backup, performance tuning, etc.) is typically supported by the IT department, while end users will ensure that financial analysis needs and requirements are met.

This chapter identifies the key issues and items you should incorporate into your analytics software planning and evaluation.

DEVISE A PLAN

The first thing to do before buying a new software package is to sit down and create a plan (see Exhibit 27.1). At a minimum, this plan should contain the following steps:

1. *Review current situation.* Review your organization's current information needs, and research and document information needs that might surface over the next few years.
2. *Choose the type of solution that best fits your needs.* Keep in mind that different types of users have different needs. This means that you might need several types of analytics tools (such as a budgeting tool, a report writer, and an OLAP-based query tool) to meet all user requirements. It is therefore important to categorize your users by their information needs and skill levels. Based on Step 1, you typically will have three choices with regard to analytics intelligence software:
   1. Upgrade your current system (if you already own a system).
   2. Build a new system based on your organization's needs.
   3. Purchase a commercial analytics solution.

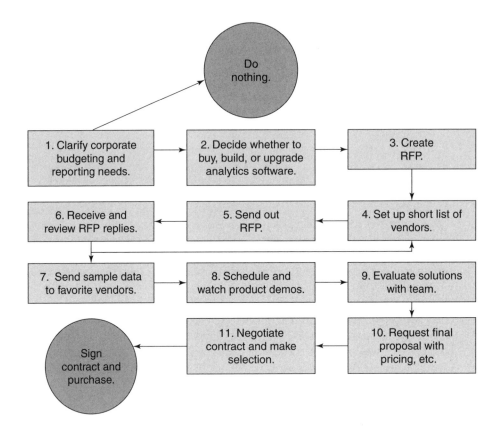

EXHIBIT 27.1   Sample Software Selection Process

Note: This chapter focuses on commercial analytics solutions, and it assumes that you are moving in this direction.

3. *Create a request for proposal (RPF)*. When considering commercial analytics solutions, it is best to approach potential vendors with an RFP before you start viewing any demonstrations or taking any other steps in the selection process. Creating this document also serves as a valuable organizational learning exercise, to motivate key people to think about what they are looking for in a product and a vendor. The RFP should describe *thoroughly* the functionality and requirements you need, in the following areas:

- Integration to your data sources and productivity tools
- Current and future data volumes
- Areas of usage (e.g., financial reporting, sales and marketing analysis, key performance indicators, annual budgeting, rolling forecast, etc.)
- Key features
- User security, access, and roles

- Implementation and training(involved parties, timelines, roles, etc.)
- Deployment infrastructure (Web, local network, single user, etc.)
- Hardware and software requirements (platforms, versions, etc.)
- Itemized cost (software, hardware, implementation, training, etc.)

Note: Don't *overstate* your requirements, or you might end up with only a few high-end tools in your final selection process, which may have functionality you don't need, be overly complicated, and end up costing your company a lot of extra money.

Follow these steps when you create an RFP:

1. Create a selection timetable.
2. Create a list of all related parties in your organization.
3. Write a short document that outlines the scope of the project.
4. Start with a sample RFP (if you have one) and modify it. Keep it as short and simple as possible. The objective is to spend most of your time actually looking at products and discussing your needs with vendors.
5. Distribute the RFP to key people and ask them to make additions and changes. (Note: Certain people might need only parts of the RFP. For example, IS staff should focus on platforms, integration, infrastructure, and general technology issues. Management, financial and accounting staff should focus on financial information and analytical features.)
6. Review, clarify, and finalize the RFP.

Note: Creating an RFP and, later, evaluating all the responses can be a time-consuming process, so it might be more efficient to engage directly in in-depth demos and needs analysis with a handful of vendors. That said, it is recommended that you create at least a "mini"-RFP, in which you describe the key requirements and address the most important questions. Take this approach only if you have experience in software selection, you have good knowledge of the analytics software market, and you are good at communicating your company's needs to vendors.

If you want to outsource the RFP and/or other parts of the selection process to a third party, there are many software selection companies that offer services in this area. If you do use a software selection company, make sure it is "vendor-neutral." If the selection company also provides implementation services for one of the software packages it recommends, that's a good sign it will be biased, and you should look elsewhere.

4. *Research vendors, create a short list, and send out the RFP.* A decade ago, before analytics software was a hot topic for businesses everywhere, only a few commercial budgeting and financial reporting software vendors existed. Today, however, you will find numerous vendors offering solutions of varying complexity, prices, and technology platforms. Because you now have so many choices, it is imperative to thoroughly research the vendors and their solutions after you receive their replies to your RFP. Depending on the time available, narrow the field down to three to five vendors, then invite each of them to make

a presentation to your organization. The following is a list of resources you can use to gather information about vendors and their solutions (see Exhibit 27.2):

- RFP
- Buyers' guides (found in accounting and financial magazines and newsletters and in other software and industry publications)
- Product brochures
- Current users
- Company background brochures
- White papers
- Third-party evaluations
- Vendor Web sites
- Third-party Web sites
- This book (see Chapter 29 for vendor list)

If you don't know a specific Web address, search the Web using keywords such as "budgeting software", "consolidation and reporting software", "analytics software", and so on. Be aware that you might not be able to get a comprehensive list of vendors from a Web search; it is dependent on the search engine you use, your keywords, and how the sites are indexed on the various search engines.

Keep in mind that many buyers' guides, publications, and other available third-party materials are not necessarily comprehensive. And too often, compa-

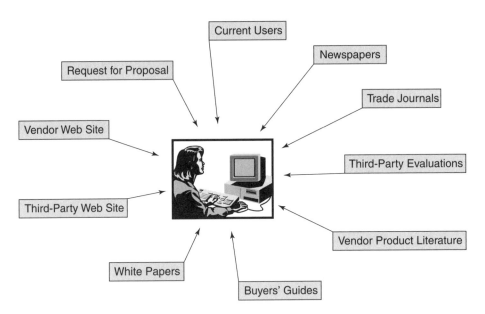

EXHIBIT 27.2   Information Sources for Vendor and Product Research

nies allow salespeople to educate them about the market, and they understandably, promote only select solutions. Finally, feature lists can be "flavored" by:

- Employee bias (used a package before, personal connections)
- Consulting company bias (experts in implementation of a particular solution)
- Vendor bias (such as an ERP vendor promoting its own BI package)
- A writer's limited understanding of complex budgeting and reporting software

Therefore, use your own evaluations (see number 8, on product Demonstrations), as well as interviews with current customers, as the basis for your software selection.

A note on distributing RFPs: Some companies send out their RFP to all the vendors they have listed and then let the vendors themselves decide (based on the content of the RFP) if their software is qualified or not. This approach can generate a large number of lengthy replies you will have to go through to find qualified candidates. A better approach is to do some vendor research in advance (to check software prices, database platforms, vendor solidity, key features, etc.) and then send your RFP to a limited number of qualified vendors. (Note: Do not forget to include a reply deadline on the RFP, to keep your evaluation process on track, timewise.)

5. *Review RFP replies.* After you have received all the information from the vendors, you and your team have to analyze and rank each reply. Normally, companies pick three to five vendors to invite on-site to present their services and solutions. If you choose too few, you could miss potentially good candidates (remember that an RFP is a written document and doesn't give the full picture of a vendor and a solution). Conversely, if you invite too many vendors, you and your team may spend weeks in presentations, which is exhausting and costly and generates biases toward vendors based on external factors such as when they presented and how busy the evaluation team was on that particular day. It is therefore recommended that you choose only a handful of vendors. If you are in doubt about certain vendors, give them a call to get the answers you are looking for.

When you study the vendors' replies to your RFP, take them for what they are: biased answers to a list of questions. And to protect yourself against "false advertising," be sure that your RFP and the final software contract state that the vendor is liable for the information provided, should you choose to purchase its solution.

6. *Send out demo material to the selected vendors.* This step is optional but strongly recommended. To get the most out of the upcoming product demonstrations, and to provide vendors with a better understanding of your information needs, it is a good idea to send to vendors sample reports, key figures, rollup structures, and examples of the different dimensions you will use. This will enable them to show you how some of your budgeting forms and reports will look and work in their software packages. This also makes it easier for your evaluation team to ask good questions, because they will be looking at a familiar model in

the presentation. Or, if you are planning to completely revamp the way you budget and evaluate your company's information, it might be a good idea to let the vendors show their own examples so you can get an impression of their standard capabilities without too much customization toward your old model.

7. *Meet with vendors and review their company and product demonstrations.* Schedule the presentations to evaluate each vendor and its solution. Ideally, have all the key people on your evaluation team present at all the demonstrations, so that they can get a complete picture before they choose their favorites. (Chapter 28 covers the evaluation process in more detail.)

   A product demonstration is your chance to get a first-hand look at the interface and features of a software package. If a skilled and experienced sales team is doing the presentation, you will get a lot of valuable information from the demonstration.

   From your RFPs, you already have information from the vendors about all of the key areas, but now is the time to see the products in action. And, if you are unclear about anything in regard to the vendor or the product, the demonstration is the forum in which to pursue these issues. You can also request a "workshop," if you need to spend more time with the software package to verify that it is a good fit for your business. Things to look for during the demonstration include:

   • Vendor/reseller background
   • Product history and future releases
   • User interface
   • Features
   • Customization/flexibility
   • Extraction, transformation, and loading of data from different data sources
   • Technology platform
   • Documentation
   • Implementation
   • Pricing

8. *Postdemonstration* evaluation. After the demonstrations, sit down and evaluate each one and select the favorite(s); if you find you need more details or additional information, request another demonstration. Use an evaluation form to rate each vendor.

9. *Request final proposal(s).* When you have found the product you feel is the right fit for your company's needs, request a final proposal with detailed maintenance, implementation, and support prices; implementation time estimates; sample project plan; and so on. If you find several vendors that might fulfill your needs at a similar level, do not hesitate to ask all of them for this information, so you can make a final, detailed comparison between them. In this case, you will also have information to help leverage your negotiations. At this point, you should also contact the references for each of your final candidates to confirm their impression of the software and to get a more objective perspective on each solution.

10. *Negotiate contracts/license agreements.* Once you have picked a favorite vendor and software solution, it is time to request a contract. This document will normally include:
    - Exact software pricing, based on number of users, number of sites, modules needed, and so on
    - Consulting and training rates and time estimates
    - Software modules, based on the functionality you have requested
    - Project outline, with main activities that must take place prior to model completion (see Appendix E for an example)
    - Hardware and software requirements
    - License agreement
    - Support plan
    - Other information that you have requested in the RFP
11. *Make final vendor selection.* Based on the response(s) to your RFP, usually you will need further conversations to discuss or clarify certain items before you feel comfortable with all the information. A major negotiation point is often pricing.
12. *Sign contract and facilitate payment.* Once your company and the vendor have addressed all outstanding issues, the last step is to sign a license agreement, and then to pay (based on payment terms), and to receive the software and documentation.

USING A SOFTWARE SELECTION COMPANY

As noted earlier, many companies solicit the services of third-party firms to help them select the optimal analytics solution. These firms range from individuals with prior experience in the budgeting and reporting software industry now working as consultants to major national/global consulting companies. Be aware that many of the large consulting companies have local, regional, or global strategic sales and/or consulting alliances with specific software vendors, or they have their own solutions. In either case, be sure to do some advance research to be assured that their recommendations are not biased in one way or another.

In general, you should consider using a software selection company if one or more of the following are true:

- You don't have time to perform a thorough vendor/solution analysis yourself.
- You are considering technologies unfamiliar to you.
- Your corporate environment is very politically "loaded," and an internal selection process will cause conflict between decision makers.
- You want a third party to assist in doing a needs analysis for your company and in matching these needs with available analytics products.

Before you engage a selection company, ask for a price quote and what the deliverables are. This will help prevent any costly surprises at the end of the engagement. Typically, costs range from $5,000 to $25,000, and delivery can take from a few days to many weeks, depending on the time the company spends analyzing your needs and participating in demonstrations and evaluations. Deliverables can include one or more of the following:

- Needs analysis
- Development of RFP document
- Selection of vendor finalists
- Participation in demonstrations

28

SOFTWARE EVALUATION: FACTORS TO CONSIDER

In general, the evaluation and purchase process for financial analytics software is similar to that of other niche software solutions, such as business intelligence software. In other words, you will require much less time for evaluations and presentations than for a typical enterprise resource planning (ERP) solution that has numerous modules (general ledger, accounts receivable, accounts payable, payroll, etc.) and affects most parts of the business.

CURRENT AND FUTURE USE REQUIREMENTS

One of the first questions you should ask during the software evaluation phase is whether you are looking for a short-term or a long-term solution. In some cases, a company must solve its budgeting and reporting issues immediately, and doesn't have time to do an in-depth analysis of long-term organizational needs or platform requirements. Perhaps this is because a "home-built" analytics model no longer works properly or is too hard to maintain. Or the reason may be related to organizational politics, and you cannot afford to wait any longer for certain parties to provide their input as to your software needs. However, in most cases, companies that invest in best-of-breed analytics software are planning to stay with it for a long time, not only because it usually represents a significant investment in terms of money, consulting, and user training, but also because of the total time involved in setting up data extraction, conversion and loading procedures, and reports. This is not a process you and your coworkers want to go through every year.

In other words, if you are seeking a short-term solution, you should not be considering the most expensive and most complex analytics packages. But if you are making a long-term investment, you should spend sufficient time looking into needs, product and vendor capabilities, and long-term maintenance costs, and focus somewhat less on acquisition and implementation costs.

Another element to consider is the *usage scope* for the near future, versus the long run. If your organization needs only a single-location implementation, and the budgeting and reporting model will be fairly simple, with few planned changes, the software selection process should be fairly simple. If, however, you are planning to expand the model and organizational usage down the road, you should spend more time looking into the required functionality of software packages and their vendors. And if you are acquiring a new software package today, and are investing in related training and implementation, make sure that the software is scalable and can grow with the organization.

Technology platforms are also important considerations if you are planning to make your new application a long-term investment. Many companies attempt to standardize on a single BI server platform, such as Microsoft SQL Server or Oracle, in order to reduce the need for human knowledge to manage the database (to do backups, troubleshooting, maintenance, etc.) and to simplify integrations and the need for third-party tools. Sometimes a current or future corporate technology/platform standardization can make your analytics software selection more difficult, especially if the software you prefer is not available on the standardized hardware platform or operating system.

At the time of this writing, the BI server platforms supported by the largest number of vendors are Windows NT and Windows 2000; somewhat fewer support UNIX and AS400. The latter two platforms have traditionally been chosen for their capability to run on hardware that can handle larger data volumes, which is not necessarily true anymore; but these software/hardware solutions are also quite a bit more expensive than, for example, a Windows 2000 platform running on an Intel-based server. This type of conflict of interest will often force you to perform a cost-benefit analysis to figure out what is most important to your company: software features or database platform. No analytics software is best at everything. If you are planning to use your new software application in several different areas of the company, it is a good idea to choose a technology platform (e.g., Microsoft or Oracle) that is supported by a number of different analytics end-user tools from various vendors, so that you are not locked into one specific tool.

WINNING COMPANY BUY-IN

If you are convinced that your company needs a new analytics package, often you will still have to convince the rest of the people who will be affected by the new software. If you move ahead on your own without conferring with the key users in the organization, chances are that few of them will support you if anything goes wrong during or after implementation, or if you have to suggest workarounds and the like.

There is no sure formula for success in achieving companywide consensus for a new software acquisition, but there are several things you can do to improve your chances.

Today, most companies that decide to look for a new analytics solution put together a project team. This team can consist of the same, or different, people as those on your general business process improvement team. However, this team should be coordinated as part of the overall BPI project. There are several advantages to this coordination. Each team member will bring special expertise and insight from his or her own area of the organization. The team will set up evaluation criteria (refer to the RFP discussion in Chapter 27) to help screen the software packages and vendors to find the best fit. The members will participate in software demonstrations to see first-hand the different products in action. (Do not, however, expect end users to be able to list every possible requirement from their area when creating the RFP, and do not push them to predict every possible need. This could easily result in an unmanageable and too-detailed RFP.) Through a point scoring system or other means of evaluation, the project team reaches a consensus and then makes the software acquisition. Whether the decision leads to the purchase of the best possible solution or not, the organizational support behind the project will be much stronger than if one person makes the decision, because the team has been part of the decision process and provided input in the areas they deemed the most important.

One of the most common problems with an organizational rollout of a new analytics software generally emerges in larger, multisite organizations. In these companies, remote offices often are not involved in software evaluation and acquisition, yet they are required to use the software as it is rolled out. This often results in less than optimal use of the new software package at remote sites, and less than ideal cooperation and goodwill in resolving ongoing analysis and reporting issues. Most companies that are successful in achieving organizationwide support do their own "sales pitch" to their divisions *before* rolling out a new analytics software. By explaining the advantages of the new solution and how it fits into the overall BPI project, and by providing sufficient training and other assistance when the software is rolled out, they improve general understanding of and goodwill toward the new solution.

COST/BENEFIT ANALYSIS

As a selection tool, a cost/benefit analysis is very helpful to assist you in focusing on the most suitable category of software, as opposed to trying to differentiate between similar business intelligence solutions. For example, it can help you determine whether your needs are better covered by one type of solution over another, such as:

- Proprietary versus open database platforms
- High-end software versus midmarket and low-end software
- Web-based versus client/server software

In addition to helping you distinguish between different software categories, a cost/benefit analysis can help you make the decision of whether to stay with what you have or to go ahead with a new software acquisition.

If you were to look at a range of companies using the different analytics packages on the market, you would see that their level of satisfaction ranges from highly satisfied to dissatisfied. The success with a particular solution is dependent on several factors:

- Software features
- Skills of implementation partner
- Training, skills, and involvement of key employees
- Long-term support and software upgrades from the vendor

In the software selection phase, matching organizational needs and constraints with software features is key to success. One of the best ways to do this is to draw up a list that weighs benefits against costs (see Exhibit 28.1). However, a tool like this often becomes rather subjective because it is hard to assign a value to many intangible items. But because each item is weighted, it is usually better than just listing items with no assigned value.

RETURN ON INVESTMENT ANALYSIS FOR NEW SOFTWARE

While a cost/benefit analysis can help you quickly establish whether the overall benefits of a new analytics solution will exceed the costs, it does not put quantitative numbers on the investment. Although a more time-consuming and difficult task, a return on investment (ROI) analysis will help you estimate the costs and the returns of a budgeting and reporting software implementation, to help you decide whether the investment is worthwhile. It is very easy to assume that installing flashy new technology is always a good decision, but unfortunately this is not the case for many companies, for these reasons:

- Cost of analytics tool compared to actual use in organization
- Purchased the wrong analytics tool for the job (poor fit for need)

Benefits	Score*	Costs	Score
Saves X labor for end users.	6	Requires $X for software and hardware.	–8
Improves control.	7	Requires X days of training/ customization.	–6
Enables better reports and smoother budget workflow.	9	Has unfamiliar user interface.	–7
Saves $X and time in distribution of budget templates and reports.	5	Needs integration to ERP modules.	–2
Saves $X over in-house programming.	7	Takes time away from other projects.	–4
Comes with good documentation.	4	Might be replaced by new technology in a few years, thus requiring additional investment.	–4
Score	**+38**	**Score**	**–28**
TOTAL SCORE			**+10**

*Scoring is from 10 to –10 for each item, where 10 is the highest score and –10 is the lowest. A total score above 0 shows that the company will most likely achieve an overall benefit by going with a new software package.

EXHIBIT 28.1   Sample of Cost/Benefit Analysis for New Software Acquisition

- Poor data quality and/or detail (due to lack of integration with data sources)
- Slow performance (due to software architecture and/or old hardware)
- Lack of usage due to poor training and/or nonintuitive user interface

To ensure the best possible investment decision, so an ROI analysis, such as that shown in Exhibit 28.2. Here, the return on an analytics investment on a three-year period is estimated at 162 percent. Unless the same capital can be employed with a higher return elsewhere, this example tells us that the investment seems to be well worth it. A follow-up analysis should be carried out each year to verify that the original estimates are accurate.

FEATURES AND FLEXIBILITY

This is almost always the primary focus of companies during the software evaluation phase. The key is to try to identify the functionality that your company needs and then try to match it against what the different software vendors have to offer. Seldom will you find a perfect match, because most of the analytics solutions on the market are built to fulfill the needs of a broad range of companies in the marketplace. That said, you might find that the lack of some features is balanced by other functionality offered by a particular software package.

At the core of a feature study is the creation of the RFP document, which specifies all the key features and requirements of a company. Rather than going into detail on specific features, the following sections offer general advice on how to evaluate software functionality.

Estimated Investment Life (Three Years)

Item	
Analytics Software (all modules)	$100,000
Annual enhancement fee ($20,000/year)	$ 60,000
Implementation	$ 50,000
Maintenance and support of model	$ 50,000
	$260,000

Estimated Return

Cost savings in report writing ($15,000/year)	$ 45,000
Cost savings in report printing/distribution ($25,000/year)	$ 75,000
Value of better decision making ($100,000/year)	$300,000
	$420,000
ROI	**$420,000/$260,000 = 162%**

EXHIBIT 28.2   ROI Analysis Example

No matter how you choose to execute your software selection process, keep in mind that it must fit the different needs of users in the organization. User categories/needs typically include:

- *End users.* Basic budget input, workflow, and reporting capabilities
- *Power users.* Full-blown functionality to set up brand new reports and budget templates and create rollup trees and business rules
- *Information recipients.* Static reports by e-mail or Web access to run reports on a periodic basis

COMPATIBILITY WITH EXISTING SOFTWARE

Software evaluation would be a lot simpler if we could ignore current systems in place and just focus on features and functionality of a budgeting and reporting package. But usually there are several other software packages that need to integrate with a company's new analytics software (see Exhibit 28.3). For example:

- General ledger(s)
- Current spreadsheet models

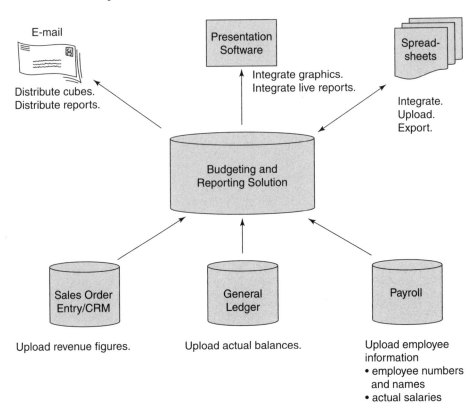

EXHIBIT 28.3   Compatibility Issues of New Analytics Software

- Payroll/human resource system(s)
- Sales order entry system(s)
- Data warehouse/data mart
- E-mail program(s)
- Presentation program

Traditionally, text files have been exported and imported as the means to exchange data between different applications. Some of the downsides of this are the extra manual work, with the inherent human errors, and slow data transfer speeds. This is rapidly changing as analytics and ERP applications vendors, as well as database vendors, build custom interfaces to each other's applications and databases, and as open standards such as XML/XBRL, ODBC, and others are adopted (see Chapter 5 for more information). When you are evaluating a new analytics package, you first need to identify which of your current and planned applications it should integrate with, and then ask the vendor to explain how this will be handled.

EASE OF USE

Needless to say, the most powerful analytics applications on the market are not necessarily the easiest ones to use. Conversely, a simple application with just a few screens and menus can probably be mastered in a few hours, but it will not have the variety of features and flexibility offered by more advanced analytics software. In particular, you will find this to be true in the areas of designing different reports (such as financial statements, key figures reports) and applying business rules (such as conditional statements (if-statements), subtotals, variance columns, calculated measures, etc.). The more you want to customize end-user reports and budget forms to fit your company's particular business model and issues, the more powerful your analytics tool will have to be. Moreover, you should expect to spend more time learning it. While most high-end applications offer full customization of reports, budget templates, and the like, lower-end software usually has limited functionality in these areas.

All modern analytics applications have graphical user interfaces, where you can use a pointing device and drill down in charts, reports, and so on; and their screens offer a variety of different fonts and colors. Online help files and context-sensitive help have also become common features to improve user friendliness. Each vendor has come up with its own unique screen layouts and user-related functions, so the best way to get a good feel for it is to watch an in-depth demonstration; or, even better, request a demo copy or a workshop where you can get some hands-on experience to determine its ease of use. The key question to ask is: Will power users as well as end users be comfortable with the application, to the degree that they adopt it readily and learn all its key features? The last thing a company wants is an application that is completely consultant-dependent or that nobody knows how to use. When a company decides that it needs the power of an advanced analytics solution, it must accept that there will be a ramp-up period to get users up to speed. In this case, the key is to provide good training and to motivate key employees to learn the software in detail.

SOFTWARE STABILITY

This is an often overlooked item during a software evaluation. The decision to purchase one software package over another can come down to small differences in features or be based on how well the vendor reps presented themselves and their product. But ascertaining the stability of the current version of the software is more clearcut: you call up references and ask for their opinions about the package, keeping in mind that the same software can run better on one database or hardware platform than on another, and that different customers using the same application on the same database and hardware platform rarely use all of the same features. Also, certain features might cause crashes, memory leaks, or other stability problems for one company, but not for another.

Therefore, to get the best possible understanding of different stability issues, ask for references that use similar hardware and software configurations as the one your company plans to use. Also check if the vendor has a reputation for producing reasonably stable software and for prompt handling of problems.

VENDOR-RELATED ITEMS

It is very easy to get buried under the small details of product selection and forget that more important than the product itself are the company and people behind it. In the past, excellent software products have disappeared from the market in the matter of a few years because the company behind it ran into problems. Such problems stem from:

- Financial mismanagement
- Human resources-related issues (such as poor retention of key employees)
- Poor strategic vision and business execution skills
- Large-scale lawsuits or legal problems

  Qualities to look for in a vendor are:

- A good reputation in the marketplace
- Long-term satisfied users
- Availability of high-quality training and support in different regions and time zones
- Strong distribution channel and/or strong direct sales and service force
- Up-to-date technology in development, products, implementation, and support
- Online customer access to support-history database
- Professional development and testing methodologies
- Strong sales and good profitability (Note: Do not fall into the trap of believing the companies with the highest revenues or most installations have the best products. Many great products came from companies that initially were small in size.)
- Well-defined future direction and strategies

- Well-developed list of third-party products that work with vendor's software (such as Web browser versions, databases, general ledgers, spreadsheet add-ins, etc.)
- Hosting services offered by the vendor itself or through application service providers

WORKING WITH AN IMPLEMENTATION PARTNER

Whether you utilize implementation services from the product vendor or a reseller or other partner, make sure that you will be working with someone who not only is trained on the product, but who has prior implementation experience. In other words, before engaging a consultant, ask about his or her experience with the product, specifically how many other implementations of this particular product the person has done. Some companies even ask for references from the assigned consultant. Other things to look for are:

- Type of implementation methodology used (project plans, prototyping, testing, etc.)
- Average implementation time for similar projects
- Knowledge of database platform
- Knowledge of integration tools (ETL) used to extract, transform, and load data from your other applications

HOW TO SELECT: SUMMARY

The process of selecting a new software is handled in a wide variety of ways at different companies, from a single person doing a quick evaluation to large project groups doing an in-depth analysis of products, vendors, consultants, and current customers. Some tips to keep in mind before you start your software evaluation process are:

- Ensure that your company has the skills to handle the evaluation. If not, engage a software selection company (see Chapter 27 for more details).
- Do a thorough analysis of your current and future analytics needs before you start looking at vendors.
- Create an RFP document to communicate your company's needs to vendors; or, as an alternative, engage directly in an in-depth dialogue with a group of preselected vendors.
- Have all key people present at the product demonstrations.
- If needed, call in vendors for repeat demos or specifically focused demos.
- If your analytics model and process are unique in any way, provide the vendors with specific information and request a customized demonstration.
- If you are in doubt about key feature areas and how your users will handle them, request a hands-on workshop.

See Chapter 27 for more in-depth information on the software selection process.

29

SOFTWARE BUYER'S GUIDE

Analytics software used in the finance and accounting area has evolved from static budget screens and reports without formatting to spreadsheets, powerful user-configurable budgeting and reporting tools attached to open databases with Web front ends. The product and vendor lists given in this chapter include a variety of different software solutions. The purpose of these listings is to give you a good starting point for your own in-depth research; they are not meant to be all-inclusive. Also, keep in mind that both vendors and their products evolve, and names, platforms, and functionality often change over time, so be prepared to also keep an eye out for new names and technologies that can support your budgeting and reporting needs.

There are several ways to categorize and group analytics tools. We have chosen to first describe reporting tools (many of which fall into the more analytical category often labeled business intelligence tools). Throughout Part Five we covered analytics solutions (see Exhibit 29.1). Here, we have broken down the reporting tools mentioned previously into four major categories: *query and reporting systems*, *decision support systems*, *budgeting and planning solutions*, and *executive (or enterprise) information systems*.

QUERY AND REPORTING SYSTEMS

Query and reporting systems allow you to look at transactional data on a row-by-row, column-by-column and cell-by-cell basis. You can search and sort your data in myriad ways, perform everything from simple to advanced calculations on your data, and output to various levels of summarization of the data, including subtotals and grand totals in reports.

Query solutions are often divided into two categories: *managed query* tools and *user-defined query* tools. Managed query tools present the data to the end users in a predefined, business-oriented manner, and the IT department typically handles the back-end logic of managing and describing the data. User-defined query tools require the end user to understand the layout of the database. Although they provide greater flexibility in terms of reporting, this category of tools is better suited for highly technical users or programmers.

Managed query and reporting tools provide flexible, user-oriented report-writing capabilities, while shielding individuals from complex programming tasks. Report writers, in particular, are ideal for producing highly formatted, presentation-quality

General Characteristics

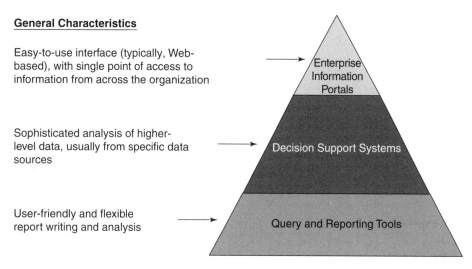

Easy-to-use interface (typically, Web-based), with single point of access to information from across the organization → Enterprise Information Portals

Sophisticated analysis of higher-level data, usually from specific data sources → Decision Support Systems

User-friendly and flexible report writing and analysis → Query and Reporting Tools

EXHIBIT 29.1   Reporting and Business Intelligence Tool Categories

financial reports, while many managed query tools are faster (because they often run on OLAP databases with data summarized at different levels), easier to use, and excellent for ad hoc reporting and analysis.

Query Tools

Several vendors of query tools are listed here:

Vendor Name	Product Name	Web Site
Brio	Brio.Report	*www.brio.com*
Business Objects	Business Objects	*www.businessobjects.com*
Microstrategy	DSS Agent	*www.microstrategy.com*
ProClarity Corp.	ProClarity	*www.knosys.com*
Oracle	Oracle Discoverer	*www.oracle.com*
Cognos	Impromptu	*www.cognos.com*
Microsoft	Excel	*www.microsoft.com*

Report Writers

High end and mid-market report writers (with consolidation functionality) include:

Vendor Name	Product Name	Web Site
Comshare	FDC Commander	*www.comshare.com*
FRx Corporation	FRx	*www.frxsoftware.com*

Vendor Name	Product Name	Web Site
Hyperion	Hyperion Enterprise	*www.hyperion.com*
Khalix	Longview Solutions	*www.longview.com*
SAS	CFO Vision	*www.sas.com*
Microsoft	Enterprise Reporting	*www.solverusa.com* and *www.microsoft.com*
SRC	Information Advisor	*www.srcsoftware.com*

Low end report writers include:

Vendor Name	Product Name	Web Site
Seagate Software	Crystal Reports	*www.crystaldecisions.com*
Synex Systems	F9	*www.f9.com*
iLytix	XL Reporter	*www.ilytix.com* and *www.xlreporter.com*

DECISION SUPPORT SYSTEMS

Decision support systems (DSS) are used for different types of analysis of business data. Typically DSS applications use summarized data derived from transactional information to allow users to analyze past results and to forecast future trends. Two common types of DSS technologies are online analytical processing (OLAP) and data mining.

OLAP

OLAP solutions are fast and powerful tools for reporting on data (as compared to data-mining tools that specialize in finding patterns in data) stored in a database. OLAP tools enable users to analyze different dimensions of multidimensional data, for example, to provide time series and trend analysis views; and to give sophisticated data analysis capabilities to end users, enabling interactive, dynamic analysis of business information.

The main component of OLAP solutions is the OLAP server, which sits between a client and a database management system (DBMS). The OLAP server understands how data is organized in the database and has special functions for analyzing the data. OLAP servers are available for nearly all the major database systems. Many of the OLAP servers come with their own user interface, and some (like Microsoft Analysis Services and Hyperion Essbase) also have a number of third-party OLAP front-end tools that integrate with their OLAP server (see the "Query Tools" section in this chapter).

Major vendors of OLAP solutions are listed here:

Vendor Name	Product Name	Web Site
Applix	TM1	*www.applix.com*
Brio	Brio Enterprise	*www.brio.com*
Cognos	Powerplay	*www.cognos.com*
Crystal Decisions	Holos	*www.crystaldecisions.com*
Hummingbird	BI/Analyze	*www.hummingbird.com*
Hyperion	Essbase	*www.hyperion.com*
IBM	DB2 OLAP Server	*www.ibm.com*
Microsoft	Analysis Services	*www.microsoft.com*
Microstrategy	Microstrategy	*www.microstrategy.com*
Oracle	Oracle 9i OLAP Services	*www.oracle.com*
PricewaterhouseCoopers	Carat	*www.pwcglobal.com*
Sagent Technologies	Sagent	*www.sagent.com*
Whitelight Systems	Whitelight	*www.whitelight-tech.com*

Data-Mining Tools

Data mining is a *decision support* process in which you search for patterns of information in data. It identifies hidden relationships in large volumes of data to provide valuable insights into key business drivers, such as buying behavior, credit usage patterns, and sources of risk.

Typically, users of data-mining tools have specialized skills, both to use the mining tools and to understand the data and patterns they are analyzing. Usually, there are only a few "data miners" in a corporation.

Major vendors of data mining tools include:

Vendor Name	Product Name	Web Site
IBM	IBM Business Miner	*www.ibm.com*
Microsoft	Microsoft Data Mining	*www.microsoft.com*
SAS	SAS Enterprise Miner	*www.sas.com*
SPSS	SPSS	*www.spss.com*

BUDGETING AND PLANNING SOLUTIONS

The number of budgeting software tools on the market is growing. We have chosen to categorize them as "higher end" and "lower end." The first category comprises higher-priced solutions that have more extensive enterprise functionality; the second category comprises lower-cost and somewhat simpler tools.

Higher-end budgeting tool vendors include:

Vendor Name	Product	Web Site
Cognos Corporation	Adaytum ePlanning	www.cognos.com
Comshare	Comshare BudgetPlus	www.comshare.com
Hyperion Solutions Corporation	Hyperion Pillar	www.hyperion.com
Longview Solutions, Inc.	Khalix	www.longview.com
MIS AG	MIS Alea	www.mis-ag.com
Oracle	Oracle Financial Analyzer	www.oracle.com
Microsoft	Enterprise Reporting	www.microsoft.com
		www.solverusa.com
SRC Software	SRC Advisor Series	www.srcsoftware.com
Timeline, Inc.	Timeline Budgeting	www.timeline.com
Walker Interactive Systems	Walker Horizon Financial Consolidation	www.walker.com

Lower-end budgeting tools vendors include:

Vendor Name	Product	Web Site
iLytix	XL Reporter	www.xlreporter.com
EPS Software	Budget 2000	www.epssoftware.com
FRx Corporation	FRx Forecaster	www.frxsoftware.com
InAlysys, Inc.	Personal Analyst	www.inalysys.com
KCI Computing, Inc.	Control	www.kcicorp.com
Planet Corporation	Budget Maestro	www.planetcorp.com
Powerplan Corp.	Powerplan	www.planningandlogic.com
Super Budget, Inc.	Super Budget	www.superbudget.com

ENTERPRISE INFORMATION PORTALS

Enterprise Information Portals (EIP) are the highest level of business intelligence applications. Typical modern EIP applications provide a highly user-friendly and customizable Web-based interface. Until recently, very few commercial EIP applications were available, so companies built their own EIPs using their IT department and/or hired developers. Vendors now offer portal software that a consultant or a trained in-house resource can set up and customize to provide easy access to all the key information sources in the company.

As portal solutions become more popular, several categories of portals are emerging. Some are more generic and are meant to interface to any type of data source; others are specialized for business intelligence. The first type of corporate portal is called an enterprise information portal (EIP); the second is often categorized as a business intelligence portal (BIP). Because EIPs and BIPs are built to present information from a wide variety of data sources with a single user-friendly interface, typically a large number of users utilize this technology in a company.

In the next list, you will find the names of some major EIP vendors and their products. Several business intelligence software vendors now also offer a BIP portal, which often can plug into an Enterprise Information Portal as key vehicles for delivery of BI specific information. For more information about BIP portal vendors, check out the individual Web sites of the BI vendors listed elsewhere in this chapter.

Vendor Name	Product Name	Web Site
Bowstreet	Enterprise Portal	*www.bowstreet.com*
Computer Associates	MyEureka	*www.ca.com*
Hummingbird	Enterprise Information Portal	*www.hummingbird.com*
IBM	IBM Enterprise Information Portal	*www.ibm.com*
Microsoft	Sharepoint	*www.microsoft.com*
Oracle	Oracle Portal	*www.oracle.com*
Plumtree	Plumtree Corporate Portal	*www.plumtree.com*
SageMaker	SageWave	*www.sagemaker.com*
Viador	E-Portal	*www.viador.com*

DATA WAREHOUSE SOFTWARE

To successfully employ an analytics tool in a larger organization, it is critical to be able to analyze and report on the data created and used in the budget process. The data must also be organized in a logical manner. A data warehouse can be composed of very large databases that involve implementation projects and software worth millions of dollars, or of smaller, less complicated databases that cost tens of thousands of dollars and more to buy and implement. These warehouses provide the accessibility and clarity of data that allows users to get the maximum value from their analytics and business intelligence tools. In short, a data warehouse is a database specially designed for decision support and business intelligence. Major vendors of data warehouse software are:

Vendor Name	Product Name	Web Site
IBM	DB2	*www.ibm.com*
Microsoft	SQL Server	*www.microsoft.com*
Oracle	Oracle	*www.oracle.com*
Sybase	Adaptive Server IQ	*www.sybase.com*
SAS	SAS Intelligent Warehousing Solution	*www.sas.com*

ETL SOFTWARE VENDORS

ETL tools are considered "middleware" (software used between two other software applications) that is required to move and convert data from one database to another, and they can be relatively inexpensive to very costly. Certainly, the time and expense of implementing an ETL tool can make the entire investment fairly large. Nevertheless, a commercial ETL tool that works with your databases will typically provide a faster and simpler way to transform and move data than something you build in-house. It is therefore important to do some research up front to make sure you choose the tool that is the best fit both for your functionality needs as well as for your budget. Some of the different ETL tools include:

Vendor Name	Product Name	Web Site
Ab Initio	MPower	*www.abinitio.com*
Acta Technologies	Acta Works	*www.acta.com*
Ascential	Data Stage	*www.aboutnewco.com*
Coglin Mill	Rodin	*www.coglinmill.com*
Cognos	Decision Stream	*www.cognos.com*
Computer Associates	Decision Base	*www.ca.com*
Constellar	DataMirror	*www.constellar.com*
Data Junction	Data Junction	*www.datajunction.com*
DataMirror	Transformation Server	*www.datamirror.com*
Decisionism	Broadbase	*www.decisionism.com*
Evolutionary Technologies	ETI Extract	*www.evtech.com*
Hummingbird Communications	Genio	*www.hummingbird.com*
IBM	Visual Warehouse/ DataPropagator	*www.ibm.com*

Informatica	Powercenter/PowerMart	*www.informatica.com*
Metagon Technologies	Dqtransform	*www.metagon.com*
Microsoft	DTS	*www.microsoft.com*
Oracle	Oracle Warehouse Builder	*www.oracle.com*
Sagent Technology	Sagent Solution	*www.sagenttech.com*
SAP	Business Warehouse	*www.sap.com*
SAS	SAS/Warehouse Administrator	*www.sas.com*
Sybase	Industry Warehouse Studio	*www.sybase.com*
Systemfabrik	Warehouse Workbench	*www.systemfabrik.com*
Taurus Software	Warehouse	*www.taurus.com*

E-LEARNING SOFTWARE VENDORS

Unless users are given proper and timely training, the return on an analytics tool investment will drop dramatically. But arranging product training classes can be expensive and often hard to coordinate. Fortunately, an electronic training medium, referred to as e-learning, allows companies (both software vendors and their customers) to develop and utilize the Internet or CD-ROMs as channels for accessing training on demand. As more organizations take advantage of online education and training, an increasing number of e-learning software options are becoming available, including:

Vendor Name	Product Name	Web Site
Centra	Centra 99	*www.centra.com*
Click2learn.com	ToolBook II Instructor	*www.click2learn.com*
Docent	Docent Enterprise	*www.docent.com*
Interwise	Millennium	*www.interwise.com*
Knowledgeplanet.com	KP 2000	*www.knowledgeplanet.com*
Learn2.com, Inc.	StreamMaker	*www.learn2.com*
MacroMedia	Macromedia Authorware	*www.macromedia.com*
RWD Technologies	RWD WILS	*www.rwd.com*
Saba Software	Saba Learning Enterprise	*www.saba.com*
WBT Systems	TopClass Publisher Studio	*www.wbtsystem.com*

APPENDIX A

SAMPLE CONFIDENTIALITY AND NONDISCLOSURE AGREEMENT (SALES/DEMO PROCESS)

In connection with discussions on July 21, 2002, and thereafter, between ABC Software, Inc., of 270 S. Peck Drive, Los Angeles, California, 91212, including but not limited to all affiliates of ABC, Inc., and XYZ, LTD, of 3110 Johnson Road, Edison City, Florida, 33090, regarding information on themselves, their relationships and transactions, and certain of their products, the parties hereto propose to provide to each other, with either in the role as "Donor" or "Recipient" (dependent upon direction of information flow as exchanged from time to time), certain confidential and proprietary information ("Confidential Information" as further defined below) for "Evaluation" or for commercial use. In consideration of Donor's providing this information, and for other good and valuable consideration, the extent and sufficiency of which is acknowledged by Recipient, Recipient hereby AGREES to the terms and conditions as follows with respect to the treatment and use of such confidential information.

1. *Definition*:
    a. Confidential Information shall mean materials, information, data and like items which have been or which may be disclosed, whether orally, in writing or within media used in electronic data processing and programs, including but not limited to information concerning (1) collection, tabulation, and analysis of data; (2) computer programming methods, designs, specifications, plans, drawings, and similar materials; (3) programs, databases, inventions, (whether or not eligible for legal protection under patent, trademark, or copyright laws); (4) research and development; and (5) work in progress. Additionally so defined is all information on any or all aspects of the business of Donor and its affiliate(s), including without limitation (6) any and all financial statements; (7) business and/or marketing plans or programs; (8) pending or threatened litigation; (9) prospective or existing contractual relations; (10) customer, vendor, or affiliate lists or identification(s), and any other information of like nature, value, meaning or significance to categories

described as 1 through 10 herein. Confidential information includes the fact of disclosure or evaluation, as well as any tangible or intangible material or information-conveying aspect, whether disclosed in oral or written form or otherwise, when and as involved in any disclosure by Donor or Recipient, and whether or not any such material or aspect is specifically marked, labeled or described as "confidential." This definition shall be subject to exclusions as appear below:

b. Confidential Information does not include any information which:

    i. is in the public domain at the time disclosed or communicated to Recipient; or which enters the public domain at the time disclosed or communicated to Recipient; or which enters the public domain through no act, fault, or responsibility of Recipient;

    ii. is lawfully obtained by the Recipient, with permission to disclose, from a third party who is not, to Recipient's knowledge, subject to any contractual or fiduciary duty not to disclose;

    iii. has been independently derived or formulated by the Recipient without reference to the Confidential Information given either before or after the effective date of this Agreement;

    iv. the Recipient can demonstrate was lawfully in its possession, free of any duty not to disclose, before the date of disclosure by Donor to the Recipient.

2. *Duty of Confidentiality.* Recipient agrees to receive the Confidential Information in confidence, to keep the same secret and confidential, to make no additional copies of same without the express written consent of Donor, and not to disclose Donor's Confidential Information to any party whatsoever, save for its officers, directors, employees, and agents, as required for evaluation hereunder or for commercial use under a coexistent Agreement, without the prior written approval of Donor. Further, Recipient shall ensure that each of its officers, directors, employees, and agents to whom Donor's Confidential Information might be disclosed under the terms of this Agreement, shall be held to subscribe to all the terms of this Agreement and to agree to be bound by all Agreement terms and conditions.

3. *Duty of Care.* Recipient shall in its protection of Donor's Confidential Information from risk of unauthorized disclosure exercise the same level of care as it does and/or would exercise to safeguard its own confidential and proprietary information, and in no event afford any less such protection and safeguarding as may be regarded as reasonable in view of the premises of this Agreement and Recipient's undertakings pursuant hereto.

4. *No License.* Nothing in this Agreement shall be construed as granting any license or right under any patent, trade secret, copyright or otherwise, nor shall this Agreement impair the right of either party to contest the scope, validity or alleged infringement of any patent, copyright or trade secret. Nor shall the parties hereto

use any part of the Confidential Information disclosed for any purpose other than furtherance of the relationship between the parties.

5. *Termination of Evaluation; Termination of Commercial Agreement.* If Evaluation is terminated for any reason, or if a commercial agreement under whose operation Donor's information has been divulged shall terminate, and in any event upon the reasonable request of Donor at any time, Recipient shall return or destroy, at Donor's option, all copies of Donor's Confidential Information and all notes, in documents or on media of any type, related thereto, as may be in Recipient's possession or under the Recipient's direct or indirect control. All such written or media-carried notes shall be subject to such return or destruction, regardless of the authorship of such notes. Recipient shall confirm in writing that it has retained no copies, notes, or other records of the Confidential Information in any medium whatsoever.

6. *Injunctive Relief: Enforcement Costs.* Recipient acknowledges that any breach of this Agreement would cause Donor irreparable harm, which would be difficult if not impossible to quantify in terms of monetary damages. Recipient consents to a granting of immediate injunctive relief to Donor upon any breach of this Agreement, in addition to all other remedies available to Donor at law or in equity. Recipient waives any requirement that Donor post a bond in connection with the any application for or order granting injunctive relief. Further, in event of legal process for breach or other cause, the prevailing party shall be entitled to recover its costs, including costs of suit, expenses, and any Attorney's fees involved in any action to enforce the terms of this Agreement.

7. *Miscellaneous.*

   a. This Agreement shall be governed by the laws of the State of California. Each party irrevocably submits to the jurisdiction of the courts of the State of California for resolution of any dispute hereunder, without regard to the conflicts of laws principles thereof.

   b. This Agreement may be modified only by a writing executed by both parties. The parties agree that this Agreement represents the entire agreement between the parties as to the subject hereof, and that all prior understanding, agreements, and representations related to the subject matter hereof have been incorporated into this Agreement. This Agreement rescinds and supplants any prior Agreement(s) as to the subject matter hereof.

   c. This Agreement shall become effective on date first written above, and remain in effect for the duration of the period of Evaluation or until this Agreement has been formally supplanted by any Subscriber, vendor relationship, financial relationship, or similar agreement between the parties which specifically absorbs, rescinds or replaces this Agreement. Failing such specific absorption, rescission or replacement, this Agreement shall remain in full force and effect for the period of five (5) years following the completion of the period of Evaluation or the expiry of any consequent Subscriber or other agreement between the parties.

IN WITNESS WHEREOF, each party agrees to and accepts this Agreement and its terms, by signature of its authorized official below.

_____   _____

ABC, Inc.   XYZ, Ltd

by:_____   *by*:_____

Title: *Title*:

Date: *Date*:

APPENDIX B

SAMPLE CONSULTING AGREEMENT

CLIENT NAME
CLIENT ADDRESS
CITY, STATE, ZIP CODE

This Consulting Agreement (the "Agreement") is entered into by and between CLIENT and CONSULTANT. The effective date of this agreement is the same date as the software agreement contract is signed.

Whereas the Client wishes to obtain the consulting services of Consultant to assist Client in connection with the design and implementation of Data Warehouse, and Consultant has negotiated the terms of such an agreement with Client and has agreed to the terms as set forth hereafter.

Now therefore, the parties hereby agree as follows:

1. TERM OF AGREEMENT: The Client hereby hires Consultant and Consultant accepts such contract work for a term for as long as PROFESSIONAL SERVICES is requested by Client, terminating when the Data Warehouse Project is completed, according to project plan, unless sooner terminated as hereinafter provided.

2. SURVIVAL OF AGREEMENT: This Agreement shall not be terminated by a restructuring of the company or of the Consultant. If either of the parties restructures but remains in the business, the contract shall survive.

3. LEGAL REPRESENTATION: Each party acknowledges that he was advised that he was entitled to separate counsel and he has either employed such counsel or voluntarily waived the right to consult with counsel.

4. NOTICES: All notices and other communications provided for or permitted hereunder shall be in writing and shall be made by hand delivery, first-class mail, telex or telecopier, addressed as follows:

> All such notices and communications shall be deemed to have been duly given when delivered by hand, if personally delivered; three (3) business days after deposit in any United States Post Office in the Continental United States, postage prepaid, if mailed; when answered back, if telexed; and when receipt is acknowledged, if telecopied.

5. ATTORNEY'S FEES: In the event that a dispute arises with respect to this Agreement, the party prevailing in such dispute shall be entitled to recover all expenses, including, without limitation, reasonable attorneys' fees and expenses, incurred in ascertaining such party's rights or in preparing to enforce, or in enforcing, such party's rights under this Agreement, whether or not it was necessary for such party to institute suit.

6. COMPLETE AGREEMENT OF THE PARTIES: This is the complete Agreement of the parties and it supersedes any agreement that has been made prior to this Agreement.

7. ASSIGNMENT: This Agreement is of a personal nature and may not be assigned.

8. BINDING: This Agreement shall be binding on both of the parties hereto.

9. NUMBER AND GENDER: Whenever the singular number is used in this Agreement and when required by the context, the same shall include the plural. The masculine gender shall include the feminine and neuter genders, and the word "person" shall include a corporation, firm, partnership, or other form of association.

10. GOVERNING LAW: The parties hereby expressly acknowledge and agree that this Agreement is entered into in the State of California and, to the extent permitted by law, this Agreement shall be construed and enforced in accordance with the laws of the State of California.

11. FAILURE TO OBJECT NOT A WAIVER: The failure of a party to object to, or to take affirmative action with respect to, any conduct of the other which is in violation of the terms of this Agreement shall not be construed as a waiver of the violation or breach or of any future violation, breach, or wrongful conduct until 180 days since the wrongful act or omission to act has passed.

12. SEVERABILITY: If any term of this Agreement is held by a court of competent jurisdiction to be invalid, void, or unenforceable, the remainder of the provisions of this Agreement shall remain in full force and effect and shall in no way be affected, impaired, or invalidated.

13. FURTHER ASSISTANCE: From time to time, each party shall execute and deliver such further instruments and shall take such other action as any other party may reasonably request in order to discharge and perform his obligations and agreements hereunder and to give effect to the intentions expressed in this Agreement.

14. INCORPORATION BY REFERENCE: All exhibits referred to in this Agreement are incorporated herein in their entirety by such reference.

15. CROSS-REFERENCES: All cross-references in this Agreement, unless specifically directed to another agreement or document, refer to provisions in this Agreement, and shall not be deemed to be references to any overall transaction or to any other agreements or documents.

16. MISCELLANEOUS PROVISIONS: The various headings and numbers herein and the grouping of provisions of this Agreement into separate divisions are for

the purpose of convenience only and shall not be considered a part hereof. The language in all parts of this Agreement shall in all cases be construed in accordance to its fair meaning as if prepared by all parties to the Agreement and not strictly for or against any of the parties.

17. WORK TO BE PERFORMED: As requested by you, CONSULTANT will develop a Data Warehouse Model using VENDOR SOFTWARE. This Data Warehouse Model will be based upon the existing spreadsheet model system used by CLIENT (Attachment X) and/or additional design specifications agreed upon by CLIENT and CONSULTANT. The Data Warehouse Model created by CONSULTANT must be capable of meeting the specifications agreed upon by CLIENT and CONSULTANT, listed in Attachment X.

18. PERFORMANCE OF DUTIES: Consultant agrees to perform at all times faithfully, industriously, and to the best of his ability, experience, and talents all of the duties that may reasonably be assigned to him hereunder, and shall devote such time to the performance of such duties as may be necessary.

19. FEES AND EXPENSES: The fee for the services provided by CONSULTANT to CLIENT will be $X/hour (not to exceed $X for all services provided). This service cost does not include any time for work performed that is not identified in Attachment X. Additionally, this cost does not include travel, lodging, meals, or incidentals. These will be billed at actual and/or per diem rates.

20. INDEPENDENT CONTRACTOR: In performing services and duties hereunder, Consultant and any person acting on Consultant's behalf shall do so as independent contractors and are not, and are not to be deemed, employees or agents of Client or any other person acting on behalf of Client. Consultant shall be responsible for meeting any legal requirements imposed on Consultant or any person acting on his behalf as a result of this Agreement, including but not limited to the filing of income tax returns and the payment of taxes; and Consultant agrees to indemnify Client for the failure to do so, if Client is required to make any such payment otherwise due by Consultant or any such person acting on Consultant's behalf.

21. REMEDY FOR BREACH: Consultant acknowledges that the services to be rendered by Consultant hereunder are of a special, unique, and extraordinary character which gives this Agreement a peculiar value to Client, the loss of which cannot be reasonably or adequately compensated in damages in an action at law, and that a breach by Consultant of this Agreement shall cause Client irreparable injury. Therefore, Consultant expressly acknowledges that this Agreement may be enforced against him by injunction and other equitable remedies, without bond. Such relief shall not be exclusive, but shall be in addition to any other rights or remedies Client may have for such breach.

22. CAUSES FOR TERMINATION: This Agreement shall terminate immediately upon the occurrence of any one of the following events:

    1. The expiration of the term hereof;
    2. The written agreement of the parties;

3. The occurrence of circumstances that make it impossible for the business of Client to be continued;

4. The occurrence of circumstances that make it impossible for the business of Consultant to be continued;

5. Consultant's breach of his duties hereunder, unless waived by Client or cured by Consultant within 30 days after Client's having given written notice thereof to Consultant.

23. COMPENSATION UPON TERMINATION: Unless otherwise mutually agreed in writing by the parties, the termination of this Agreement due to any cause other than that specified in Paragraph 22.4 shall not relieve Client of its obligation to make any payment of money or any delivery of shares or securities which would have been required, or could have been required by Consultant, pursuant to Paragraph 19, if this Agreement had not been so terminated.

IN WITNESS WHEREOF, the parties have executed this Agreement on the date above.

Signature:

_____   _____

_____   _____

(Printed Name)   (Printed Name)
For CLIENT   For CONSULTANT

APPENDIX C

SOFTWARE VENDOR LISTING

The Buyer's Guide in Chapter 29 has more information on the products offered by each of the vendors listed in this appendix.

Vendor Name	Web Site	Addresses
Ab Initio	*www.abinitio.com*	2001 Spring Street Lexington, MA 02421 Tel: (781) 301-2000 Fax: (781) 301-2001
Acta Technologies	*www.acta.com*	1667 Plymouth Street Mountain View, CA 94043-1203 Tel: (650) 230-4200 Fax: (650) 230-4201
Applix	*www.applix.com*	112 Turnpike Road Westboro, MA 01581 Tel: (508) 870-0300 Fax: (508) 366-2278 Toll-free: (800) 8-APPLIX
Ascential	*www.aboutnewco.com*	50 Washington Street Westboro, MA 01581 Toll-free: (800) 966-9875 Tel: (508) 366-3888 Fax: (508) 366-3669
Bowstreet	*www.bowstreet.com*	343 Sansome Street 9th Floor, Suite 950 San Francisco, CA 94104 Tel: (415) 262-4300 Fax: (415) 262-4333
Brio	*www.brio.com*	4980 Great America Parkway Santa Clara, CA 95054 Toll-free: (800) 879-2746 Tel: (408) 496-7400 Fax: (408) 496-7420

Vendor Name	Web Site	Addresses
Business Objects	www.businessobjects.com	3030 Orchard Parkway San Jose, CA 95134 Toll-free: (800) 527-0580 Tel: (408) 953-6000 Fax: (408) 953-6001
Centra	www.centra.com	430 Bedford Street Lexington, MA 02420 Tel: (781) 861-7000 Fax: (781) 863-7288
Click2learn.com	www.click2learn.com	110 110th Avenue NE, Suite 700 Bellevue, WA 98004 Toll-free: (800) 448-6543 Tel: (425) 462-0501 Fax: (425) 637-1504
Coglin Mill	www.coglinmill.com	421 First Avenue SW, Suite 204 Rochester, MN 55902 Tel: (507) 282-4151 Fax: (507) 282-4727
Cognos	www.cognos.com	67 South Bedford Street Burlington, MA, 01803-5164 Toll-free: (800) 426-4667 Tel: (781) 229-6600 Fax: (781) 229-9844
Computer Associates	www.ca.com	One Computer Associates Plaza Islandia, NY 11749 Toll-free: (800) 225-5224 Tel: (631) 342-6000 Fax: (631) 342-6800
Comshare	www.comshare.com	555 Briarwood Circle Ann Arbor, MI 48108 Toll-free: (800) 922-7979 Tel: (734) 994-4800 Fax: (734) 213-2161
Constellar	www.constellar.com	3100 Steeles Avenue East, Suite 1100 Markham, Ontario Canada, L3R 8T3 Toll-free: (800) 362-5955

Vendor Name	Web Site	Addresses
Crystal Decisions (formerly Seagate)	www.crystaldecisions.com	895 Emerson Street Palo Alto, CA 94301-2413 Toll-free: (800) 877-2340 Tel: (604) 681-3435 Fax: (604) 681-2934
Data Junction	www.datajunction.com	2201 Northland Drive Austin, TX 78756 Toll-free: (800) 580-4411 Tel: (512) 452-6105 Fax: (512) 459-1309
DataMirror	www.datamirror.com	3100 Steeles Avenue East, Suite 1100 Markham, Ontario Canada L3R 8T3 Toll-free: (800) 362-5955 Tel: (905) 415-0310 Fax: (905) 415-0340
Docent	www.docent.com	2444 Charleston Road Mountain View, CA 94043 Tel: (650) 934-9500 Fax: (650) 962-9411
Evolutionary Technologies	www.evtech.com	816 Congress Avenue, Suite 1300 Frost Bank Plaza Austin, TX 78701 Toll-free: (800) 856-8800 Tel: (512) 383-3000 Fax: (512) 383-3300
FRx Corporation	www.frxsoftware.com	4700 S. Syracuse Parkway, Suite 700 Denver, CO 80237 Toll-free: (800) FRx-8733 Tel: (303) 741-8000 Fax: (303) 741-3335
Hummingbird Communications	www.hummingbird.com	480 San Antonio Road, Suite 200 Mountain View, CA 94040 Toll-free: (877) FLY-HUMM Tel: (416) 496-2200 Fax: (416) 496-2207

Vendor Name	Web Site	Addresses
Hyperion	*www.hyperion.com*	1344 Crossman Avenue Sunnyvale, CA 94089 Tel: (408) 744-9500 Fax: (408) 744-0400
IBM	*www.ibm.com*	1133 Westchester Avenue White Plains, NY 10604 Toll-free: (888) SHOP-IBM
ILytix	*www.ilytix.com* *www.xLreporter.com*	270 N. Canon Drive #1166 Beverly Hills, CA 90210 Tel: (310) 444-9633 Fax: (310) 477-7113
Informatica	*www.informatica.com*	3350 West Bayshore Road Palo Alto, CA 94303 Toll-free: (800) 653-3871 Tel: (650) 687-6200 Fax: (650) 687-0040
Interwise	*www.interwise.com*	2334 Walsh Avenue Santa Clara, CA 95051 Tel: (408) 748-7800 Fax: (408) 748-7801
Khalix	*www.longview.com*	1974 Sproul Road, Suite 402 Broomall, PA 19008 Tel: (610) 325-3295 Fax: (610) 325-8851
Knowledgeplanet.com	*www.knowledgeplanet.com*	11490 Commerce Park Drive, Suite 400 Reston, VA 20191 Toll-free: (800) 646-3008 Tel: (703) 262-6600 Fax: (703) 716-0237
Learn2.com, Inc.	*www.learn2.com*	1311 Mamaroneck Avenue, Suite 210 White Plains, NY 10605 Toll-free: (888) 339-8898 Tel: (914) 682-4300 Fax: (914) 682-4440
MacroMedia	*www.macromedia.com*	600 Townsend Street San Francisco, CA 94103 Tel: (415) 252-2000 Fax: (415) 626-0554

Vendor Name	Web Site	Addresses
Metagon Technologies	*www.metagon.com*	PO Box 2810, Matthews, NC 28106-2810 Tel: (704) 847-2390 Fax: (704) 847-4875
Microsoft	*www.microsoft.com*	One Microsoft Way Redmond, WA 98052-6399 Toll-free: (800) 426-9400 Tel: (425) 882-8080
Microstrategy	*www.microstrategy.com*	861 International Drive, McLean, VA 22102 Toll-free: (888) 537-813 Tel: (703) 848-8600 Fax: (703) 848-8610
Oracle	*www.oracle.com*	500 Oracle Parkway Redwood Shores, CA 94065 Toll-free: (800) ORACLE-1
Plumtree	*www.plumtree.com*	500 Sansome Street San Francisco, CA 94111 Tel: (415) 263-8900 Fax: (415) 263-8991
PricewaterhouseCoopers	*www.pwcglobal.com*	1301 Avenue of the Americas New York, NY 10019 Tel: (646) 471-4000 Fax: (646) 394-1301
Proclarity, Inc.	*www.proclarity.com*	500 S. 10th Street, Suite 100 Boise, ID 83702 Tel: (208) 344-1630 Fax: (208)343-6128
RWD Technologies	*www.rwd.com*	10480 Little Patuxent Parkway RWD Building, Suite 1200 Columbia, MD 21044-3530 Toll-free: (888) RWD-TECH Tel: (410) 730-4377 Fax: (410) 964-0039
Saba Software	*www.saba.com*	2400 Bridge Parkway Redwood Shores, CA 94065-1166 Tel: (650) 581-2500

Vendor Name	Web Site	Addresses
SageMaker	www.sagemaker.com	1301 N. Elston Chicago, IL 60622 Toll-free: (888) 412-7177 Tel: (773) 394-6600 Fax: (773) 394-6601
Sagent Technologies	www.sagent.com	800 W. El Camino Real, 3rd Floor Mountain View, CA 94040 Toll-free: (800) 782-7988 Tel: (650) 815-3100 Fax: (650) 815-3500
SAP	www.sap.com	3999 West Chester Pike Newtown Square, PA 19073 Tel: (610) 661-1000 Fax: (610) 355-3106
SAS	www.sas.com	SAS Campus Drive Cary, NC 27513-2414 Tel: (919) 677-8000 Fax: (919) 677-4444
Seagate Software	www.crystaldecisions.com	895 Emerson Street Palo Alto, CA 94301-2413 Toll-free: (800) 877-2340 Tel: (604) 681-3435 Fax: (604) 681-2934
Solver	www.solverusa.com	270 N. Canon Drive, Suite #1166 Beverly Hills, CA 90210 Toll-free: (800) 281-6351 Tel: (310) 444-9633 Fax: (310) 477-7113
SPSS	www.spss.com	233 S. Wacker Drive, 11th Floor Chicago, IL 60606-6307 Toll-free: (800) 543-2185 Tel: (312) 651-3000 Fax: (800) 841-0064
SRC	www.srcsoftware.com	2120 SW Jefferson Street Portland, OR 97201 Toll-free: (800) 544-3477 Tel: (503) 221-0448 Fax: (503) 223-7922

Vendor Name	Web Site	Addresses
Sybase	*www.sybase.com*	6475 Christie Avenue Emeryville , CA 94608 Tel: (510) 922-3500
Synex Systems	*www.f9.com*	1444 Alberni Street, 4th Floor Vancouver, British Columbia Canada V6G 2Z4 Toll-free: (800) 663-8663 Fax: (604) 688-1286
Taurus Software	*www.taurus.com*	1032 Elwell Court Palo Alto, CA 94303 Tel: (650) 961-1323 Fax: (650) 961-1454
Viador	*www.viador.com*	2000 Charleston Road, Suite 1000, Mountain View, CA 94043 Toll-free: 877-VIADOR1 Tel: (650) 645-2000 Fax: (650) 645-2001
Whitelight Systems	*www.whitelight-tech.com*	Brooklands Close Windmill Road Sunbury-on-Thames Middlesex, TW16 7DX Tel: 44 (0) 1 932 724 034 Fax: 44 (0) 1 932 724 200
X.HLP	*www.xhlp.com*	610 Lincoln Street Waltham, MA 02451 Tel: (781) 663-7500 Fax:(781) 890-4505

APPENDIX D

SAMPLE CHART OF ACCOUNTS

NATURAL ACCOUNT SEGMENT

Assets

Current Assets

Cash

Operating Account	10100
Deposit Account	10200
Payroll Account	10300
Petty Cash	10400

Accounts Receivable

Accounts Receivable—Trade	12000
Allowance for Doubtful Accounts	12010
Employee Receivables	12100

Intercompany Receivables

Intercompany—Trade	13100
Intercompany—Management Fee	13200
Intercompany—Commissions	13300
Intercompany—Interest	13400

Inventory

Finished Goods	14100
Work-in-Process	14200
Raw Materials	14300
Reserves	14500

Prepaid Expense

Prepaid Rent	15100
Prepaid Insurance	15200

Prepaid Taxes	15300
Prepaid Other	15900

Fixed Assets

Fixed Assets

Computer Equipment	16100
Machinery and Equipment	16200
Furniture and Fixtures	16300
Vehicles	16400
Leasehold Improvements	16500
Land and Buildings	16600

Fixed Assets—Accumulated Depreciation

Computer Equipment	17100
Machinery and Equipment	17200
Furniture and Fixtures	17300
Vehicles	17400
Leasehold Improvements	17500
Land and Buildings	17600

Other Assets

Intangible Assets

Goodwill	18100
Goodwill—Accumulated Amortization	18150
Other Intangibles	18200
Other Intangibles—Accumulated Amortization	18250

Other Assets

Other Assets	19000

LIABILITIES

Current Liabilities

Accounts Payable—Trade	20100
Accounts Payable—Other	20200
Accrued Expenses—Salaries and Benefits	20910
Accrued Expenses—Other	20920

Taxes Payable	21000
Long–Term Debt, Current	22000
Notes Payable, Current	22500
Capital Leases, Current	22600
Other Current Liabilities	23000

Long-Term Liabilities

Long–Term Debt, Net of current	25000
Notes Payable, Net of current	25500
Capital Leases, Net of current	25600
Deferred Taxes	28000
Other Long–Term Liabilities	29000

EQUITY

Common Stock	31000
Paid-in Capital	32000
Treasury Stock	33000
Retained Earnings—Beginning	35100
Retained Earnings—Current	35200
Dividends Declared	36000
Translation Adjustments	37000

REVENUE

Gross Sales	41000
Intercompany Sales	41500
Returns	43100
Refunds	43200
Reserves	44100
Discounts	44200
Allowances	44300
Other/Miscellaneous Revenue	49000

COST OF GOODS SOLD

Direct Expenses	51000
Intercompany COGS	51500

Material Purchases	52000
Inventory Reserve	52100
Direct Labor	53000
Freight, Transportation	54000
Depreciation	57000
Other Cost of Sales	59000

OPERATING EXPENSES

Personnel Related

Salaries and Wages	61000
Overtime	61100
Bonuses	61200
Payroll Taxes and Benefits	61300
Contractors/Temporary Help	61400
Payroll Services	61500
Commissions	61600
Travel and Entertainment	62000
Seminars, Conferences, etc.	63000
Training	64000
Relocation	65000
Other	69000

Other Operating Expenses

Advertising and Promotion	71100
Selling Expenses	71200
Printing and Supplies	71300
Professional Fees	71400
Communications	71500
Consultants	71600
Rent	71700
Security	71800
Legal	71900
Permits/Fees	72000
Supplies	72100
Utilities	72200

Contributions	72300
Repairs and Maintenance—Building	73100
Repairs and Maintenance—Janitorial	73200
Repairs and Maintenance—Other	73300
Property Taxes	74000
Insurance	74100
Intercompany Expenses	75000

OTHER INCOME AND EXPENSES

Bad Debts	76000
Gain/Loss on Disposal	76100
Foreign Exchange Gain/Loss—Unrealized	76200
Foreign Exchange Gain/Loss—Realized	76300
Depreciation	77000
Amortization	77100
Interest Income	78000
Interest Expense	78100
Other Income	78200
Miscellaneous	79000

TAXES AND EXTRAORDINARY ITEMS

Federal Income Tax, Current	81100
State Income Tax, Current	81200
Other Income Taxes, Current	81300
Other Taxes, Current	81400
Federal Income Tax, Deferred	82100
State Income Tax, Deferred	82200
Other Income Taxes, Deferred	82300
Other Taxes, Deferred	82400
Extraordinary Income	85100
Extraordinary Expense	85200

STATISTICAL ACCOUNTS

| Headcount, etc. | 9XXX |

DEPARTMENT SEGMENT

Sales and Marketing

Selling	100
Internet Sales	110
Advertising	120
Marketing	150
Promotions	160
Printing	170

General and Administrative

Accounting	200
Finance	210
Tax	220
Legal	230
Distribution	240
Maintenance	250
Human Resources	260
IT	270
Warehouse	280
Quality Assurance	290
Administration	300

Other

Allocation Departments	700
Miscellaneous	900

PRODUCT SEGMENT

Product Group 1	100
Product Subgroup 1	110
Product Group 2	200
Product Subgroup 2	210
Product Group 3	300
Product Subgroup 3	310

LOCATION SEGMENT

North America	1000
United States—East	1100
United States—South	1200
United States—Midwest	1300
United States—North	1400
United States—West	1500
Canada	1600
Mexico	1700
Central America	2000
South America	3000
Europe	4000
Asia Pacific	5000

GLOSSARY

Accountability matrix   A matrix that maps the project work requirements to individuals who are responsible, identifying roles and decision-making responsibilities (advisory, need to know, and support); assures that each element of the project is assigned to a responsible individual. (Often referred to as a *responsibility matrix*).

Activity   A name process, function, or task that occurs over time and has recognizable results. Also, activities combined to form business processes, or a task or series of tasks performed over a period of time.

Activity analysis   The analysis and measurement (in terms of time, cost, and throughput) of distinct units of work (activities) that make up a process.

Activity-based costing   A set of accounting methods used to identify and describe costs and required resources for activities within processes.

Activity-based management (ABM)   A system of management that seeks to optimize the value-added activities performed by the enterprise, while minimizing or eliminating the nonvalue-added activities, resulting in overall improvements in the effectiveness and the efficiency of the enterprise in serving its customers.

Activity measure   A performance value assigned to an activity's primary output.

Activity, nonvalue-added   Any activity that provides a negative return on the investment or allocation of resources to that activity. Within broad limits, the enterprise benefits by allocating fewer resources to nonvalue-added activities.

Activity, value-added   Any activity that contributes directly to the performance of a mission and that could not be eliminated without impairing the mission.

Alignment   The degree of agreement, conformance, and consistency among organizational purpose, vision, and values; structures, systems, and processes; and individual skills and behaviors.

"As-is" process model   A model that portrays how a business process is currently structured. In process improvement efforts, it is used to establish a baseline for measuring subsequent business improvement actions and progress.

Baselining   Obtaining data on the current process that provide the metrics against which to compare improvements and to use in benchmarking.

Benchmark   A measurement or standard that serves as a point of reference by which process performance is measured.

Benchmarking   A structured approach for identifying the best practices from industry and government, and comparing and adapting them to the organization's operations. Such an approach is aimed at identifying more efficient and effective processes for achieving intended results, and at suggesting ambitious goals for program output, product/service quality, and process improvement.

Benefit-cost analysis   A technique for comparing the various costs associated with an investment with the benefits that it proposes to return. Both tangible and intangible factors should be addressed and accounted for.

Best practices   The processes, practices, and systems identified in public and private organizations that performed exceptionally well and are widely recognized as improving an organization's performance and efficiency in specific areas. Successfully identifying and applying best practices can reduce business expenses and improve organizational efficiency.

Bill of activity (BOA)   A structured listing of the sequence of activities performed to produce a unit of a product or service. Similar in concept to a bill of materials (BOM), which is a structured list of the components of a product.

Business case   A structured proposal for business improvement that functions as a decision package for organizational decision makers. A business case includes an analysis of business process performance and associated needs or problems, proposed alternative solutions, assumptions, constraints, and risk-adjusted cost/benefit analysis.

Business process   A collection of activities that work together to produce a defined set of products and services. All business processes in an enterprise exist to fulfill the mission of the enterprise. Business processes must be related in some way to mission objectives.

Business process improvement (BPI)   The betterment of an organization's business practices through the analysis of activities to reduce or eliminate nonvalue-added activities or costs, while at the same time maintaining or improving quality, productivity, timeliness, or other strategic or business purposes as evidenced by measures of performance. Also called *functional process improvement.*

Business process reengineering (BPR)   A systematic, disciplined improvement approach that critically examines, rethinks, and redesigns mission-delivery processes in order to achieve dramatic improvements in performance in areas important to customers and stakeholders.

Change management   Activities involved in (1) defining and instilling new values, attitudes, norms, and behaviors within an organization that support new ways of doing work and overcoming resistance to change; (2) building consensus among customers and stakeholders on specific changes designed to better meet their needs; and (3) planning, testing, and implementing all aspects of the transition from one organizational structure or business process to another.

Contingencies   Stated risk factors that, if they occur, may significantly affect the successful completion of a program initiative, project, or task.

Continuous process improvement   An ongoing effort to incrementally improve how products and services are provided and internal operations are conducted.

Core, or key, process   Business processes that are vital to the organization's success and survival.

Cost center   A function in a business where the cost of producing a product or service is tracked and personnel are held accountable for performance.

Critical path   The series of interdependent activities of a project that, connected end to end, determine the shortest total length of the project. The critical path of a project may change from time to time as activities are completed ahead of or behind schedule.

Cultural assumptions   Beliefs about the internal workings and external environment of an organization that, because they worked well in the past, have gradually come to be taken for granted and that provide the basis for group consensus about common events and circumstances. Cultural assumptions function as the unifying themes of organizational culture.

Customer   Groups or individuals who have a business relationship with the organization; those who receive and use or are directly affected by the products and services of the organization. Customers include direct recipients of products and services, internal customers who produce services and products for final recipients, and other organizations and entities that interact with an organization to produce products and services.

Cycle time   The time that elapses from the beginning to the end of a process.

Database   A collection of related data organized to serve one or more independent applications, stored with security, privacy, and integrity controls.

Data repository   A specialized database containing information about data and data relationships. Used to provide a common resource of standard data elements and models.

Decomposition   The breakdown of a process into subprocesses and activities.

Deliverable   An interim by-product of completed project work that is measurable and observable.

Driver   The root cause of a condition or measurement that is felt downstream in a process, as in cost driver and quality driver.

Economic analysis   A formal method of comparing two or more ways of accomplishing a set objective, given a set of assumptions and constraints and the costs and benefits of each alternative, such that the analysis will indicate the optimum choice.

Executive steering committee   The top management team responsible for developing and sustaining the process management approach in the organization, including selecting and evaluating reengineering projects.

Fishbone diagram   A graphic technique for identifying cause-and-effect relationships among factors in a given situation or problem. Also called *Ishikawa diagramming.*

Fixed cost   A cost that does not vary with the amount or degree of production. The costs that remain if an activity or process stops.

Function   A set of related activities that are part of a process; often known as a *subprocess* within a process. Organizations often divide themselves into functional units, such as purchasing, product development, order fulfillment, and so on.

Functional management   A philosophy of management that organizes an enterprise by type of work performed. *See also* Process management.

Gantt chart/bar chart   A graphical representation of the tasks comprising a project, and the relative duration of each. Tasks are typically arranged in sequential order sorted by start date and/or precedence.

Goals   The desired, measurable outcomes of program initiatives and/or a project. Project goals are intended to be measurable and observable.

Improvement initiative   A set or package of planned improvements resulting from the analysis of baseline processes, inspection of strategic and business plans, and benchmarking results that, if implemented, will result in process improvement.

Improvement opportunities   Situations that can be changed to produce a more effective or more efficient process or product. Improvement opportunities may involve processes, business rules, or both. Opportunities are often packaged together as an improvement initiative.

Information engineering   An approach to planning, analyzing, designing, and developing an information system with an enterprisewide perspective and an emphasis on data and architectures.

Information technology investment review process   An analytical framework for linking information technology investment decisions to strategic objectives and business plans in organizations. The investment process consists of three phases: selection, control, and evaluation. This process requires discipline, executive management involvement, accountability, and focus on risks and returns using quantifiable measures. For guidance on the investment review process, refer to the Office of Information and Regulatory Affairs guide, "Evaluating Information Technology Investments: A Practical Guide, Version 1.0"; and the GAO guide, "Assessing Risks and Returns: A Guide for Evaluating Federal Agencies' IT Investment Decision-making, Version 1," (GAO/AIMD-10.1.3, February 1997).

Input   The financial and nonfinancial resources the organization obtained or received to produce its outputs.

Integrated Definition for Function Modeling (IDEF)   Modeling techniques designed to capture the processes and structure of information in an organization. IDEF0 is a process modeling technique; IDEF1X is a rule- or data-modeling technique.

Investment justification   A functional economic analysis indicating that it is better to do a certain action than not to do it. Investments may be compared and ranked by various criteria, including return on various categories of capital, risk-adjusted discounted cash flow, affordability, internal rate of return, and so on.

Just-in-time (JIT) policy   A policy calling for the delivery of materials, products, or services at the time they are needed in an activity or process. Used to reduce inventory, wait time, and spoilage.

Life-Cycle Management (LCM)   A management process that governs a process or system from conception to final disposition. Also called Life-Cycle Management of Information Systems, LCMIS.

Manpower planning   The process of projecting the organization's labor needs over time, in terms of both numbers and skills, and obtaining the human resources required to match those needs.

Migration system   An existing information system that has been officially designated to support standard processes and is intended to be the means of arriving at a target system or architecture (as in open systems architecture).

Milestones   A readily identifiable point in time that marks completion of work. Milestones are used to monitor progress and costs throughout a project life cycle. It is measurable, observable, and independent of time.

Model   A representation of a set of components of a process, system, or subject area. A model is generally developed for understanding, analysis, improvement, and/or replacement of the process.

Modeling or flowcharting   Graphically depicting the activities and subprocesses within a process, and their interrelationships.

Nonvalue-added activity   An activity performed in a process that does not add value to the output product or service, which may or may not have a valid business reason for being performed. Similarly, nonvalue-added cost.

Objectives   The predetermined results of a project; the end toward which effort is directed. Objectives should provide direction in project decision making and state to what end the project will be managed; objectives should be hierarchical, observable, attainable, and consistent.

Outcome   The ultimate, long-term, resulting effects—both expected and unexpected—of the customer's use or application of the organization's outputs.

Performance gap   The difference between what customers and stakeholders expect and what each process and related subprocesses produce in terms of quality, quantity, time, and cost of services and products.

Performance measurement   The process of developing measurable indicators that can be systematically tracked to assess progress made in achieving predetermined goals, and using such indicators to assess progress in achieving these goals.

Predecessor task   Defines the interdependence of tasks. The start date of other tasks (called *successor tasks*) is dependent upon the completion of this task. Predecessor tasks must be completed before their successor tasks can start.

Process   A set of activities that produce products and services for customers.

Process management approaches   Approaches, such as continuous process improvement, business process redesign, and reengineering, which can be used together or separately to improve processes and subprocesses.

Process owner   An individual held accountable and responsible for the workings and improvement of one of the organization's defined processes and its related subprocesses.

Problem report   A report that documents a problem and the need to find a solution; documentation that focuses on deviation of key control parameters, noted events, or variances that impact the attainment of the original project plan.

Productivity   The measurement of labor efficiency when compared to an established norm or baseline. Also used to measure equipment effectiveness and utilization.

Project life cycle   The duration of a project from start to finish, composed of sequential phases in time through which work passes. The phases may be further broken down into stages, depending on the area of project application.

Project team   The core group, headed by the project manager, which is responsible for the successful outcomes of the project strategies.

Risk analysis   A technique used to identify and assess factors that may jeopardize the success of a project or achievement of a goal. Risk analysis also helps define preventive measures to lower the probability of these factors from occurring and identifies countermeasures to successfully deal with these constraints when they develop.

Root cause analysis   A technique used to identify the conditions that initiate the occurrence of an undesired activity or state.

Sensitivity analysis   Used to determine how sensitive outcomes are to changes in the assumptions. The assumptions that deserve the most attention will depend largely on the dominant benefit and cost elements and the areas of greatest uncertainty of the program or process being analyzed.

Simulation modeling   A computer program that replicates the operations of a business process and estimates rates at which outputs are produced and resources are consumed. Simulation models test the consistency of the facts, logic, and assumptions used by planners to design a proposed business process, to compare alternative business processes, or to test the sensitivity of a process to changes in selected assumptions. These models help decision makers assess the potential benefits, costs, and risks of alternative processes and strategies.

Stakeholder   An individual or group with an interest in the success of an organization in delivering intended results and maintaining the viability of the organization's products and services. Stakeholders influence programs, products, and services. Examples include congressional members and staff of relevant appropriations, authorizing, and oversight committees; representatives of central management and oversight entities, such as OMB and GAO; and representatives of key interest groups, including those that represent the organization's customers and interested members of the public.

Strategic plan   The document that specifies the organization, tactics, and methodology to be followed throughout the project life cycle.

"Stretch" goal   A goal that requires a significant change in the performance (quality, quantity, time, cost) of a process.

Subprocess   A collection of related activities and tasks within a process.

Successor task   Defines the interdependence of required tasks that precede a given task. All tasks that depend on a prerequisite task are called successor tasks. A successor task cannot begin until all of its predecessors have been completed.

Task   The fundamental element of a project. Each task has a distinct beginning, end, and time duration. The nature of the work being performed shapes the definition of a task.

"To-be" process model   A process model that results from a business process redesign/reengineering action. The "to-be" model shows how the business process will function after the improvement action has been implemented.

Total Quality Management (TQM)   An approach that motivates, supports, and enables quality management in all activities of the organization, focusing on the needs and expectations of internal and external customers.

Value-added activities   Activities or steps that add to or change a product or service as it goes through a process; the activities or steps that customers view as important and necessary.

Variance analysis   The difference between the budgeted and actual cost of work performed. Variance can be calculated based upon time as well as cost.

World-class ("leading") organizations   Organizations that are recognized as the best for at least one critical business process and are held as models for other organizations.

Workflow   A graphic representation of the flow of work in a process and its related subprocesses, including specific activities, information dependencies, and the sequence of decisions and activities.

INDEX

Software selection (*cont.*)
  sample process, 226
  using a company for, 231–232
Standard Query Language (SQL), 26
Statistical accounts, 196
SQL. *See* Standard Query Language
Systems. *See* software

Technology trends, 23–41
Terminology, inconsistent use of, 14
Trees, intelligent hierarchies, 36

Web portal, 44–46

XBRL. *See* eXtensive Business Reporting
  Language
XML. *See* eXtensible Markup Language

Virtual close. *See* closing procedures

Workflow
  design, 92
  goals, 92
  management, 92
Workflow diagramming, 143–144; 178–179

Zero-based budgeting, 133